BEING INFINITE

AN ENTHEOGENIC ODYSSEY INTO THE LIMITLESS ETERNAL

A MEMOIR FROM AYAHUASCA TO ZEN

BY

MARTIN W. BALL, PH.D.

Being Infinite:
An Entheogenic Odyssey into the Limitless Eternal

A Memoir from Ayahuasca to Zen

Martin W. Ball, Ph.D.

Kyandara Publishing
Ashland, Oregon

ISBN-13:
978-1500108342

ISBN-10:
1500108340

Author's Note:

The names of some individuals have been changed to protect anonymity. Otherwise, this is a true story.

TABLE OF CONTENTS:

Preface:

I want to tell you the story of how I accepted the truth that God is the only reality, including you, and including me. I want to tell you the story of how I learned that everything that exists is one, universal, all-embracing, loving being, and how all sense of separation or distinction from this one being is an illusion created by the mind and human ego. I want to tell you how I learned this truth within myself, and have subsequently learned to live with this reality as an individual who has been profoundly and permanently transformed by this truth.

Perhaps despite appearances, this is not a tale of spirituality, religion, or anything of the kind – if anything, it is a tale of overcoming and moving beyond the inherent limitations of religion and spirituality as constructs of the human ego. It is a tale of truth, personal discovery, and liberation and transformation. It is a very personal story with universal ramifications, and as such, it is timeless.

I want to tell you of how I discovered myself, and in doing so, also discovered you.

I've told bits and pieces of this story in books that I've published, interviews I've given, articles I've written, and through my podcast, "The Entheogenic Evolution" – and have shared the story with countless people who have come to visit me, curious about how I've learned the things I share publically. Ever since my personal liberation and transformation in early 2009, I've been intending to write the complete story down, and in some respects, have been putting it off, especially over the past year (the first year in a decade that I have not undertaken a large writing project), but the time feels right, and thus here I am, typing these words, preparing to bare all for those who desire to know what I went through, what I learned, how it has changed me, and how I now understand myself, the world, and everything in it.

Readers will, no doubt, find much of what I write here challenging, perhaps even unbelievable. I can sympathize. I doubt that I would accept a great deal of what is in these pages as true if it hadn't happened to me. It did, however, and my aim is to tell it as it happened, and I leave it to readers to make up their own minds about what I have to share and what conclusions they may draw from it. Regardless, it is my story, and at the very least, I hope you find it intriguing, and perhaps, it just might help you find your own clarity, your own center, and the truth of your being, and as such, serve in your own awakening and ultimate liberation. I hope so, for I love you as myself, for that is what you are – we are all each other, in the most profound and intimate way.

Who could you be
Other than God
Wrapped in flesh
Nestled into human form
Holding so many possibilities
In these two hands
Seeing with these two eyes
The infinite
Looking out upon infinity
With a quickened pulse
The heart of the fractal of universal being
Informing and birthing the individual that you are
Unique
Yet merely part of the pattern
The spiraling into matter
Of consciousness rendered perspectival
Giving you every right
To proclaim
I Am Here
So be the fractal that you are
Experience yourself as the timeless
Enraptured by time
By choice
By will
By love
Attachments and projections
These are the only illusions
Trust the Real
And know the infinite
As yourself
What you have always been
And what you will always be
It is you, my Love
It is you

In the Hall of Infinite Mirrors
With no beginning
And no end
Which one
Is the Real You?

Chapter One

The Early Years

In my 2008 book, *The Entheogenic Evolution: Psychedelics, Consciousness, and Awakening the Human Spirit*, I concluded with a final chapter entitled, "My Journey." At the time, I was in the middle of a profound process of personal transformation and awakening, largely facilitated by my use of 5-MeO-DMT (and also augmented by ayahuasca in the form of *Daime,* and also *Salvia divinorum, psilocybin* mushrooms, and N,N-DMT). When I wrote that book, I didn't know where the process was taking me, or what the end results would be. That process was to come to a dramatic climax in the spring of 2009, some months after I published *The Entheogenic Evolution.* This book is intended as a completion of what was written in that earlier book, revealing both what led up to that profound process (the details of which were scant in that publication), as well as what has transpired in the time since. This is my first attempt at putting all of this down in written form, and as such, it is something that I am currently very much looking forward to. So, let the process begin!

To reveal the punch line of my story, so to speak, in the spring of 2009, I found that I could no longer convince myself that this one fundamental truth was not genuine and real: I accepted the fact that I was God. It sounds grandiose, I know, but it was the conclusion that resonated with every aspect of my being. Try as my ego might to convince me that this could not possibly be true, reality won out, in the end, because for me to accept anything less would require that I lie to myself, and I decided that I was no longer going to engage in such practices of self-deception, no matter what the truth might be. So I accepted the truth that I was God, and that changed everything for me – though ironically, it also changed nothing, for I was merely accepting what had always been the case. What changed was my personal clarity on the matter, and subsequently, my experience of living in the world changed dramatically, as well as my personal sense of identity. The world, however, is still the same, for it has always been what it is. It is my perspective, and sense of being, that has been altered. Living in truth has a profound effect on one's experience of being, but in many important respects, it changes nothing, for it is only a revealing of that which has always been and always will be.

Lest the reader assume that I am making a unique claim for myself in the person of Martin W. Ball, let me clarify from the start that my acceptance of the truth of my being God is not limited to this individual here, this particular human being. This is a truth that applies to all, equally, without any exception. God is the only reality, and we are all expressions and embodiments of this one universal being. As I like to describe it, there are countless characters that fill the mirrored funhouse and ongoing drama of reality, but there is only one actor, and that actor is God, playing all the various parts simultaneously.

What changed for me was directly discovering this truth within myself, not because I believed it, or because I received some profound teachings from a guru or teacher, or because I advanced along some spiritual path. I discovered this truth within myself through my personal explorations of my energy and my being, and in the end, it was the only conclusion that accounted for everything that I had encountered, experienced, and learned. In the process, I had to let go of every supposed spiritual truth, every belief, and all constructs of identity and sense of self. My awakening to this truth was unconventional, to say the least, and it has provided me with a perspective that I have yet to encounter fully in other versions of the self. I've met plenty of people who *believe* this truth, and others who have glimpsed it, or experienced fleeting, transcendent moments of it, but none who have given themselves to it in the manner that I've personally experienced. I've encountered plenty of people who react and become deeply offended when I make such claims, but as I've said, I've given up the practice of being self-deceptive, either internally or externally, so my only aim is tell it like it is. If that offends someone else, that is his or her issue to grapple with, not mine. I'm only interested in truth.

Setting such concerns aside, I'll tell you my story, and you can make of it what you will. It matters not whether you believe what I share. Maybe it will give you hope. Maybe it will inspire you. Maybe it will make you want to burn this book and write the author off as a nutcase. The choice is yours. My advice, always, is to choose wisely, and be honest with yourself. Self-honesty, and self-love (which are really the same thing), is what brings about liberation, and that, I think, is something everyone could use.

****

I am a universal being. In fact, I am the universe. I am reality itself. There is nothing that is not I, for I am That Which Is. I am a being of infinite energy and limitless love. I am God. I am the person writing this, that which is written, that which it is written on, and also the person reading these words. I am all of these things, and more. The only limits I experience are the ones I have created for myself in order to facilitate the ongoing experience of reality. Reality is my experience of myself, and it is a game – a game that allows me to experience myself as both subject and object simultaneously, and it is the expression of my being and life. It is who and what I am.

But this is intended as a personal story – the story of how one version and embodiment of myself, Martin, came to realize who and what he truly is, and how he learned to accept this within himself. So, let me tell you his story. It is my story, in the form of Martin. From the perspective of where I find myself now, I only partially identify as "Martin." "Martin" is just one of many characters that I play within reality, but for the purposes of this book, and to make things simple, I will write from the first person perspective as Martin, sharing his/my personal story. Once one has accepted universal being, and existing as an infinite expression of energy and love, pronouns can become a bit tricky. I, you, we, him, her, they – these are all just permutations of the one essence and being that we all share. Conventionally, and for communicative purposes, distinguishing ourselves dualistically into subject and object, self and other, serves its purpose. All communication assumes duality – one who communicates, and another who is communicated to. Thus duality is built into the very fabric of language and words, and as such, language cannot fully articulate the true, nondual nature of being. To share requires convention, however, and the limitations of language. So, I will take up the convention and write personally in order to share my story as Martin.

I began the process of fully waking up to my true nature in the late summer of 2007 with a cascade of events that transpired at, and rippled out from, Burning Man. Realistically, this process had been working through me for my entire life, but it was circumstances at Burning Man that really brought it to a head, and initiated a complete transformation in my self-understanding and sense of being. In order to understand the how, the why, and the what, I'll need to tell you more of my life – what led up to that crucial week at Burning Man, and why things happened the way they did in the fallout from that week. It was, personally, a pivotal moment, and as with so many things, context is vital to understanding its significance. So we'll get to that week, and all that came after, but first, I need to tell you about my life – where I came from, who I understood myself to be, and everything that brought me to the breaking point at Burning Man. Then, we can address what has come after.

To begin, I was born as Martin Wilmarth Ball on November 26, 1972, in Goleta Valley Community Hospital in southern California at 11:41 am. My parents, David and Andrea Ball, were living in Isla Vista at the time, a small community of students, immigrants, and staff and faculty, just beyond the borders of the University of California, Santa Barbara, where my father was doing research as a chemist. Prior to my birth, my father was pursuing research at the university in Santiago, Chile, where my parents adopted my sister, Jessica, who was just over a year old when I was born. We lived in a duplex that was owned by a UCSB chemistry professor, a few blocks from the beach, and close to my father's work.

We moved away when I was still young, relocating to Chico, a small town in northern California, where my father got a job teaching organic chemistry at Chico State University, so I have no memory of those early years in Santa Barbara. For the first couple of years that we lived in Chico, we would live in Santa Barbara in the summers so that my father could continue his research at the university, and these summers I do remember, with fond memories of hanging out at the beach.

There was one beach in particular that I liked to visit, for it had an ample collection of driftwood, which served as ideal habitat for western fence lizards. I'd go there regularly to catch lizards, sometimes with a friend, sometimes by myself. There was also a park near our home in Isla Vista that featured a pond, and I would go there to catch crawdads, frogs, and turtles. Today, there's a fence around the small pond, something I don't recall from my childhood. Maybe I climbed the fence, or maybe it just wasn't there.

After a few years of this summer arrangement, my father began teaching chemistry summer school at the University of California in Santa Cruz, where he was to continue to teach summer classes up through my time in college. The majority of my summer memories are of Santa Cruz, where I was a jr. lifeguard. That ended when I went to college, and then spent the summers first in Chico, watching the house and family dog while my father and step-mom were in Santa Cruz, and then later in Berkeley with my girlfriend and her family when her mother was dying of breast cancer. I have countless excellent memories from my summers in Santa

Cruz, and in many ways, it was a world away from Chico, and something I always looked forward to every summer – and not just for getting out of the heat in the Sacramento valley, but culturally, as well.

Chico was a small college town with a strong agricultural and rural feel and culture. In the colloquial, there were a lot of "hicks" in Chico. Santa Cruz, by contrast, also a relatively small college town, was far more tapped into the west coast counterculture with punks, Rastas, hippies and other "alternative" types, and my father credits (or blames) my interest in altered states of consciousness and unconventional thinking to my time spent in Santa Cruz. This may or may not be true, but I certainly enjoyed the many summers spent in Santa Cruz, and it was there that I first cultivated my love for reggae and world fusion music, as well as my enjoyment of marijuana.

My parents were both Californians. My father was raised in a Mormon household in San Francisco, and my mother was from Berkeley. They originally met while attending UC Berkeley in the 60's, though neither was a "hippie" or "counterculturalist." My father rejected Mormonism when he was a child, telling me that he decided that "it was all bullshit," and he never considered himself a Mormon – something that was true for his two brothers, as well. His two sisters remained within the fold of the church, however, a fault line that runs along the divide of my father's side of the family.

My father can perhaps best be described as a scientific materialist and atheist – something I too identified as for a long time, and I still hold many sympathies for this worldview. Despite my claims to be God, I don't hold any religious or spiritual views, and my own understanding of reality is far more in line with the scientific than it opposes or challenges it. At any rate, I'm very grateful that I was not raised Mormon, and in fact, didn't even know that my grandmother was Mormon until much later in life. I appreciate my father instilling in me a strong sense of skepticism and a desire for rational argument, proof, and experimentation and confirmation.

According to my paternal grandmother, we have some interesting family history, and given that she was a Mormon (Mormons, of course, being deeply invested in family lines), she was probably accurate. According to her, we are related to Martha Washington, wife of George Washington, and also John Wilkes Booth, assassin of Abraham Lincoln. Personally, I cannot confirm whether either of these two bits of trivia is true or not, but they make for colorful family history.

On my mother's side, there is more interesting family history. When I was young, my mother was given a medal by the Daughters of the Revolution for having had a distant relative who came to the New World on the Mayflower, so our family line there traces back to the beginnings of the European conquest of North America. More recently, her grandfather, Harold Ickes, was Secretary of the Interior under Franklin Roosevelt. Because of his position and job, her father, my maternal grandfather, spent many years growing up on Native American reservations in the U.S., as development issues on reservations fell under my great-grandfather's responsibilities.

My grandfather was raised in Chicago, and one winter, while on break from school, he attended an Ojibwa ceremony somewhere around the Great Lakes. As my grandfather described it to me, he was approached by an Ojibwa elder at the conclusion of the first day of dancing and was invited to return the next day. When my grandfather returned, the old man who had spoken to him the day before had a ceremonial vest for him. The old man urged him to put it on and go out and dance, which my grandfather did. At the end of the day, he was encouraged to return again the following day.

The next day, he was given a set of ceremonial armbands. Then the next, ceremonial leggings. To complete the regalia, on the final day, he was given ceremonial bags. All the items were intricately beaded in traditional Ojibwa designs. When the dance was all done, the old man who had originally approached my grandfather suggested that he get in the canoe with the rest of the family and head up river for a couple weeks. My grandfather asked his father if this would be OK, as he would likely miss a few days of school, and he was told that, "You'll learn more with them than you will in school, so go," and he did. Those "couple weeks" turned into a year and a half spent with the Ojibwa in their traditional territory, where my grandfather became fluent in the language and was initiated into the *Midewinwin*, the Grand Medicine Society.

This was to initiate my grandfather's life-long interest in and connection to Native American cultures. From the Ojibwa, he ended up moving down to New Mexico where he lived with the Navajo, becoming fluent in the language and being initiated as a ceremonial singer. Then, he went on to Oklahoma, where he lived with Lakotas, being introduced to the vision quest, sweat lodge, and Native American Church use of peyote, and also became fluent in Lakota. He later went on to become proficient in numerous other languages.

From my grandfather, my mother learned to distrust what he called "organized religion," and developed a respect for indigenous cultures and their worldviews and lifeways. My grandfather carried several medicine bags, which he wore under his shirt until the day he died. When I was young, I assumed we (my mother's side of the family) were Native Americans – an illusion that was dispelled one day when a neighbor boy told me his tribal affiliation and I promptly went home to ask about ours. It was then that my mother informed me that we were of European descent. This came as a great surprise, given that my grandfather's multi-story house in Berkeley was filled from top to bottom with Native American artifacts, and my grandfather would sing and drum Navajo songs in the living room. His house was like a museum, and when I was young, it gave me a bit of the creeps. Some of the Native American masks were scary (or so I thought), for one. My grandfather also had a large collection of snakeskins, including one anaconda skin that stretched across several walls in one room upstairs. Near the dining table, he had a collection of stuffed owls – maybe 30 or 40 in all. There was a tiger skin on a banister, and a reindeer hide on a chest near the dining room table. In the living room were a variety of Navajo rugs and a large collection of drums. One room upstairs was dedicated to ammunition, marksmanship awards (many of which were my grandmother's), and boxing trophies. Something that I was not to learn until after my grandfather's death, and the publication of my book, *Mushroom Wisdom*, was that my grandfather also collected local psychoactive mushrooms, which he dried and kept in jars in his basement. My grandfather had lived quite the old-school adventurer's life.

My mother isn't spiritual or religious at all, and was clearly influenced by her father in this regard. Somewhat following in his footsteps, she had been an anthropology major at Berkeley. She also read tarot cards, but as a parlor game and entertainment. She enjoyed playing with self-proclaimed psychics and fortunetellers by using fake accents and pretending to be foreign, just to throw them off and see if they could see past her deceptions (they couldn't). My earliest memories of my mother in regards to religion are all dismissive. I can recall one time that my sister and I were playing out in front of our house in Chico and we were visited by proselytizers. They went to the door, only to have my mother slam it in their faces, which she then promptly reopened to shout, "And stay the fuck away from my children!" having seen them start to approach my sister and me. I also remember my mother standing up for me when I refused to pray over our daily allotment of toast at my Montessori preschool. Prayer was a strange and foreign practice for me, and still is.

I did pray once, as a child. I forget my age, but it was prior to my parents divorcing when I was nine. Before going to bed one night, I got down on my knees and folded my hands together, just as I had seen in images of children praying on TV, like on "Little House on the Prairie." I remember attempting to talk to God, and saying something along the lines of, "I just can't believe in you, so I'm going to need to proof that you exist. I can't do blind faith." Ironically, it was many years later that I got the proof I needed, and it wasn't at all what I expected. The joke, in a sense, was on me.

Two weeks before my parents divorced, it occurred to me that virtually all of my friends' parents were divorced or separated. At the time, I was attending Hooker Oak Elementary School in Chico, in what was called the "open classroom" – basically, countercultural-style education with very little structure. We didn't have desks, and were allowed to create our own schedule for the week. I was always a self-motivated and responsible individual, so I'd do all my "work" early in the week, and schedule myself plenty of time to draw by the end of the week. We had a central carpet where we'd all sit around cross-legged, and there were "loft" play structures in the rooms. It wasn't until after the divorce and my mother moved with my sister and myself to Sonoma, California, that I encountered a school desk for the first time, as well as a more hard-edged school year with far more serious bullies than I had endured in Chico.

Leading up to the divorce, my parents would get into awful arguments and shouting matches. I can recall one night when my father, in his anger, threw a full bowl of salad at my mom. Another night (or perhaps even the same one, I don't know), he took my mom's favorite plant and threw it into the fire. Personally, I decided that it would probably be best if my parents followed suit with the majority of my friends' parents and get divorced. They certainly didn't seem happy. And I didn't like the fact that the fighting made my sister cry. I blamed my dad for that and was angry with him. Especially when he threw the plant in the fire.

It was a weekend day that I learned my parents were going to divorce. My mother had dropped me off at a soccer field for a game I was to play that day, though she inadvertently dropped me off several hours early – the result of an unnoted schedule change. I wandered around, looking for my teammates, but they were nowhere to be found. Incidentally, it was a terrible team. We lost every game that season, with the exception of two that we tied. Winners, we were not! Even on that team, I was still an odd one out. When it came time to choose our jersey numbers, I got it in my head that I wanted the infinity symbol, which seemed much better than any random number, to me. Of course, that wasn't an option, so I settled for two zeros placed closely together. No one on my team got it, and other players liked to give me a hard time about my "infinity."

Personally, I wasn't ever much of a sports player. I did *Jujitsu*, and also enjoyed the swimming that was part of being a jr. lifeguard – it was one of the few sports I excelled at and regularly won races – but I was mostly a chubby, awkward kid. I never did well with team sports, and this soccer team was no exception. It wasn't until jr. high school that I realized part of my awkwardncss was due to the fact that I'm ambidextrous, though not interchangeably so. My realization was prompted by my P.E. teacher passing out catching mitts on the first day of softball. He asked who was left-handed. I raised my hand, and received a left-handed mitt (for my right hand, so I could throw with my left). It didn't work for me, because I threw right-handed, despite the fact that I wrote left-handed, and also batted left-handed. I'm still very much mixed, with half the things I do being left-handed, and the other half right-handed.

My father wasn't ever around much. His thing is playing with chemicals in the lab, and he spent most of his weekends there – and still does, despite being "retired" from Chico State. The university wasn't far from the soccer field, so I made my way over to his office to see if he was around and could take me home. It took me awhile to find his office door, but I eventually did and knocked on it. Much to my surprise, my mother opened the door. She had clearly been crying. She whisked me away and took me to her car, driving me back to the soccer field to find out what was going on with my game.

It was then, in the car, that she told me about the impending divorce. She probably expected some kind of reaction from me, but my take on it was, "It's about time." My sister took the news much harder and was far more affected by the divorce than myself. I credit the fact that I had already reached the conclusion that they would be better off divorced a couple weeks prior for my nonchalant reaction to the news.

First my dad moved out, and then my mom, my sister, and I moved to Sonoma. For the first time, my mother was working full-time as a teacher and we were in a new place where we didn't know anyone. The overall culture of Sonoma was harsher than that in Chico. On my very first day at my new school, in 5th grade now (sometime in October, already into the school year), I was approached by some boys on the playground at recess who promptly informed me that they were "calling me out." Probably to their surprise, I looked blankly at them. I'd never heard the expression before and didn't have a clue that it meant that they were challenging me to a fight. When I didn't react properly, they eventually gave up, though the offer did return several more times over the coming months. I never got into a full fight with anyone there, though I did pin a boy up against the wall while choking him. Every day he'd greet me with "Martin's fartin' balls!" and one day I'd had enough. I pulled my best Darth Vader move on him and informed him that I never wanted to hear him say that to me again. I didn't, so apparently the choking and threat worked. To this day, that's the most violence I've ever shown anyone or personally been involved in.

My mother was very emotionally unstable, and I found her difficult to live with. Before the school year was out, I had decided that I would go live with my father, who had spent the year in Santa Cruz, but would be moving back to Chico in the summer. It was a friend who let the decision slip out and made my plans known to my mother while she was driving us around after school. The friend said something about me moving away, which was news to mom. Needless to say, she wasn't happy. She was of the opinion that my father was "brainwashing" me – a view she wasn't reticent to share with me, along with the claim that my father "has his head stuck up his ass!" My sister wanted to go too, but she didn't have the courage, so she stayed with my mom. In high school, she started having major drug and behavior problems and eventually came to live with us in Chico, and then with my uncle, and then grandmother, in Stockton, eventually moving to the streets, where she still lives today, somewhere in the vicinity of Chico, having abandoned her two kids at my father's house a decade ago.

Overall, my mother took the divorce pretty hard, and she struggled with it emotionally for years. In some ways, I became a surrogate target for her emotional distress. She was convinced that I wasn't old enough to make up my mind for myself, so she always suspected some duplicitous meddling by my father whenever my desires conflicted with hers. There were periods in my later teenage life when I refused to speak with her or have anything to do with her. One time was for a year. The other was for a year and a half. When I got divorced from my first marriage in 2007, my mother and I still had some issues to work out, for she still saw me as my father and saw echoes of her own divorce in mine – an interpretation that I thoroughly disagreed with.

My father remarried first, to a former student. Somewhat surprisingly, his new partner was religious, having been raised in a Pentecostal household where speaking in tongues and inspired prayer and healing were regular features of daily life. Still as a young boy, probably when I was in sixth grade and sparing with the religious kids in my class who gave me a hard time for accepting Darwin's theory of evolution, I told my step-mom my theory that one day people would evolve beyond their belief in God, because it really was just a mental crutch to answer questions that hadn't been fully addressed by science and reason. She disagreed. Around the same time, I remember overhearing other kids talking about me on the playground while I was in the restroom, expressing their disbelief that I thought that humans had evolved from apes over millions of years of gradual changes, and that I didn't believe in Jesus and the Bible. After that, I decided to write "Atheists Rule!" prominently on my school binder, just so there'd be no confusion about where I stood on the matter.

My childhood was thus relatively religion-and-spirituality-free, something for which I am tremendously grateful. My conclusion, from my current vantage point, is that all religion and spirituality is a construct of the human ego, and as such, is based on incorrect premises about the nature of the self, God, and being. This conclusion is not a result of my upbringing, however, for I certainly experimented with religion and spirituality, as I will discuss later in this book. Rather, this conclusion is based on my own understanding of the nature of the Self and is a direct result of my own awakening. This is a challenging position for many people to hear, for there are many in the counterculture, and increasingly in mainstream culture, who disavow "religion," but express deep passion, sincerity, and interest in being "spiritual," presumably because being "spiritual" is seen as being better than being "religious." Well, they're both constructs of the ego and sense of self-identity, and are both equally problematic. Being spiritual doesn't make someone any more enlightened than the most hardened religious fanatic, and in some ways, it's worse, because the people who create such identities for themselves *think* that they're enlightened, or evolved, or however it is that they chose to self-identify. But I'm getting ahead of my story. We'll return to these themes later.

It was in late high school that I began my first explorations into religion and spirituality. In one of my English classes, we studied the Bible as literature – not as a religious document, but as a collection of stories and narratives. I found this approach refreshing, and enjoyed getting to know some of the material in the book without having someone tell me that I had to believe all this make-believe crap. As a document on reality, I felt it had almost no value. As a collection of stories, it was interesting, and accessible. Also, around the same time, we started studying philosophy in English, and that hit me like an epiphany. My thought was that it sounded like the perfect job for me – sitting around, thinking about stuff, and trying to distinguish the real from the false. A profession that sought for clarity and understanding. That sounded about right for me, and eventually inspired me to become a philosophy major in college.

There was also an interesting turn of events in my physics class. One day, while we were studying Einstein's theory of relativity and discussing the eccentricities of the speed of light, my teacher, almost off-handedly, mentioned that this strange book I had never heard of, *The Tibetan Book of the Dead* (more accurately translated as *On Liberation Upon Hearing in the Between* in reference to the fact that the book is to be read to corpses while the individual's consciousness inhabits the *Bardo*, or space "between" death and rebirth), describes the absolute nature of the mind as pure white light, and had some similarities to Einstein. I made a mental note and decided that I'd have to get my hands on a copy of this esoteric book and see for myself what it had to say.

It was also around the time of high school that I started to develop an interest in Rastafarianism, mainly through my interest in reggae music, and of course, the herb. I was 14 when I first tried marijuana – on my birthday, actually. Every four years, my birthday falls on Thanksgiving, and otherwise, comes either just before, or just after, this holiday. It was also a day after my grandmother's birthday. When I turned 14, the family was gathered at our house in Chico for the holiday, and various relatives were coming in from across California. One relative, my cousin Tim, drove up from L.A. and arrived around 10 pm the night of my birthday. Only my sister, who was 15, and I were up at the time. Seeing that everyone else was asleep, Tim asked us if we wanted to come out to his car to try out his bong (which he kept in the passenger seat so he could take bong rips while driving). My sister was experienced with herb, but this was my first time, and it showed. After smoking (my first time smoking anything), we went back inside to watch TV. I was engrossed. I couldn't believe how entertaining whatever it was we were watching was. I also noticed that I was glued to the TV, not moving at all – I felt like a statue, and very much "stoned". When I tried to tell my cousin and sister that I wasn't moving, they laughingly pointed out that I was moving to talk to them. Definitely a novice.

That summer, when we went back to Santa Cruz for my dad's research and summer teaching, my good friend Alex, a fellow jr. guard, had also been turned on to pot. We spent a good many afternoons, after our morning session of jr. lifeguards, back at his place in Scott's Valley, up in the forested hills from Santa Cruz, smoking pot and playing "Tupperware wars," where we took all the lids of his mom's Tupperware collection and used them as flying disks as we ran wildly about his three-story house, flinging them at each other.

It was that summer that I first saw Ziggy Marley play at the Santa Cruz Civic Auditorium, my first real introduction to reggae music and Rasta religion and philosophy. At the show, I was standing next to a group of young people smoking pot. Suddenly, this girl shoved a loaded pipe into my hands and walked off. I was high, and a bit dumbfounded, but quickly understood why she had done what she did when a burly security guard came up and informed me that there was no smoking in the auditorium. "It's not mine," was my lame response. He just shook his head and walked off without incident. The girl quickly reappeared and claimed her pipe and disappeared into the crowd.

I was a bit confused by reggae and Rastafari. I loved the music and the rhythms, but was never sure of the religious content of the songs. After my introduction to Ziggy, I learned about Bob Marley, and spent a lot of time carefully listening to the music. I deeply appreciated the social and political consciousness of the music that was steeped in Rasta philosophy, which was so different from the various religious views I had been exposed to previously. Religion had always seemed to be a conservative force, but here it was progressive and talking about equal rights, justice, and righting the wrongs of history. For the budding liberal that I was becoming, it seemed a good fit.

But I didn't get the Halie Selassie thing – Rastas claiming that this man was Jesus returned to liberate all black people. For one, he was dead, and for another, he was a dictator who watched his people starve in Ethiopia while he was rumored to feed his dogs steak dinners. Didn't seem like much of a messiah to me, even if he did have some good things to say, such as his speech that was used to create the Bob Marley song, "War." And, it all seemed rather contradictory, for what's a messiah for only one race, anyway – not to mention that Bob Marley had a white British father? Still, the idea of the West as being "Babylon" that sought to mentally enslave its subjects resonated with me. I appreciated Bob's message that "None but ourselves can free our minds." I just didn't necessarily agree with the Rastas about what we were supposed to be freeing our minds for or to. I certainly wasn't going to adopt Halie Selassie as my messiah, though I probably would have grown dreadlocks, had my hair been more amenable to dreading.

Later, some of my high school friends started hanging out with the local Rastas, and attending their *Nyabhingi* sessions, complete with copious consumption of the Holy Herb. I was interested, but never attended myself. At any rate, these friends became the go-to folks for getting high, as they tended to have a good supply of herb on hand. Some of them started to adopt the Rasta identity – others just wanted to get high and have a little spirituality to go along with it.

Of course, though I didn't know it at the time, if one wanted to develop a spiritual identity around the use of marijuana, one could choose to look to the historical antecedents of Rasta – ones that are generally overlooked by Rastas themselves. Religion, in all its many forms, is an expression of the ego, and as such, is primarily concerned with identity, the exclusive focus of the ego. Black Rastas in the Caribbean created a religious, spiritual, and cultural identity that set them apart from both their White colonial rulers as well as more criminal and complacent identities in the Black community. By becoming Rastas, they were able to claim the religion of Christianity as more authentically their own, and their interpretation of history and the Bible became more valid than that of their White overlords. As such, it was important for Rastas to create the image and identity of an "authentically" Black form of Christianity that supposedly originated in Black Africa. However, their use of the term *ganja*, smoking it out of a *chilam,* and their penchant for wearing their hair in dreadlocks belies the true historical origin of much of the look and feel of Rasta culture and identity. Religion isn't about historical accuracy, though – it's about identity, and therefore the true historical influences are left out entirely in the self-generated story of the origins of the Rasta movement.

Ganja, the Rasta term for their herbal sacrament, and the pipes they smoke it in, the *chilam*, are words of *Sanskrit* origin and come from the Hindu culture of India, not Africa. When the British imported workers from India to the Caribbean, they brought with them their ancient practice of smoking ganja, largely to honor and worship the Hindu god Lord Shiva. Like depictions of Lord Shiva himself, his Shaivite followers wear their hair in dreadlocks and regularly partake of Shiva's favorite magical plant, marijuana. Even today, the way one celebrates Lord Shiva's birthday, *Shivaratri,* is to smoke ganja. Though he is known for many things, one of Shiva's main identities is the god of magical plants and substances. In the ancient Hindu sacred texts, the *Vedas,* there is a god known as Soma, which is also a sacred substance that is called *amrita,* or the divine nectar of immortality. Though many of the Vedic gods have fallen out of fashion over the millennia, Shiva has taken up the mantel of the god of *soma* and *amrita,* and still today in India and Nepal, Shiva is known for his use and association with all kinds of mind-altering plants and fungi, with marijuana being one of the more popular and common, though he is also associated with psilocybin and amanita mushrooms as well as the more dangerous and potentially deadly datura (another *Sanskrit* word).

Looking even further back in time, before the time of Shiva and the Vedas, we can also see through anthropology and archaeology that these forms of Hindu identity and religious practice actually find their antecedents in pan-Asian shamanism. The word "shaman" itself comes to us via Russian anthropologists who took the term from the Tungustic peoples of Siberia, where the amanita mushroom was used by shamans for trance, divination, and healing. Tellingly, Siberian shamans, and northern hemisphere shamans in general (including Inuit cultures in the "New World"), traditionally wore their hair in long dreadlocks, unlike other members of their cultures. It's highly likely that these shamanic cultures were also well familiar with marijuana, one of the oldest cultivated crops of humankind. In this sense, Rasta use of ganja for altering consciousness and the adoption of dreadlocks actually traces all the way back to archaic religion and spirituality, and has very little to do with African expatriate religious and cultural identity, though that is the role that it came to serve in the construction of Rasta culture.

Somewhat ironically, the Rasta identity has found a welcome home among White counterculturalists in the U.S. – not because they are the descendents of Black slaves that are looking to establish a revolutionary identity that has its "roots" in Africa, but because the emphasis on "consciousness" and rebellion speaks to the desire to construct a "spiritual" identity that is at odds with "Babylon" and mainstream culture, thinking, and forms of cultural and religious identity. The fact that it comes with smoking marijuana, a Western countercultural staple and badge of identity, is a bonus.

Around this same time, near the end of my time in high school, I started going out with a girl who was a thorough Born-Again Christian. Needless to say, she wasn't very supportive of my appreciation for the herb. I remember one time we were talking about evolution, and I was astounded to hear that she believed the earth was only a few thousand years old, and that dinosaurs apparently never existed. "You can take chicken bones and put them together any way you want," was her response to my challenge of how she could explain fossils. That was a real eye-opener about how self-deluding religious believers could be, and how they could willingly deny evidence that contradicted their beliefs, even when it was right in front of them.

Another girlfriend I had in high school was goth (back then, we just called it "alternative"), and while not a "religion" *per se*, it is a socially constructed identity, just like Born-Agains, Rastas, and everyone else who decides that they are some *thing* or *kind* of person in particular. It comes complete with culture, music, art, personal attire, symbolism, idols, places of worship, etc., just like a religion. I flirted with the goth identity, spending some time dressing in black and listening to dark music. Like with reggae and Rasta, I still enjoy the music style and some of the aesthetics, but never became a full-fledged goth. Just to be a troublemaker, I wore some Rasta clothes to go see Depeche Mode, which definitely stood out in the sea of black. It was when I went to see Peter Murphy, former lead singer of the goth band Bauhaus, that I really decided that it was all a bit silly. There we all were, out in the hot Sacramento Valley, and all these kids were walking around dressed completely in black with white face paint and dark eyeliner. It all seemed too excessive to me and too dependent on an outer style to communicate a mysterious identity that was a complete construction (as are all identities).

I learned a bad habit with this goth girlfriend. She was a real manipulator and a bit off. When I had had enough and I decided to break it off, she came over to my house and started cutting herself. I felt so helpless and out-of-control that I just broke down crying. Much to my surprise, she responded immediately to this turn of events, stopped cutting herself, and promptly left. The bad habit I learned was that I could get the results I wanted from people if I played the victim and tried to make someone feel sorry for me. She was my first fully sexual relationship, so it set the tone for me in ways that were to ripple out through my adulthood. I also learned the dangers of making other people feel bad, as her cutting had showed me. She ended up on a two-week suicide watch at the local hospital. That taught me that ending relationships was dangerous – as if that lesson hadn't come through clear enough with my parents' tumultuous divorce.

I started making music when I was 15, around the same time that things ended with the girlfriend mentioned above. Given my influences, I wanted to do something that sounded like Bob Marley and The Cure – not necessarily two sounds that went together. Having not committed to either being Rasta or goth, I just decided to go for both, at least musically speaking. I hooked up with an older boy at my high school and started learning how to play the guitar, accompanied by more experimenting with marijuana. One day when I came over to his place to play music, he informed me that, "As artists, it's our social duty to experiment with drugs and get high. We owe it to the people." I liked the sound of that, and it made music much more fun and expressive.

Heavy metal and Led Zeppelin were all the rage at my high school, so my musical preferences kept me on the outskirts with the other outcasts and oddballs. I refused to learn how to play "Stairway to Heaven" on the guitar, and my fellow musicians were of the same opinion. We were the unpopular smart kids and were comprised of skaters, wannabe Rastas, punks, goths, atheists, a Jew, a couple Iranians, and outright geeks and nerds. We celebrated and embraced our outcast status by being provocateurs, even going so far as to create an underground magazine, originally started by kids a couple years ahead of me, called "Hardcore Mag." It pissed plenty of people off, and entertained others. I eventually became the editor for the mag, and even had my dad make photocopies of the publication after he discovered some of our fictitious stories discarded in a trashcan. My father decided to print it on yellow paper, telling me that it was a pun for "yellow journalism." I didn't get the joke.

I also learned a lot about homophobia as a high school student. I was the first boy in my high school to wear an earring and have long hair, and that didn't sit well with the jocks and religious crowd. Not a day went by that I wasn't yelled at or harassed for being a "fag" or "fairy." It definitely taught me how deeply fear of the "other" can run, especially when that "other" challenges peoples' identities and belief systems. It gave me a lot of sympathy for people who, unlike myself, were actually gay, so those with "alternative" tendencies were welcomed in my circle of friends and misfit outcasts.

Overall, I couldn't wait to get out of high school. It was profoundly boring, for one, and I certainly didn't feel that I fit in. Most of the classes were pathetically easy and just felt like a waste of time. Socially, most people just wanted to go out and drink and get drunk. I got drunk enough to vomit once, and decided at that point that drinking just made me feel stupid and sick, so I didn't really drink after that. College, for me, was the light at the end of the high school tunnel, promising the possibility of real education and learning. Personally, I wanted a challenge other than the social problems of a small town high school. I wanted to learn big and think deep thoughts. By the time graduation came, I was ready to get out of there. As Peter Gabriel sang, I was ready for my own experience of the "Big Time."

The day after graduation, I stopped by my former English and drama teacher's office – one of the few adults at the school who I felt understood and knew me – just to say hi. On her desk she had a book, *Zen Mind, Beginners Mind.* I picked it up and leafed through it. My former teacher noticed and immediately commented that she thought I would like it, knowing that I had enjoyed our studies of Herman Hesse. She urged me to take the book home, give it a read, and return it to her when I was done.

That was the point that I started to become interested in religion and spirituality in earnest, and began the next phase of my life as a "spiritual seeker," an identity that I eventually dropped after my own awakening in 2009. But, I get ahead of my story . . .

CHAPTER TWO

THE ZEN OF COLLEGE

In the fall of 1990, I loaded up my Volkswagen bug with everything I owned and headed south on I-5 to Los Angeles. My primary choices for college were UC Berkeley, Reed College in Oregon, and Occidental College in L.A. Apparently, Occidental liked me enough to offer a pretty good financial deal that would make it possible for my father to pick up the rest of the price tag of attending a private school, which was substantial.

I was 17 when I started Occidental. I had always been a bit ahead in school, generally the youngest of my class. I felt profoundly free to be away from home, living in the biggest of big cities. Chico had about 30,000 residents when I was a teenager, and living in a city of millions had its appeal to me – an appeal that was soon to wear off when I found that the 15 mile trip to the beach in Santa Monica could take up to an hour and a half because of the terrible traffic, but initially, at least, I was thrilled to be living in L.A.

I was also excited to be attending a school that claimed to be one of the most ethnically and racially diverse in the U.S., where "multiculturalism" was celebrated, embraced, and sometimes, enforced. That didn't stop students from largely congregating into racially and identity-bound groups, however, and the student quad at lunch time was always telling – no matter how much "multiculturalism" we got, everyone still segregated themselves into clearly distinct cliques. For the most part, students didn't cross racial, cultural, and identity lines when it came time for socializing.

I learned my educational preferences very early on at Occidental – my very first term, actually. I had placed out of needing to take any math classes as I had taken calculus at Chico State my senior year at high school. For some reason, I let my academic advisor talk me into taking a class called "Discrete Mathematics," something I'd never heard of, which was supposedly something that one could take after completing calculus, though the subjects were not related. The class was at eight in the morning, my first class of the day. Out of the thirty or so students in the class, there was only one, a young man who was literally a mathematical genius, who ever understood what in the hell the teacher was trying to teach us. He sat up in the front, in the very middle of the class, and attentively nodded along to everything the teacher said, never needing to take notes. The rest of us were thoroughly confounded by the subject matter. Somehow, I received a "B" in the class. The teacher *must* have been grading on a very generous curve, because I personally felt that I had failed every assignment and test. The entire class was an opaque mystery to me.

To make matters worse, probably because I didn't understand anything that was happening in the class, I found that I was threatening to fall asleep in virtually every class meeting. However, my second class of the day, starting at 9 am, was my very first philosophy class. I found that I would immediately perk up upon entering the class, and was so taken with the subject matter that I just ate it up, loving every minute. It was then that I had the idea that philosophy really was a good fit for me, and perhaps I could let the math thing slide. When that term was done, I never took another math class again, though I did take a year's worth of physics. Still, it was the philosophy classes that really got me going, so before long, I declared as a philosophy major.

The workload was enormous, and far more than anything I had ever experienced in high school. I learned very quickly that the vast majority of students at Occidental didn't bother to do all the reading every week, which stretched into the hundreds of pages. I, however, ever the diligent student, read every word and every page. My typical day was to get up around 9, eat breakfast, go to class, finish in the afternoon, and then start reading, with a break for dinner, up until 10 pm. Then, I'd give myself an hour of playing guitar. 11 pm was time to get high and play Ultimate Frisbee out on the lawn in front of the dorm with fellow students, then inside for one more bowl just before midnight, finish off the day with old-school *Star Trek* with Captain Kirk and Mr. Spock from 12 am to 1 am, and then bed.

My social life was essentially non-existent. That was the price of actually doing all the work that was assigned. The only time I took off was on Fridays (philosophy classes never met on Friday). I'd sleep in, take a late breakfast, and then get high and spend the afternoon playing guitar. That was my Friday thing and the only time I spent not working diligently as a student. Occidental is also built on a hill, called Mt. Fiji by students, and I used to spend my Fridays wandering around the hillside, a little slice of nature. I'd often go up there at night, as well, and discovered that there were great horned owls living up there, so I'd go up there just to hang out with the owls. I'd also take trips into the mountains on Fridays to go hiking in Angeles National Forest and found some nice swimming holes.

My main social outlets were my cousin Tim and his partner, Kenji, living nearby in Pasadena, my then-girlfriend, (who didn't really consider herself my girlfriend since I hardly ever saw her, given that I was so busy being a student) and a friend of mine from high school, Devon, who was going to UC Irvin a little further south. Devon and I first met in jr. high school, but didn't really become friends until high school, and mostly bonded our senior year when we were into smoking pot together. Devon always had some herb, and carried around a backpack with a bong in it wherever he went. Our first priority, whenever he came up to Occidental to visit, was to break out the bong and get high. I also purchased my first bong at this time and would smoke out with my roommate, Chris, whose favorite bands were Depeche Mode and

Metallica. I loved listening to Depeche Mode high. Fortunately, Chris always changed out the Metallica to something that was more to my liking when I was in the room.

Music was a major outlet for me in college – and still is, though I don't sit around simply playing guitar the way that I used to. I started performing with a guitarist that I met through hearing the sound of his playing coming out of his dorm window. The acoustic "coffee house" thing was just starting up then, and many of the dorms on campus would host "unplugged" shows, so we regularly performed around campus. My friend, Kevin, was into Bob Mould, and he'd probably be happy to admit that he was a bit of a music snob. Due to personality issues, our collaboration lasted a couple years, and then fell apart. My second year of college, I also put together a reggae band, but the fellow members of the band ended up not liking Occidental and transferred to other schools at the end of that year.

I actually had a fairly intense period of guitar withdrawal my first year of college. In the spring, my girlfriend and I decided we'd take part in a school program where a group of students would go down to Mexico for the weekend and build a house for a homeless family. The entire event was a complete fiasco, largely due to the incompetence and flakiness of the professor leading the trip. It both started and ended badly, and over the course of the weekend, my guitar, which I had brought with us for campfire entertainment, had been stolen.

The result was that I no longer had a guitar – that, and the fact that my one trip ever to Mexico was a total disaster (the details of which I won't go into). My main expressive outlet was gone, and it wasn't until I got home that summer that I was able to purchase a new guitar. That was a hard couple of months and made me realize just how much making music was an essential part of myself and how I dealt with life.

It was that summer home from college that I first experienced psilocybin mushrooms and some major shifts in my sense of the spiritual. I had been cultivating my budding spirituality throughout the year by joining a Zen meditation group at Occidental, which I continued with throughout my time as an undergrad. Ever since reading *Zen Mind, Beginners Mind,* I had become increasingly fascinated with Zen Buddhism. To put it mildly, I was completely astounded when I read that first book on Zen, for this was not at all like what I had experienced of religion, and certainly was nothing like the Christianity of my fellow students. There were no obviously untrue myths presented as fact; there was no divine savior to believe in; there was nothing about heaven or hell; no sin, no judgment, no reward or punishment – just you, your breath, and cultivating clarity of mind and presence. It was clean, straightforward, and totally rational. No mysticism, no magic, no make-believe. And what was more, it all made sense to me, and really resonated with how I already looked at the world and the values that I held. Zen seemed like something of a miracle to me: a religion that actually made sense and wasn't overloaded with a bunch of nonsensical crap that I could never bring myself to believe in. In fact, there was nothing that I saw in Zen that required any belief whatsoever. It was a practice of finding clarity and centering in on reality. It seemed perfect for me.

The Zen meditation group was lead by a Pure Land Buddhist priest who had formerly been a student at Occidental. He was Japanese-American and had decided, upon completing his schooling, that being a Buddhist priest sounded like a better deal than going to fight in Vietnam via the draft, so he chose religion, more for practical reasons than anything else. When we first met, I didn't know the difference between Zen and other forms of Buddhism, like Pure Land, and I was ignorant enough about Buddhism to mistakenly think that it had originated from Japan.

Zen is a form of *Mahayana* Buddhism, or "Greater Vehicle" Buddhism. To distinguish itself from earlier, and perhaps arguably more "authentic," forms of Buddhism, as based on the original teachings of the historical Buddha, *Mahayanists* coined the term *Hinayana* for the earlier schools of Buddhism, which translates as "Smaller Vehicle," and gave themselves the more auspicious title of being "Greater," and therefore better. The distinction was that *Mahayana* developed a new metaphysics that was not present in the original teachings of the Buddha of the "three Buddha bodies," or *Trikaya,* which, in contradiction to early Buddhist teachings, posited that the Buddha (despite his death, and his insistence that with his death and achievement of *parinirvana* and fundamental extinguishing and thereby being "gone") was still "out there" in a visionary realm called the *Shamboghakaya* and as the absolute nature of mind and being, called the *Dharmakaya.* *Mahayanists* also adopted the ideal of the *Bodhisattva* – an enlightened being who would forgo *parinirvana* until all sentient beings of the universe were liberated from suffering and delusion. At the practical level, *Mahayana* Buddhism opened up the identity of being a "Buddhist" to many more converts as it became open to acts of worship, prayer, and religious service that were disavowed as not serving enlightenment and liberation as defined and identified by the historical Buddha.

Our meditation leader, Noriaki Ito, whom we called Nori, was a priest at the Higashi Honganji Buddhist Temple in downtown L.A. in a section known as Little Tokyo. As this was a Zen meditation group, he never taught us too much about Pure Land. As forms of Buddhism, Pure Land and Zen couldn't be much more different from each other. Zen is known as the "meditation school," and puts virtually all its emphasis on the practice of mediation. Zen also tends to eschew philosophy, which is popular in Buddhism – probably the most philosophical of all the world's religions – and also is ritualistically very sparse, whereas other forms of Buddhism might have elaborate rituals and practices, such as with *Vajrayana*, or focus on devotion, such as in Pure Land (in contrast, Zen Buddhism advocates that "When you meet the Buddha on the road, kill him" – not a lot of devotion and worship going on there!). To my mind, Zen is very clean, aesthetically open like the iconic *enso*, and no-nonsense – you're either in "monkey mind" or you're not.

Pure Land Buddhism is all about devotion to Amitabha Buddha, or Amida, as he his known in Japan. It was a later development of Mahayana Buddhism, and the main doctrine is that these are degenerate times when people are not disciplined enough to gain the merits of pure meditation, and thus need to rely on a benevolent outside force in the form of Amida Buddha, who, if you recite his name in acts of devotion, will let you be reborn in your next life in his "Pure Land" where you will be able to make more progress with your meditation. In my imagination, I can hear the original Buddha responding with a forceful, "What the fuck?" to this form of Buddhism, for the Buddha originally taught that *only you* can liberate yourself and no "outside" agents or beings can assist you in this process. The development of Pure Land, or devotional, Buddhism was part of the Mahayana program to bring Buddhism to more people and make it more accessible for them, for not everyone can devote his or her life to meditation and the rigors of monastic life, as Buddhism was originally conceived. Thus meditation is not emphasized in Pure Land Buddhism and instead all the emphasis and focus is put on a future life granted by a benevolent deity that takes pity on you and extends his infinite grace to you through your devotion. Though Zen Buddhism also came about through Mahayana Buddhism, it seems much more in line with the Buddha's teachings, which rejected the devotional and ritual practices of the Brahmanical Hindus of the historical Buddha's day as ineffectual, and possibly damaging, in the quest for liberation and enlightenment.

The advent of Zen is credited to the Indian monk, Bodhidharma. According to tradition, Bodhidharma came to China and introduced the teachings of *Chan*, or "meditation only" to Chinese Buddhist converts (called Zen in Japan). He is generally depicted iconographically with big, bulging eyes, for according to tradition, he cut off his eyelids so that he wouldn't fall asleep while meditating. Unlike other Mahayana schools, Bodhidharma urged his followers to simply meditate, rather than focusing on prayer, ritual, and worship of the Buddha (or Buddhas, as they were conceived in Mahayana), as this was, in his great big eyes, the true path to liberation and enlightenment.

These days it's popular for "spiritual" people to claim that all the various religions and "wisdom traditions" of the world speak of the same fundamental spiritual truths, but this is a wildly inaccurate statement, and generally reflects ignorance about the true diversity of religious views, metaphysical propositions, and core teachings of various traditions. Zen and Pure Land Buddhism do not teach the same fundamental truths, for example. And Buddhism itself was originally highly critical of Brahmanical Hindu practices as being delusional and counter-productive to enlightenment. Hindus believe in a creator God: Buddhism denies the existence of a creator God. Hindus believe in the power of ritual sacrifice and offerings to the gods: Buddhism rejects these practices. Hindus believe in the existence of an immortal soul: Buddhism teaches the doctrine of "no-self" or "no-soul" (Sanskrit, *anatman*; Pali, *annatta*). Such doctrinal issues are not merely a matter of opinion or perspective – either a creator God exists, or it doesn't – either we have souls or we don't. The big difference between Buddhism and Hinduism is that Hindu doctrines are based on the "divine revelations" of the ancient texts, the *Vedas*, whereas Buddhist doctrine is based on the insight of one man, Siddhartha Gautama Sakyamuni. His insights found the Hindu doctrines to be fundamentally flawed, and thus he introduced his teachings of the Middle Path that rejected the majority of Hindu teachings as erroneous and incorrect. How anyone could claim that these two religions are about the "same truth" boggles my mind, for they are clearly at odds with each other. In fact, most new religions start as critiques and rejections of pre-existing traditions – Buddhism, Jainism, Sikhism, Islam, Christianity, New Age religions, etc., are all examples of such. When you really study religion, what you find is diversity, rather than any core similarity or some supposed *perennial philosophy*.

So I nurtured my budding spirituality by attending weekly *Zazen* sessions at the Occidental Interfaith Center with Nori and a revolving handful of other students. There were times when Nori couldn't make it, so I would lead meditation as well as the follow-up discussions that were part of our practice, as I was busy reading pretty much everything I could get my hands on about Zen. I always looked forward to it, and even got my own *zafu* so I could meditate on my own – something I practiced regularly for many years. I flirted with the idea of actually calling myself a Zen Buddhist, but never went so far as to fully take on that identity. Zen was something that I did, but it wasn't who I was.

I also enjoyed smoking marijuana and then practicing meditation, which tended to make it more intense, and more profound. That was one of the reasons that I didn't feel comfortable calling myself a Zen Buddhist, for most forms of Buddhism reject the consumption of mind-altering substances (though it is quite possible that *Vajrayana* contains a secret history of mind-alterants in the form of *amrita*, a ritual drink known as the "divine nectar of immortality"), and I wasn't about to give up my enjoyment of marijuana for Zen, even if Japanese Zen monks are notorious for their love of *sake*.

Something that is far more effective for generating radical altered states of consciousness than either meditation or marijuana is, of course, psychedelics. As I mentioned above, my first experience with psilocybin mushrooms came in the summer after my first year of college Zen meditation. It was my girlfriend, Rachel, who left Occidental after her first year, who first suggested that I might enjoy the psychedelic experience afforded by psilocybin. She pointed out another student who had magic mushrooms on his shirt once at a concert that was held on campus and urged me to go talk to him about mushrooms. I only ever got pot from my cousin, or someone else I already knew, and the idea of approaching someone I didn't even know and asking him for drugs seemed beyond the pale, so I didn't act on that advice. It wasn't too long after that, however, that summer came around, and so did some mushrooms. Rachel also suggested that I read Andrew Weil's book, *Natural Mind*, which was my first time reading specifically about drug-induced altered states of consciousness, and I found his approach compelling and reasonable. It made me reflect on my own childhood experiences of altered states, such as lying on the floor and watching the spackled ceiling ebb and flow, my imaginary friends (of which I had several when I was younger), and my desire for insight into the nature of being.

I returned to Chico for the summer. My responsibility was to watch over the house and care for the family dog while my father and step-mom were in Santa Cruz for my dad's annual stint of chemistry research. It was hot – my first summer spent in Chico – my friend Devon was back in town, and I was free of parental supervision. I was working at McDonald's in the drive through, and tended to work nights. When it was time for me to get off work, Devon would come around and we'd either go to the cemetery across the street and smoke a bowl (we had many good times laughing hysterically in that cemetery), or go back to my place to get high and sit up on the roof and look at stars for a few hours.

We also spent a lot of time with our friend Gary, who was tight with the local Rastas and seemed to have an endless supply of herb. It was Gary who told us about this upcoming festival that was going to happen out in the hills of California called "Gathering of the Vibes," and he suggested that we all go and camp out for the weekend. I arranged time off from work, made sure not to tell my parents where I was going or what I was doing, and we headed out for the hills and my very first hippie festival.

These days, summertime is festival season on the west coast. Much of the current scene is inspired by Burning Man and neo-tribalism. Now, in addition to Burning Man, there's Lightning in a Bottle, Beloved, Symbiosis, Enchanted Forest, Fairy Worlds, Mystic Garden, and seemingly countless others. The scene was different back when I was younger. Burning Man was still in its obscure, nascent phases, and the big gatherings were the Rainbow Gathering – an all-hippie event – which is still around, and Reggae on the River. The Gathering of the Vibes was a new entry onto the scene, and promised a weekend of reggae and world beat music with camping, a river to swim in, and vendors. Sounded great, so we went.

The drive out was a bit crazy. Gary was driving, and didn't bother to get directions to where we were going, so we missed our turnoff by at least an hour, and had to turn around and retrace our route. Then, in driving through winding mountain roads, Gary had a serious case of tailgating with the old couple in front of us while he repeatedly took his hands off the steering wheel to light his pipe and take tokes. I found it unnerving and kept thinking about how unhappy my father would be if he knew where I was, whom I was with, and what I was doing. We were committed, however, so there was no turning back.

We finally arrived at the festival site many hours after we had planned on getting there. We took our place in a long line of cars that were seeking entry and settled in to the festival vibe. While still in Gary's vehicle, a man came up to Gary's window and said one word, "Shrooms?" He also held out a bag that was filled with what I now know were just stems and no caps. Gary eagerly purchased the bag and stashed it away for later use. We eventually got parked and set up camp for ourselves, and then went out to enjoy the first night of the festival.

It was located along the Russian River in northern California, and despite the fact that I had gone to Bob Marley Day in Long Beach and Sunsplash at the Hollywood Bowl earlier that year, I had never seen anything like this. To my mind, it was like a scene right out of the 60's. Hippies were everywhere, and many of them were naked, or covered in mud from the river. People were openly bathing in the river, completely unclothed. This was my first experience with public nudity. I couldn't believe that this kind of thing was still happening, as I had mistakenly thought that the 60's ethos had died before my time. I was clearly utterly wrong about that.

People were openly smoking pot everywhere. Even at Bob Marley Day, people were circumspect about pot smoking, as security guards would come and stop you, and possibly get you in trouble, if they saw you. But here, there were no security forces, no police, and everyone was just doing whatever they wanted openly and without a care. It was great. I felt like I was in a time warp or had entered an alternate dimension.

I think it was probably on our second night of the festival that we ate the mushrooms, Gary passing out the stems among the three of us. We munched away and settled in to let the journey begin. Not long after the mushrooms got going, I got separated from Gary and Devon and spent some time wandering around the festival trying to find them. I felt lost, alone, and disoriented. I know now that the mushrooms weren't all that strong, but for my first time, it was unnerving.

Without the presence of my friends to ground me and give me something to reference, I felt adrift. I didn't let it show, but inside, I was quite nervous. I kept forgetting who I was, in a sense, and people seemed so strange and odd. Overall, that was my first impression of mushrooms: just a strange, odd experience. Looking into peoples' eyes, I felt like I could see through them, or see into their deepest thoughts. It was both menacing and strangely attractive and fascinating, and panic threatened to well up at any moment. I kept my cool, however, and wandered around long enough until I found Devon and Gary sitting in the crowd watching the bands play on the main stage. I felt so relieved when I found them. I joined them and sat back to listen to the music. In my relaxation, I started to notice the visual distortions of the mushroom more than I had previously in my search for my friends. Colors were glowing and everything in my vision was breathing and flowing with the music and my breath. I didn't enjoy it as much as I enjoyed marijuana, however, and wondered what the real appeal of mushrooms was when marijuana was, to my mind, so much more pleasant. Mushrooms just seemed strange and alien. I was glad when the experience finally wound down at the end of the night and I felt that I had made it through a minor ordeal. I didn't like the panicky, out-of-control feeling, and it challenged me in ways I hadn't expected.

I was intrigued, however, and wanted to give mushrooms another try. It was maybe a couple weeks later that Devon and I went over to Gary's apartment on the far side of town for another go at the magic fungi. This time things were different in the sense that we weren't out at a festival and we were able to start things in a more controlled environment – well, except for Gary. We ate a decent amount of mushrooms in his small apartment with Gary's ubiquitous dub music pumping out of his sound system. I could tell almost right away that this was going to be stronger than the previous mushroom experience at the festival. It all started with waves of energy building up and crashing in my being. It put the previous experience in perspective and thus I was able to understand it a little bit better.

Just as things were starting to get going, Gary proclaimed that he needed to drive to 7-11 to get something, I forget what. I was never a supporter of Nancy Reagan's "Just Say No" crap, but the thought of getting in a car with someone tripping mushrooms behind the wheel just seemed stupid and dangerous to me, so I declined to join in the outing. Devon was game for the run to the convenience store, however, so the two left me alone in Gary's apartment. That's when the mushrooms really opened up for me.

Though minor in comparison to later journeys I was to have, what unfolded there by myself was a revelation, at the time. Unlike my first mushroom experience, this was strongly visual. At first, just the carpet was growing and waving like tall grass in the wind, but the flowing eventually transformed into intricate geometric patterns, much like an M.C. Escher drawing. Initially, the patterns were confined to the surfaces of things, but they expanded into seemingly empty space, creating complex geometric structures that I felt I was somehow a part of, or inside of. Quite strikingly, and much to my surprise, the intricate interlaced patterns looked distinctly like Celtic knots.

My reaction was something along the lines of, "Oh! This is what all this artwork is about!" Furthermore, the web of knots and geometry all seemed to be alive and conscious, somehow, and also seemed to be interacting with me, which led to the thought of, "This is what people mean by spirits and the spirit world. This is where fairies and sprites come from. This is what all those old stories are about!" It seemed so obvious. There was clearly something more to old fairy tales than just entertaining stories. There were real experiences that they were based on. While I wasn't prepared to make any ontological judgments about the full reality of my experience and insights, the experiences themselves were clearly very real, even if the contents of the experiences might just be reflections of my own mind and consciousness. In other words, while I didn't come away with the view that spirits were real, I certainly now understood that *experiences* of spirits and other forms of consciousness were certainly real.

I was delighted by this, and though still a bit nervous about the whole thing, was enjoying myself more than the previous experience, and also reached the conclusion that taking stronger doses was better than mild doses, as the effects of the mushrooms were more obvious and therefore made more sense. Whereas my first experience I just characterized as odd and strange, this was profound, and quite beautiful, as well. And it just made more sense to me. Rather than merely feeling altered and strange, here I could contemplate and fully immerse myself in the experience, and as such, it felt far more accessible and intelligible, which was certainly counter to any expectations I might have had.

My state of personal revelation and immersion was abruptly interrupted by Gary and Devon's return from 7-11, and typical of Gary, they weren't alone. Gary had randomly invited some college students off the street (He lived on the college side of town, and most of the apartments nearby were filled with Chico State students. At the time, Chico State had a reputation as a major party school, and packs of students tended to wander around from one drinking engagement to the next on weekend nights. Chico State was even named the #1 party school in the nation by *Playboy* and MTV.). Gary had offered to smoke them out. I wasn't too appreciative, as the last thing I wanted was a bunch of strangers hanging out with us while I was undergoing these profound revelations. Fortunately, they only stayed long enough to get high and then move on. I declined partaking of the herb, as I wanted to just experience the mushrooms and not mix them with anything. I wanted to keep the experience pure.

After they left, Gary suddenly realized that he couldn't find his bag of mushrooms, and reached the conclusion that the guys he had just smoked out had stolen them. In a fury, he rushed out of the apartment to go find them, asking people on the street if they had taken a bag of mushrooms. Now I was really uncomfortable. Gary eventually came back in, and promptly found his bag of mushrooms just where he had left them.

It was then that we decided to go for a bike ride. Now that was interesting! We rode out into the local orchards. The only light was that produced by the stars and the lights on our bikes. Such an interesting experience to cruise down the road with so much geometric activity taking place in the beam of my headlight. It made it difficult to tell if there were obstacles in the road or not, but I trusted that the road was open and I was just seeing stuff that wasn't there. When I relaxed into it, it was exhilarating.

We eventually stopped somewhere well out of town. Gary wanted to look at the stars, so he plopped down in the middle of the road, lying on his back, gazing up at the amazing stars. Devon joined him, but I couldn't bring myself to do it. My ever-responsible inner dialog said that lying in the middle of the road on a dark night was a good way to get run over, and was a classically stupid kids-on-drugs kind of move, so I sat down in the orchard and enjoyed the view from there. No cars ever came, so my fear was unwarranted, but it did highlight the difference between Gary and myself and our approach to the experience in general.

After that, we went over to a friend's house. By this time, the mushrooms were well past their peak, and their psychedelic ebb and flow would come and go. *Star Trek the Next Generation* was on, so we sat back to watch some TV. I spent most of my time watching the art on the walls breathe, and found that the more I relaxed into it and focused on the experience, the more intense it became, and that it could almost instantly be dispelled if I shifted my focus and pulled myself together. The evening ended with smoking *bidis* out on the balcony. Overall, I felt that it had been a great mushroom experience, and I was very glad that I hadn't just written mushrooms off as strange and uncomfortable. Clearly, they were something special, and quite profound.

A little later that summer Devon and I got together to enjoy some mushrooms at his house, this time *sans* Gary, something I appreciated. I liked Gary, but he was somewhat unstable, and was always trying to push people into doing things. I was looking forward to being able to experience mushrooms without his anxious and quick-to-overreact presence. Our plan was to watch Val Kilmer's take on Jim Morrison in the film *The Doors.* We munched our mushrooms and settled in with the film.

Right about the time the mushrooms were really coming on (when Val was portraying Jim tripping on peyote), Devon's mom showed up at home. It was awkward. I tried to be casual, sinking back into the couch and avoiding direct eye contact, but she could tell that we were pretty altered. Fortunately, she just let us be and didn't say anything at the time. Things sure would have been different had a similar encounter happened at my house with my dad!

Watching the movie was great. I loved it. No big revelations or insights for this journey – just a very comfortable and entertaining time.

Toward the end of the summer, I bought a bag of mushrooms to take with me to Occidental, intending to share them with my roommate, Chris, who I'd be rooming with again for another year. I thought he'd love them, and was eager to share the experience with a novice. I could hardly wait to eat them, I was so excited.

Chris was game, so we ate them one Friday or Saturday night, very early in the term. I had imagined that we'd spend the evening tripping together, but just as the mushrooms were coming on, Chris disappeared down the hall and was gone. Geometry was everywhere and things were really starting to get going, but now I was all alone and not sure what to do with myself. Obviously my plan to spend the evening with my friend and share that space with him was not going to happen, and I didn't want to just sit in my room, so I decided to stop in at a party I knew was happening at another friend's room in a dorm across campus. Heading over there was fine, but things got weird when I actually got in the room. It was fully lit, for one, and it appeared way too bright to me. It was also crowded with people who were drinking, so I really felt like the odd one out. One student had a pre-release record that he was playing by a band no one had heard of – some band from Seattle called Nirvana and their song, "Smells Like Teen Spirit." The music was a harsher vibe than I was looking for, at that point, though it occurred to me upon listening to it that this was something that was going to change the music scene.

My sense of awkwardness reached its peak when I encountered difficulty taking an overshirt off and attempting to tie it around my waist. I just couldn't accomplish this simple task and, at least to my mind, other students were looking at me and laughing at my strange inability. At that point I left, starting to feel self-critical and far too self-conscious for my liking.

I wandered around campus in the dark with this relentless critical inner dialog of self-doubt and judgment. I just felt like a fool. This wasn't at all the joyous mushroom experience I had been looking forward to. It wasn't necessarily a "bad trip," as I wasn't freaking out or anything – just beating myself up internally.

After what felt like an endless time of this, I made it back to my dorm room, hoping that I might find my roommate there so I could share my experience with him, but alas, no one was there. So, I sat there in the dark playing my guitar with the door open. Some girl was visiting a dorm mate who lived across the hall, and she ended up sitting in my room listening to me play. That went on until the mushrooms finally wound down and things returned back to "normal." I was a little shaken by the experience and was grateful that the relentless inner criticism had finally abated. Playing guitar had helped. Socially, I had long felt like an oddball, and with the guitar, I felt free to express and explore myself in a way that I generally didn't in my social and interpersonal interactions.

My relationship with mushrooms took a turn toward the greatly disturbing shortly thereafter. My girlfriend of the previous year, Rachel, had left Occidental, and with her departure, so ended our relationship. Fairly early on that second year at Occidental, I had noticed this very attractive woman who lived on the floor below mine on the other side of the dorm. It was still my practice to smoke a bowl at midnight and sit down in the dorm lobby and watch old *Star Trek*. One night as I was sitting down there watching by myself, she walked by, stopped, looked at the TV and then back at me and said, "You like *Star Trek*?" clearly not a fan herself. My response was that I found it campy and very entertaining, plus, it had good messages, so yes, I liked Star Trek. I was drinking a cup of instant mocha, and when she asked me what I was drinking, I told her, and offered her a sip. She came down from the landing and sat with me awhile and tried my drink and watched her first episode of *Star Trek.* I learned that her name was Phoebe.

A couple nights later, I was high once again and down in the lobby watching *Saturday Night Live* with a bunch of other students. I was sitting off to the side, by myself, and suddenly there was Phoebe, plopped down next to me, asking me what my plans were for the night. I informed her that I was just getting ready to make one of my nightly trips out to Mt. Fiji to go hang out with the great horned owls up on the hill. She said that was something she'd like to see, so I offered to bring her along, and she agreed. Apparently her roommate urged her against going out with some strange guy she didn't know in the middle of the night, but she disregarded the advice and soon reappeared, ready to head out.

We made the trek up to the top of Mt. Fiji and sat down in front of a dead Eucalyptus tree that the owls favored. Sure enough, one of the owls came and perched on a branch right in front of us, much to Phoebe's delight. Then, as if on cue, a shooting star streaked through the orange L.A. night sky, just beyond the owl. "Kiss her, you fool! Do it now!" I told myself, so I turned to Phoebe, and did it. It was perhaps my most forward advance on a woman in my life at that point. Happily, she responded warmly and we dove deeply into the kiss that night up on Mt. Fiji with the owl and the shooting star.

And that's how Phoebe and I met. I was 18. She was a couple years older, a year ahead of me in school, a psych major, and came from Berkeley. She was adopted and had a sister who was 11 years older who raised horses in northern California. Her mother was a ceramic artist and her father worked for a tech company in the Bay Area. From that point on, we were a couple. Of course, schoolwork kept me busy, so I usually didn't see Phoebe until dinner time, and then again later at night, after 10, when I had completed my studies for the day. Soon after we got together, her roommate quit school and I basically moved in with her, spending most nights in her room, though still I used my room for studying and practicing guitar.

One night, some months later, my relationship with all forms of altered states of consciousness got weird. We were in Phoebe's room watching *The Doors* with some other students. I rarely drank alcohol, but that night we were sipping wine while watching the movie. Phoebe and I were sitting on her bed and I had my back to the wall. We came to the point in the movie where the mushrooms had really kicked in when I had watched the movie with Devon that summer, and I suddenly recalled what the movie had looked and felt like while on mushrooms. Suddenly, everything shifted for me. I thought my head was melting into the wall I was resting it against, and my visual field became fractaled and geometric. It was unmistakable: I was tripping.

In a panic, without saying anything, of course, I got up, excused myself, saying I needed to go to the bathroom, and went into the restroom to splash some water on my face. It didn't help. My heart was racing and energy was bubbling all through my being. Everything in my vision was moving and breathing. Internally, I was railing against myself. "You've really done it now! You've fucked yourself up with drugs, and now you're having a flashback that you can't control and you're losing it!" I had never felt so out of control in my life, and I didn't like it at all.

After some time, I re-entered the room and sat back down to continue watching the film. I was too embarrassed to say anything to anyone and didn't want to let on that internally, I was completely freaking out. The sensation of tripping continued throughout the rest of the film, and gradually subsided after it was over and I was no longer being reminded of that previous mushroom trip. Little did I know, however, that the doors had been opened, and this was to be anything but a one-time-event.

Following this initial onslaught, virtually anything that reminded me of tripping mushrooms could set me off. In order to keep myself grounded, I had to swear off any kind of mind-altering substances. I wasn't a big drinker, only rarely having any kind of alcohol, so that wasn't a problem, but even one hit of herb could set me off, and thus I stopped smoking pot for the remainder of that school year. What was worse, however, was that I didn't need any kind of mind-altering substances to bring on the mushroom experience. Anything that exhibited geometric and fractal forms would do it. Looking at the patterns of leaves on a tree could set me off. Looking at the grass could do it. Looking at rugs with intricate, repeating patterns could do it. It also regularly occurred when I went to meditate.

The episodes were generally accompanied by a wildly racing heart. I was basically having panic attacks, and I even considered that there might be something wrong with my heart. I ended up at a cardiologist's in Pasadena, who kept asking me if I was a cocaine user, which I wasn't. He didn't seem to believe me, however, as he asked me the question repeatedly. He never asked if I had taken psilocybin mushrooms, so I didn't volunteer that information. After receiving a couple heart scans, I was diagnosed with micro-valve prolapse, a heart murmur. It was a convenient diagnosis for the doctors, but was most likely completely bogus. No later doctors have ever heard anything in my heartbeat that would suggest a heart murmur.

Personally, I concluded that these were the fabled "flashbacks" that I had heard about that could afflict psychedelic users. My fear was that I had permanently opened some door that was never going to shut, and that I would be afflicted by these fear-inspiring flashbacks for the rest of my life. The only person I felt I could talk to about it was Devon, who knew my history and I could speak openly with. I certainly didn't want to talk to my doctor, or my family, or my friends at Occidental. So I spent a lot of time with Devon on the phone discussing the issue.

By this time, Devon had left UC Irvine and was now attending the University of Oregon in Eugene. With my permission, Devon consulted with his father, who had been a physician (but lost his license due to drug related issues). Contrary to my fear, Devon's father assured him that I would not suffer debilitating flashbacks for the remainder of my life. I was happy to hear that, though it didn't seem like it, as it was happening to me virtually all the time. I had to muster all my energy to "keep it together" and carry on as though I wasn't undergoing this major, and constant, ordeal.

I think meditation helped, despite the fact that it tended to bring the episodes on. Mostly the shift in consciousness would occur at times that I didn't want it to occur, and this was one of the most disturbing factors of the whole thing. However, when meditating, I was setting aside time to go into myself and my experience, so it was a bit more manageable as there wasn't anything else that I was trying to do, like interact normally with people, or do my school work, or enjoy a conversation. While meditating, it was just myself that I had to grapple with. I wanted to talk to Nori about it, but didn't want to share my drug use with the Buddhist priest, so I said nothing and just endured.

Toward the end of the school year, I eventually learned to simply relax and not freak out when these episodes occurred. It helped when I finally talked to an older student about my episodes, who responded with, "Are you kidding? Free ride, man! Just enjoy it." I found that if I simply relaxed into the sensation of shifting perception and energy, it would generally come in the form of a wave that would slowly peak and then fade away. It was my internal reaction to the events that was causing the racing heart and panicky feelings. It was my own desire to control myself that was really causing the problem, not the shifts in perception. It was up to me to choose how I was reacting. Once I learned to accept this, things got much better. I still had the shifts in awareness, but they weren't freaking me out anymore. I felt so much better. When they happened, they happened, and I just let them be. I still had occasional moments when things pushed me to my edge, but as long as I just stayed calm and accepted what was happening to me, they would come and go and I could carry on. And I no longer felt that I had to hide my internal panic, as it was mostly no longer there. What a tremendous relief!

Looking back on this time now, I see it very differently than when I was going through it. As I now understand it, this was an important part of my process of breaking through my "ordinary" sense of being and perception, and it was vitally important for me to learn to relax, trust, and just let myself be, no matter what my state. I also would not describe these episodes as flashbacks, and would rather describe them as spontaneous openings and endogenous releases of tryptamines in my system. Back then, I had no idea that the human body produces things like DMT and 5-MeO-DMT, or that there was such a thing as an "endogenous release" of psychedelic compounds in the human system. In fact, I now doubt that there really is such a thing as a "flashback" that is triggered by previous use of a psychedelic. Many years later, I was to undergo a very similar process, though it was many orders of magnitude stronger, and in fact, became permanent in many important respects. These days, I can go into a full endogenous 5-MeO-DMT release at the drop of a hat, and it's something that I've become completely comfortable with. I went through several months where I felt as though I were constantly using 5-MeO-DMT, though it was all produced from within. I'll return to this later in my story, as it was still many years from the time I'm describing now.

My relaxing into my new state of being came just in time for summer. My father and step-mom were spending the summer in Santa Cruz again, and I was to watch the house and take care of the dog once more. This time, Phoebe came with me to Chico and stayed with me. Devon also came back from Eugene with his new girlfriend, Jana, and they brought with them Devon's first homegrown crop of marijuana. They brought over a large jar full of some of the best looking pot I had ever seen, and kept it in a cupboard in my kitchen. Whenever we wanted to get high, we simply reached in the jar, loaded up the hookah, and took a toke. It was a fantastic summer of herb, a return to the next Gathering of the Vibes festival (no mushrooms that time, however), and hanging out in Bidwell Park in Chico, lounging in the creek and swimming and hiking. Ah, the carefree days of youth.

Returning back to Occidental in the fall, it was now my third year of college. As I progressed through school, I found that I was increasingly drawn to taking classes in religious studies. Occidental was all about diversity and multi-culturalism – a real bastion of liberal "politically correct" thinking – and I had become somewhat jaded on my studies in philosophy. "Philosophy" basically means "Western philosophy," and is exclusively Euro-American in focus. I felt that this was too limited, and also disrespectful of other cultures and their philosophical systems. The more I learned about Buddhism, the less viable this distinction appeared. My concern was cemented one day when I asked my favorite philosophy professor why we didn't look at the philosophy of other cultures and traditions in our classes, and she answered that, "Only Western culture has philosophy. Other cultures have religion." OK. So I promptly became a religious studies minor while continuing my education in Western philosophy.

The distinction, of course, is completely and utterly bogus and makes absolutely no sense. While much Western philosophy can be distinguished from theology, it was still largely grounded in the religious assumptions and views of the various European cultures from which it came. Take Descartes, for instance. He's very concerned about God and the soul. He wasn't a theologian, but he was clearly writing with basic Christian assumptions about the nature of the world and reality, even if he also served to challenge some of those assumptions. I couldn't accept my professor's claim that this was "philosophy" that was distinct from "religion," whereas Buddhist thinking was purely religious. It was an invalid distinction. But that was how the educational system was set up, and largely still is, with "philosophy" departments teaching Western philosophy and religious studies departments covering everything else from every other culture and tradition. It's an artificial divide and one that deserves to be overcome. Later, when I was a graduate student at UC Santa Barbara and I told my professor, Ninian Smart, about this comment from my previous philosophy professor, his sarcastic, yet playful, response, in typical Ninian fashion, was, "Oh – she must have read a lot of Indian philosophy to be able to reach the conclusion that it didn't count as philosophy." To my knowledge, the professor who originally made the philosophy/religion comment had never read any Indian philosophy, either Hindu or Buddhist.

Thus I increasingly dove into religious studies while also pursuing my undergraduate degree in philosophy.

Inspired by my interest in Buddhism, and my concern for the environment, in addition to focusing on Asian religions, I read everything I could find on Deep Ecology, Environmental Ethics, and Buddhist approaches to the environment, such as the work of Joanna Macy. I was deeply concerned with how people dissociated from "nature" and how the wild had been essentially demonized in Western cultures as the realm of the devil, sin, and wickedness. I was interested in learning about how different senses of self-identity and self-conceptualization created the environment as an "object" that was dissociated from what was taken as "the self" or as "the sacred." It seemed clear that the transcendent focus of much of Western religion, philosophy, and culture was a large part of the problem, whereas the more mystical and more eminent focus of other systems of thought seemed more amenable to addressing environmental problems. To my mind, the Buddhist sense of no-self, co-dependent origination, and impermanence, seemed like the best route for overcoming our collective and individual sense of separation from nature and the world around us.

It was also at this time that I learned about "shamanism," and that there was a whole genre of literature out there about the roles of entheogens in shamanism. That third year of college, I was a resident advisor in one of the dorms, and down the hall there was an interesting fellow who I first met early on in the school year when I passed by his open door and saw him sitting in the middle of the floor, smoking a bong. I was very open about my love for marijuana, and had a reputation as a legalization advocate, passing out information and leaflets and telling people about hemp and the medical value of marijuana – something I knew from personal experience. (After my parents got divorced, I started suffering from seasonal allergies upon returning to Chico to live with my dad, and part of that suffering included very severe asthma. I had tried all kinds of inhalers and asthma medicines, none of which ever seemed to do me any good, and I could go through seriously frightening bouts of asthma where I could barely breath and would be coughing up massive amounts of phlegm, fearing that I would suffocate. As a teenager, I discovered, much to my delight, that whenever I felt an asthma attack coming on, all I needed to do was take a couple hits of pot and the asthma would immediately abate, allowing me to breathe and function normally. Personally, I do not know of any pharmaceutical that is as effective in treating asthma as marijuana.) I also arranged to have Jack Herer, author of *The Emperor Wears No Clothes,* come and speak at my dorm. He smoked me out in the parking lot of my dorm, and also brought some tasty hemp seed brownies for us to enjoy as edible, but non-psychoactive, treats.

Despite my openness about marijuana, I couldn't just let some guy openly smoke his bong with the door open, so I approached the student. As it turned out, he wasn't smoking pot – only white sage – and he invited me to give it a try. So, we got to talking, and after a few conversations, he told me about this writer, Carlos Castaneda, whom he thought I would really enjoy reading. I made a note that I'd look for his books on my next trip to the Bodhi Tree bookstore in Hollywood. I did look, and I did find them, in the non-fiction section, of course, and thus began my avid consumption of Carlos Castenada books. I became aware of the controversy around the authenticity of Castaneda's works early on, but there was a professor at Occidental who had known Carlos, and he told me that he thought the books were genuine. Later, as a grad student, one of my professors had also known Carlos Castenada, and she told me that she had outright asked Carlos whether the books were true or not, and he confessed to her that he had invented the character of Don Juan and that indeed, they were largely fiction.

Nevertheless, the books were sold and marketed as non-fiction, and still are. Really, they belong in the fantasy section of the bookstore. They aren't even remotely true, anthropologically speaking. Carlos Castenada was an anthropology student at UCLA, and there's pretty damning evidence that he stole materials and plagiarized his fellow anthro students such as Barbara Myerhoff and Peter Furst, both of whom where studying with the Huichols of Mexico. Carlos invented this "Yaqui Indian Sorcerer" of Don Juan Matus, and just ripped off materials from other students, as well as from his eclectic reading collection. He created this wild New Age fantasy of the "the second attention" and about being a "man of power," all marketed toward gullible New Age readers – and they are terribly gullible. You can tell New Agers virtually anything and they are likely to believe it if it seems to fit within their patchwork worldviews of mix-and-match metaphysics and spirituality. Especially if you tell them it comes from an ancient or indigenous culture, or was channeled, or revealed in some vision, or any other exotic claim. Masters of discernment New Agers are not. They're like Fox Mulder's poster in his FBI office on the *X-Files*: they want to believe.

The modern New Age movement finds its roots in the 19th century Theosophy movement in Europe, which had a deep fascination with all things "esoteric" and "Oriental." It is from Theosophists, for example, that we derive the contemporary fascination with the "chakras" in New Age circles (which are almost universally mispronounced as "shakras"). Spelled properly as *cakras,* and pronounced with a "ch" sound (as in "chicken"), most contemporary New Agers assume that cakras are real things and are often equated with what is characterized as Indian "mind science" and "esoteric wisdom." According to New Agers, following in the footsteps of Theosophists, the cakras exist as part of the "subtle body" and are associated with rainbow colors, are seven in number, and have specific *mantras* that are associated with each, and they are understood as a fundamental aspect of human spiritual makeup. These days, you can go into virtually any New Age bookstore or yoga center and find a seven-cakra model with rainbow colors, and this formulation is prevalent in many examples of New Age art and iconography as well.

There are several problems with this cultural trend. For starters, there is the assumption that these cakras are somehow "scientific." They are not. In order for something to be classified as scientific, it must be open to observation and confirmation by non-biased observers, and such cannot be claimed for cakras. It is quite telling that in Indian traditions, there is *no uniformity in either the number or quality of cakras*. Some Indian systems claim that there are seven cakras; others claim that there are nine; still others claim that there are five; and some claim that there are three. Furthermore, there is *no*

Indian source that depicts the seven cakras as associated with rainbow colors – *this is purely an invention of Western enthusiasts.* In other words, this system is clearly a creation, not a scientific discovery in any sense, and it is not even backed up by actual traditions that come from India. It is a contrivance of the West.

The situation is made even more problematic when one learns that not even all the Indian traditions that posit the "existence" of cakras consider them to be objectively real in any sense. In some schools of Buddhist *Tantra,* for example, the cakras are largely understood to be conventional constructs of the mind that are useful for meditative purposes, but are not understood to have any inherent existence outside of the contrivance of the meditator's mind. In this case, they are understood as a projection and not objectively real. In this sense, they are understood more as an art than as a "science."

Furthermore, there is no uniform agreement among Indian traditions about how the cakras work, what mantras are associated with each, what colors best represent them, or even how they are associated with supposed subtle energies. According to *Kundalini* practitioners, a serpent energy awakens at the base of the spine and progressively moves up the cakras to the crown to produce an experience of enlightenment. According to Tibetan Buddhists, subtle drops of consciousness exist in the base and crown cakra that must be drawn into the heart cakra, where, when combined, produce an experience of enlightenment. These two systems are in complete disagreement with each other over how these supposed subtle energy centers function, how one is to go about manipulating them, and how one generates effects from them. If it were scientific, there would be more agreement. Instead of verifiable scientific objectivity, what we find are subjective formulations that are contradictory, incompatible, and largely disparate. There is no universal "system" here – just different collections of metaphysical beliefs and practices.

However, in the modern New Age West, the seven-cakra rainbow system is largely assumed to be simply "true," "valid," and "universal," and those who would reject their objective existence are deemed to be "closed-minded" and "ignorant" of subtle bodies and energies. Moving beyond any Indian sources, many New Agers have also expanded on this formula to invent various forms of "color" and "sound" therapies that supposedly coincide with the colors and "vibrations" of the cakras, and also includes various forms of crystal therapy – none of which has any basis in Indian metaphysics. Furthermore, this model is greatly simplified from the various Indian versions where the individual cakras are described and depicted in intricate detail, where each cakra is a complex mix of colors and iconography rather than the simplified rainbow version. In Tantric Buddhism, for example, practitioners are only expected to be able to effectively visualize the cakras in minute detail and all their complexity after many years of intense training in visualization techniques. In this context, the cakras are understood as mental constructs, not an objective reality, and are intentional manipulations of the highly malleable human energetic system.

Overall, in the western context, especially, cakras are an invention that has no basis in scientific observation or inquiry, is purely a contrived metaphysics, and is not objectively true in any sense. None of this, however, stops anyone from believing in them, for it fits New Age identities as being "enlightened" and tuned in to subtle energies.

Like other New Agers, Carlos Castaneda found inspiration in the writings of the Theosophists and used their works to help create the fiction of Don Juan, the imaginary "Yaqui sorcerer." Real anthropologists and students of Native American cultures will tell you that there is absolutely nothing authentically Yaqui about anything in Castaneda's books. As such, it is a fantasy of projection of the "mystical other" that is completely divorced from Yaqui reality, history, or identity. Though it *seems* to be supportive of "indigenous views," it is actually an extension of colonial hegemony through projection and cultural appropriation. Additionally, aside from these cultural problems, whole passages are obviously plagiarized from other, non-Native, sources, sometimes even copied word-for-word from other authors' works. It's total bullshit, marketed as "ancient wisdom," eagerly consumed by white folks looking to be spiritual and "enlightened," un-encumbered by the "dominant paradigm" of rationality, logic, and scientific materialism. It's ready-made for people looking to forge an eclectic and multicultural spiritual identity, and as such, is excellent fodder for the naïve ego.

What can I say? Like many other spiritual seekers, I bought it. I loved the books and gobbled them up, one after another. His first book fascinated me as it dealt with accounts of consuming mushrooms, the extremely dangerous datura, and peyote. Despite his reputation, it was really only that first book, of nine, I believe, that dealt with entheogens to any degree, and there's essentially no mention of entheogens in the following books. I found this disappointing, as I was hoping to learn more about what I had gone through in the previous year with my own "flashback" issue. I also found that the books were increasingly inconsistent as they went along, with conflicting timelines, characters, and an excessively confusing metaphysical mumbo-jumbo presentation that just got stranger and stranger. Still, it was interesting reading, and for the next two years, I read all of Castaneda's books between my heavy load of school-related readings and assignments, though with each subsequent book, my suspicion that it was all bullshit continued to grow. I finally accepted this in my first year of grad school with the comment from the aforementioned professor that she had confronted Castenada about the truth of his books and he had admitted their fictional nature. Up until then, I thought that there might be elements that were true, and even hoped were true.

I think it was my fourth and final year as an undergrad that I then moved on to reading Terence McKenna, after getting my fill of Carlos Castenada. I was reading everything I could find about shamanism, psychedelics, and altered states of consciousness. I don't remember if someone suggested McKenna to me, or if I just came across him in one of my regular trips to the bookstore to find new materials to read, but somehow I found his *Food of the Gods*, and read it enthusiastically. He seemed academic enough to be legit, and certainly had a lot of footnotes and citations, unlike Castenada (McKenna later admitted that he had constructed this book intentionally as an "academic Trojan horse," filling it with obscure footnotes and citations simply to throw academics off). I was also reading Peter Furst, Barbara Myerhoff, and Marlene Dobkin De Rios. My father, keeping track of my interests, had purchased the book, *The Shaman's Apprentice,* by Mark Plotkin, and gave it to me as a gift (I think he thought this book was more scientific than some of the other stuff I was reading, and thus was doing his part to try and keep my interests academically legitimate). Pretty much everything I was reading was exotic – I had only ever experienced psilocybin mushrooms, and I was reading all these materials about datura and peyote and ayahuasca and the like, but I read it all with great enthusiasm and wondered why we didn't get to read stuff like this in school, or why there were no classes being offered specifically on shamanism or entheogens in religion and spiritual traditions, for clearly this existed out there in the world, but no one taught it or included such materials in their syllabi. Why couldn't we learn about this in school?

These readings also led me to Michael Harner's book, *Way of the Shaman,* which I originally read in the summer between Occidental and starting graduate school at UC Santa Barbara in the fall of 1994. All of these readings, and my own bout with spontaneous psychedelic experiences, started to make me think that perhaps I had the natural inclination to be a shaman myself. Maybe Zen Buddhism wasn't the fulfillment of my spiritual aspirations that I had thought. Maybe shamanism was the thing for me.

Shamanism and Zen are not necessarily compatible. Whereas Zen is a practice of self-exploration and analysis that focuses on the fundamentally nondual nature of being, shamanism is thoroughly dualistic and would be regarded by Zen practitioners as indulging in *samsara* and the realm of *maya,* or illusion. The historian of religion, Mircea Eliade, identified shamanism as an "archaic technique of ecstasy," and by "ecstasy," he meant "soul" or "out-of-body" travel. Shamanism is predicated on the belief in souls and spirits that reside in a nebulous "spirit world" that can be contacted for knowledge, healing, and insight, and can also inhabit the shaman's body in states of possession, channeling, and mediumship. Unlike Zen, shamanism generally posits that there is a "fundamental" spiritual self that travels between worlds and can make meaningful contact with other "fundamental selves" in the forms of spirits. There is an ontological divide between "self" and "other" in shamanism – indeed, the entire practice is built around contact with the "mysterious other." Zen seeks to go beyond such illusory dualistic distinctions so that the meditator can enter directly into the natural, nondual state of awareness where the divide between subject and object disappears and reality is experienced from its most fundamental and authentic level – it is this experience that leads to enlightenment. Shamanism is not concerned with enlightenment – it's about working with spirits. Historically, Buddhists have regarded shamanic practice as steeped in superstition and false thinking, and Buddhists made a strong effort to convert the shamanic cultures of Asia to their way of thinking, practicing, and identifying.

Despite these incompatibilities, my interest in shamanism grew; largely because here was an identity and practice that, while not universally, commonly accepted entheogens as a legitimate route to knowledge and practice. Inspired by the urgings of people like McKenna to forge a new practice of neo-shamanism that would serve as an "archaic revival" that would be fundamental in saving the world from the folly of Western civilization, I thought that shamanism might be the path for me.

McKenna, like many other New Agers and counter-culturalists, promotes a fairly common narrative that goes something like this: Western culture is bad for the reasons of X, Y, and Z, and Indigenous and Non-Western cultures are good because they are more in balance with the earth and possess deep esoteric wisdom, and by following their ways, we Westerners will be able to heal our relationship with the earth, usher in a new age of enlightenment and peace, and will evolve into a new form of human that is "galactic" in nature. While the specific characters change, the basic narrative stays the same. However, in this story, most of what is taken as Indigenous or Non-Western wisdom is largely a projection and fabrication of Western observers, so really, it's all a self-reflection and critique that has very little to do with the exotic other and is more a self-generated fantasy. As such, it is a narrative and discourse that is generated and sustained by the ego, and has very little to do with any kind of objective or verifiable reality. The recent New Age fascination with "2012" is a perfect case in point, and is merely another example of projection and ego-based storytelling.

Like other naïve spiritual seekers, I didn't understand any of this at the time, and psychedelic gurus like Terence McKenna really spoke to me – or more specifically, spoke to my ego and my budding sense of spiritual identity. I, too, was critical of what I perceived as the shortfalls and defects of "Western" civilization, and I, too, found inspiration and "wisdom" in the Non-Western world. It was a perfect fit for my chosen identity as someone who saw through the deceptions of his culture and who wanted to identify with the dispossessed and disrespected "other," whether that be Non-Western religions or Indigenous spirituality. It helped me to construct an identity that said, "I'm not *that* bad stuff, I'm *this* good stuff. Because I care deeply about the fate of the world, I'm a *shaman.*" It was ego-based dualism, through and through, and miraculously, it was all built around the image of being non-egoic in nature, for it was "enlightened" and "selfless." Ah, the ego will believe just about anything, especially if it paints itself as being on the enlightened side of the equation!

Meanwhile, there started to be trouble in my relationship with Phoebe. Looking back now, what was probably the high point (no pun intended) in our relationship was a trip we took to Eugene on the spring break of my jr. year, her senior year, of college. We made the long drive to Oregon to visit Devon and Jana, and made plans to take mushrooms – Phoebe's first time. It started out as a grueling experience for Phoebe. Almost immediately, all kinds of fear started arising within her. We all went outside as the mushrooms were coming on, thinking that some fresh air might help Phoebe relax. It didn't, as she kept seeing demonic, mocking faces in the leaves of a nearby tree. So we went back inside, and the panic was just welling up within her. Jana was the "sitter," so it was only Devon, Phoebe, and myself who were taking the mushrooms. I remember Jana hovering over Phoebe and myself – she seemed all Cheshire Cat smiles and too many eyeballs to me, and Devon just sat and stared at Phoebe with a big grin on his face, trying to help her feel more comfortable. Eventually, Jana took Devon into the shower, and when Devon exclaimed that Phoebe really should try the shower herself, we moved off the couch and into the bathroom where Phoebe started playing with the water in the sink. She loved it and finally relaxed into the mushroom experience. She had suddenly found the joy of the altered state of perception, and now, after several hours of suffering, she was finally having a good time.

From the bathroom we moved into the bedroom and lounged on the bed, staring at a tapestry on the wall. For a time, there in Devon and Jana's bedroom, it felt like we were one being, sharing the same reality, and that there were no barriers between us in any way. We were two different people, but essentially the same being, simultaneously enjoying itself from two different, though intertwined, perspectives. It was profoundly beautiful and touched me in a way that no previous experience with another person ever had. I had never felt such intimacy or closeness to another human, and it just felt right. We had never before been so close, and we were never to be that close again. In a sense, it was all downhill from there, though it took many more years for our relationship to fully dissolve.

The trouble really started that summer. Phoebe had finished her undergraduate studies and I still had one more year to go. She had applied to, and was accepted in, the M.A. in Education program at Occidental, where she was going to get her teaching credential. Because she would be continuing on at Occidental, we had decided to take a student trip together for the summer. The plan was to participate in a program that would take us to west Africa, doing good and helping to save the world and all that kind of thing. However, Phoebe's mother was suffering from breast cancer, and the diagnosis didn't look good, so we cancelled our plans in order for Phoebe to be closer to her mother and not be on the other side of the world, should something happen. Looking back now, I think that had I decided to go to Africa anyway, things might have turned out differently for Phoebe and myself – maybe, maybe not. There isn't much use in second-guessing the past, and I certainly do not regret in any way how things turned out, so it isn't that I'd like things to have gone differently. I only note this as it was part of my habit of compromising myself for the sake of others, or relationships, in ways that were not actually authentic to my own desires. I wanted to go to Africa, not Berkeley. For the sake of our relationship, and to support Phoebe, I chose to go with her to Berkeley for the summer.

Something that I had "learned" from my parents' relationship and divorce was that making waves in a relationship was not good, and that making compromises to help someone else feel good was desirable. My studies of Buddhism and the emphasis on compassion and doing for others also played into this decision I had made of how to be in a relationship. So, I chose not to act on my desires and instead agreed to go to Berkeley for the summer because that was the "selfless" thing to do.

It was there that our relationship started to suffer, and it began our downhill slide into disconnection, frustration, and lack of fulfillment in each other and ourselves. We were staying in Phoebe's childhood room in the two beds in which she and her sister used to sleep. For the past couple years, we had shared a bed, and now, we were in a sleeping arrangement that was like something out of a 50's sitcom. That meant that any sexual contact between us had to be intentional rather than spontaneous and natural, and the issue was compounded by the fact that Phoebe was not comfortable having sex in her parents' house or in her childhood bed. Thus began the "not now" response from Phoebe. Prior to this time, we had had a robust sexual relationship. Much to my personal amazement, I would regularly orgasm two or three times per love making session, and we had sex at least once a day. We also regularly kissed passionately and tended to sleep in each other's arms. The arrangement at her parents' house put an end to all of that. I don't recall if we ever had sex that summer. If we did, it certainly wasn't memorable. Rather, what comes to mind is my increasing frustration and feelings of being constantly rejected.

The situation was made worse by Phoebe's mom encouraging her to read her personal journal. In it were numerous accounts of how Phoebe's mom wished that Phoebe was more like this child, or that child, and how she felt that Phoebe wasn't interested in the arts, like herself, and how she enjoyed spending time with other peoples' children more than Phoebe. Reading this devastated Phoebe, and it hurt her tremendously, feeling that her dying mother had never understood her, nor given her a chance. It seemed to Phoebe that her mother regretted having adopted her, and her sense of self-worth and value was plummeting, all while she was doing her very best to care for her cancer-inflicted mother.

At any rate, a distance grew between us that summer that we were never able to transcend, despite the fact that we were to go on to marry a few years later and have two children together. Realistically, our romantic and loving relationship was over by the end of that summer, and if I had been stronger in my commitment to caring for and loving myself, I would have ended our relationship sometime during my senior year of college. The thought of dumping someone whose mother was dying of cancer seemed cruel, however, and the last thing I wanted was to be the cause of someone else's heartache and suffering. So, I took it on as my "spiritual" burden to help me be more compassionate, more giving, more selfless. I used every tool at my disposal to convince myself that this lackluster relationship was actually good for me and was serving me spiritually. In other words, I lied to myself in order to rationalize why I was too afraid to act on my desire to end the relationship and move on, and instead of following my heart, I held on to my self-constructed image of what I thought a spiritually aware person would do. The last thing I wanted was to be the "bad guy," or do anything that might be perceived by others as being selfish and uncaring. Also, as the reader may recall, there was that girlfriend in high school that had become suicidal upon our break up, so I knew what emotionally vulnerable people were capable of when rejected (not to mention my mother's reaction to her divorce). It wasn't as though I thought Phoebe would react similarly, but the experience had made a deep impact on me, and I tended to treat relationships tenderly and with caution, never being sure of how to end things when they were already over.

With the coming conclusion of my time as an undergraduate, it was time for me to start looking for a grad school. It had always been my assumption that I would go on to grad school and get my advanced degree. The idea of "taking time off" never occurred to me, and I didn't know what I'd do, anyway, if I did. Going to grad school was simply the next obvious step, so that's what I planned on doing.

By this time, I was spending more and more time in the religious studies department, and went to my professors there for advice on where to apply for grad school. My choices came down to the following: Stanford (which was a long shot), The University of Hawaii, where there was a program in their philosophy department that offered a degree in Buddhist philosophy, and the University of California, Santa Barbara.

Stanford came back as a rejection. I was accepted to the University of Hawaii, and waitlisted at UCSB. For a time, it looked like I would be going to Hawaii, and if I had, it might have been the end of my relationship with Phoebe. She insisted that she would not be coming with me to Hawaii, as she didn't want to be that far away from her ailing mother. So if I was going to go, it was going to be on my own. I think she was surprised when I responded that if that was going to be the way of things, then so be it. Regardless of what she wanted to do, I was going to go to graduate school. This was one area in which I had no intention of compromising.

Phoebe was relieved, and I was very happy as well, when my waitlist number finally came up for UCSB, which was my preference over Hawaii anyway, and I was accepted into the program. At the end of that school year, we packed up our things from Occidental and made the move up the coast to beautiful Santa Barbara, the American Riviera, and I once again returned to the place of my birth. I reunited with an old childhood friend, Rod, whose parents had befriended my parents first in Santiago, Chile, and then had moved to Santa Barbara with my parents upon their return from South

America. Rod was a deadhead, a philosophy major at UCSB, and an avid pot smoker. It was like coming home and reuniting with a long-lost brother. Despite the lackluster relationship that Phoebe and I shared, things were otherwise looking good, and I was ready to embark upon the next stage of my educational journey and search for That Which Is.

CHAPTER THREE

THE TRIALS OF GRADUATE SCHOOL

Phoebe and I moved into a small apartment just beyond Isla Vista in Goleta, outside of Santa Barbara proper. After living four years in L.A., it was heaven. Just down the street, the apartments came to an end, and beyond was a marsh, groves of Eucalyptus trees, and then bluffs and the beach. From the bluffs, we could regularly see dolphins and whales, along with sea lions and all kinds of shorebirds. The open fields were populated by foxes, kites, red tail hawks, and kestrels. There was, and still is, a grove of trees that are regularly inhabited by migrating Monarch butterflies nearby, and many trails and paths wound their ways through the fields and trees. It was only a short bike ride to campus from our place, and a 7-11 was just up the street for midnight snack runs. It was great.

I started working with a political activist group, Peace Action, which was going door-to-door in the area to work on issues of nuclear proliferation, U.S. weapon sales, and the grossly over-bloated U.S. military budget. One day, when seeing me off to work, Phoebe and I shared our first passionate kiss in over a year. It was also the last real kiss we ever shared, despite the fact that we would be together for more than a decade beyond this point and were still to get married and have children together.

That summer, prior to starting school, was when I first got into Michael Harner's book, *Way of the Shaman.* It seemed to me that thing called "shamanism" might be a good fit for me, as in some ways, I fit the profile. I had had several "imaginary friends" as a child, had a strong visual imagination, had a proclivity for altered states of consciousness and lucid dreaming, had a strong sense of empathy and desire to help others, and through my bout with the "flashback" issue, had undergone a traumatic mental break and reintegration that somewhat fit the "self-healed" archetype of the shaman. After we moved into our place in Goleta, I started practicing Harner's "core shamanism" program of going on "shamanic journeys" to "discover my power animal" by sealing myself in our closet with rapid drum beat tracks while I closed my eyes and let the inner journey unfold.

Phoebe was rather skeptical of the whole thing, asking me what I was doing, and why. My answer was that I wanted to see what would happen, and what I might learn. It was something of an experiment, and a way for me to explore my own spirituality.

Honestly, it never felt that authentic to me. Most of what came up in those closet sessions seemed purely self-generated, like consciously directing a dream or fantasy. It never really felt "real."

There were some interesting developments, however. Early on in this process, I identified the golden eagle as my "power animal" and shape-shifting alter-identity. I would often experience myself as an eagle, flying about and doing various things. I liked that, as I had gotten into bird watching and was an avid sky-watcher, always looking out for the next bird of prey or species of bird I hadn't yet checked off my life list. During that first year in Santa Barbara, I performed these shamanic journey sessions once a week, generally after spending 20-30 minutes meditating. I took copious notes afterward, which I probably have stashed away somewhere in a box in the garage. Mostly the material that was generated from these sessions seems largely irrelevant now, except for my final time performing these specific practices.

In that last session, I found myself looking out on what seemed to be the surface of a planet, somewhere out in space with a cosmic backdrop. Looking out at the stars, I saw my eagle start to approach where I was standing, or where my point of view was located. The eagle flew up and landed on the ground, and where it landed, all these mushrooms suddenly sprouted up. The eagle bent over and munched away at the mushrooms. It then turned into rainbow light that swirled around the disappearing image of the bird, and then formed into a rainbow light image of myself, standing and facing me. The rainbow me then said, "If you want to visit with the eagle, eat the mushrooms." Message received. That was the last time I ever bothered to shut myself up in a dark closet and do Harner's "core shamanism" practices, and looked forward to my next journey with the mushrooms, as that was unambiguously the thing I was telling myself to do.

The school year started off with a bang. Occidental had seemed like a heavy study load, but now that I was in grad school, Occidental appeared light and relaxed. Now I had some serious reading to do, and once again, unlike most other students, I read every word of every page, always the diligent and devoted student.

In my first term, I was delighted to be able to take a class on "Comparative Mysticism." Now *this* was the kind of education I had been looking for! It was in this class that there was an interesting turn of events that was to shape much of my life to come, both as a student, and beyond. For this class, all the students were required to do a research report and presentation on a mystic. For the assignment, the professor had compiled a list of different mystics from different traditions. He passed the list around the class, asking us all to sign up for one. The paper was going clockwise around the table and the woman sitting just to my right chose Nagarjuna, the only Buddhist on the list. When the paper came to me, I asked if it was OK for me to do Nagarjuna as well, for I wanted to focus on Buddhist philosophy in grad school and wanted to dive right into my chosen subject. The professor answered that it was to be only one student per mystic, and that I'd have to choose someone else. I wasn't inspired by any of the other names on the list – most I had never even heard of – so it was then that I proposed that I could do a Native American mystic, something that was absent from the list. Privately, I was thinking I could do Don Juan of Carlos Castenada fame. The professor liked my idea, but said that I'd need to go meet with the professor who taught Native American religions to get suggestions about a good Native American mystic to use for my research project.

I got the professor's name, found her office, and noted her office hours. A few days later, we met for the first time. I'll call her "Professor X," for reasons that will become clear. Her specialty was the female initiation ceremony of the Mescalero Apache people, a group she claimed to share ancestry with. It was many years later that I was to learn that many Mescaleros living on the reservation didn't share this opinion of Professor X, somewhat disparagingly referring to her as, "A Mexican," but I knew nothing of this at the time that I began working with her and took her claims of Mescalero ancestry at face value and without any skepticism. When we first met, she had been working on a book on what Mescaleros called "The Big Tipi," a ceremony held for girls upon reaching puberty that would initiate them into adulthood and educate them in the history, culture, and traditions of the Mescalero people. She had been working on the book for 20 years when we first met in 1994. To my knowledge, the manuscript remains incomplete and is as-yet still unpublished.

Mescalero Apaches live on a reservation in south-central New Mexico. The tribe (they don't refer to themselves as a "nation") is comprised of several originally distinct Apache cultures: Mescalero, Chiricahua, and Lipan Apache. The reservation is located in the heart of traditional Mescalero territory. The Lipans were originally from areas around the Texas/Mexico border. Most were killed, and only a small band survived the conflicts of the wild west to eventually join with the Mescaleros on their reservation. The Chiricahuas came to Mescalero after they were released as extended prisoners of war by the U.S. Federal government. Geronimo, a renegade medicine man (he was never a chief, despite this common erroneous assumption), had led an ongoing revolt among the Chiricahuas, protesting their confinement to a reservation in Arizona among the Western Apaches. There was a time when one quarter of the standing army in the U.S. was running around the Southwest trying to capture Geronimo and his small band of followers. The army was not successful, however, and the U.S. ended up hiring other Chiricahuas to hunt down and capture Geronimo. When they brought Geronimo in, along with his 29 followers, the entire population of Chiricahuas was taken as prisoners of war, even those who lived peacefully on the reservation, and were shipped off via train to a prison in Florida. To add insult to injury, the Chiricahuas who served as Apache Scouts in the army, and who had brought in Geronimo, were also shipped out as prisoners with the very people they had helped to capture. Every last man, woman, and child among the Chiricahuas thus lived some 25 years as prisoners of war. When they were finally granted release, they were given the choice of living in "Indian Territory" in Oklahoma, or they could return to New Mexico, not on their own reservation, but could live with the Mescaleros on theirs. Some, such as Geronimo, chose to remain in Oklahoma, and others went to Mescalero. In the long run, it was those who returned to Mescalero who were able to hold onto their language, culture, and traditions, whereas the descendants of those who remained in Oklahoma lost their language and ceremonies, mostly becoming farmers and ranchers.

Today, most everyone on the Mescalero reservation is of mixed ancestry between these various Apache groups, and there have been numerous intermarriages with Navajos and other Native peoples of the Southwest, with a great deal of Pueblo blood in the mix as well. Collectively, they are known as the Mescalero Apache Tribe. Their name does not come from the tribe being fond of peyote, as some people assume, and they are not named after mescaline. There are a variety of different plants in the Southwest that share the name "mescal." The Mescaleros got their name originally from Spanish explorers who first encountered them and found that their main food staple was the mescal plant, or agave. Mescaleros harvest mescal in the desert and then cook it in an earth oven for four days. It can then be eaten warm, or dried out and stored for later use. Today, many people are familiar with the taste of mescal due to the recent popularity of agave nectar as an alternative sweetener, and it is readily available in most grocery stories in the baking aisle. The Mescaleros are, therefore, the people who eat mescal, and are not peyoteros.

I had first read about the Mescaleros in Winston LaBarre's book, *The Peyote Cult,* the summer prior to starting grad school. In that book, LaBarre describes Mescaleros as a transitional culture in the spread of what was to become the Peyote Church, or Native American Church, a pan-Indian religious practice that combines elements of indigenous peyoteism and Christianity. Peyote grows in the desert in northern Mexico and parts of Texas. Pre-contact, its use was mostly confined to cultures in those areas and was not popular throughout Native America, as it is today. In the early reservation period, Mescaleros began experimenting with peyote, and through them, use of the cactus spread into more northern parts of the Southwest. I've now been to a few different peyote meetings with a local branch of the Native American Church, and to my ears, I can hear influences from Mescalero traditional songs in many of the peyote songs that are sung in ceremony today. The Mescaleros, however, decided that peyote use conflicted with their traditional religion, and use on the reservation eventually declined.

Today, there are many Mescaleros who still participate in the Native American Church, but tipi meetings are not held on the Mescalero reservation, and thus they travel north to Navajo country where the Native American Church is openly practiced on the sprawling Navajo reservation. During my time of fieldwork research at Mescalero, I also learned through one of my medicine teachers, an old medicine woman named Meredith Begay, that the Lipan Apache had their own distinct form of peyoteism that was not connected to the Native American Church, but it had died out with the destruction of their culture by Texans and Mexicans. One of my medicine teachers, Willeto Antonio, considered peyoteism to be "make-believe religion," though he had only attended a peyote ceremony once, and had not eaten any of the medicine, so he wasn't speaking from personal experience. Also, Mescalero medicine people all keep mescal beans (which come from yet another plant) as part of their ceremonial regalia and ritual tools, but despite the fact that the red, orange, and purple mescal beans are psychoactive, they are not used in that way by the Mescalero, for whom they are more symbolic.

To return to my story, Professor X suggested Lame Deer, a Lakota, as a good Native American mystic to research for my project in the Comparative Mysticism class, and I eagerly took her advice. This was my initial foray into studying Lakota culture, which was eventually to become the focus of my Master's thesis. It was then that I was introduced to the Sun Dance, vision quests, Yuwipi ceremonies, sweat lodge, dreaming, and the acquisition of helping spirits in the cultures of the American Great Plains. As usual, I read everything I could find on the subject and found it to be more than suitable for my Comparative Mysticism project.

This was also the beginning of my tutelage under Professor X, something that was to shape the entire trajectory of my time as a graduate student at UCSB. Somewhat ironically, the professor of that Comparative Mysticism class who originally directed me to Professor X pulled me aside in the hallway one day after I started working with her more and gave me a stern warning. "She screws students over," he warned me. "My best advice is not to work with her. You'll regret it. Stay away from her." My own sense of being "special" got in the way, and I dismissed the stern warnings. "She wouldn't be like that *with me*," I foolishly told myself.

It seemed hard to believe. Here was a professor I could be completely open with. I told her all about my experiences with mushrooms, my interest in entheogens and shamanism, and my desire to cultivate my own spiritual abilities. "Well," she had responded, "it sounds like it's about time you met some real medicine men then." And with that, she invited me to go out to Mescalero with her that summer and meet some people. Nothing bad could come from that, could it?

It was also from those early conversations with Professor X that I learned that Carlos Castaneda was considered a fraud, charlatan, and plagiarist by most academics who worked in the field of Native American studies. She gave me names and titles of works to research that definitively showed the fraud in his work, and after that, I considered the case to be settled. In Native Studies circles, Castenada was considered to be a prime example of how non-Natives appropriate Native cultures, traditions, and identities to sell books to a non-Native and largely ignorant New Age audience. He wasn't the only one, and there were plenty of other examples, such as Lynn Andrews, who was also popular, at the time. Despite these authors' popularity among New Age readers, they were widely disparaged in the Native Studies community, and Professor X urged me away from reading such material. She also let me know that Terence McKenna fit into this camp and was considered a pseudo-academic, at best, and was yet another author who was using Native spirituality to sell books and construct a countercultural image for himself with his interest in entheogens, shamanism, and ayahuasca. Anyone familiar with countercultural and New Age authors today, almost 20 years later, can easily see that nothing has changed, and indigenous cultures and traditions are still widely appropriated by non-Natives to construct identities and sell books. The recent 2012 obsession is a perfect case in point, with authors like Daniel Pinchbeck heralding it as the return of the "Mayan" (Aztec, actually) deity, Quetzalcoatl, basically picking up where Terence McKenna left off with his fantasies about 2012 being the "end of time and history," something supposedly supported by indigenous "prophecy." For indigenous cultures, the history of oppression and cultural appropriation is still very much a reality and something that they continually struggle against.

My first meeting with members of the Mescalero Apache tribe came early that spring in Santa Cruz. Professor X's daughter was attending UCSC at the time and had arranged to bring out a group of Mescalero Apache Mountain Spirit dancers and ceremonial singers to perform a ceremony on the UCSC campus. My uncle owned a home in Aptos, not far from UCSC, so I made arrangements for a group of us students to stay there for the weekend and attend the ceremonies at the university. It was then that I started to learn that hanging out with students of Professor X was like joining a therapy group for children of abusive parents, for virtually everyone had stories to share about how they had been frustrated by their work with her. However, they all wanted to learn about Native American religions and cultures, and Professor X was the only professor who taught the subject (something that is very seldom taught in religious studies departments and is generally confined to ethnic studies programs). It was thus deal with Professor X, or choose a different academic focus. Many of the students were Natives themselves, and thus had no intention of changing their focus, and others had come to UCSB specifically to work with Professor X, having transferred from other programs. All were frustrated and disillusioned. I still hoped that my own situation with the notorious professor would be different. Maybe I would be the exception to the rule.

This was my first introduction to what would become the focus of my Ph.D. dissertation research: the Mescalero Apache Mountain Spirit tradition. There are several different areas of traditional religion and practice among the Mescalero that are all somewhat distinct, and also somewhat intertwined. One major tradition is the female initiation ceremony of the "Big Tipi," so named because of the large tipi that is constructed of oaks and evergreens for the purpose of initiating girls into womanhood. Mescaleros belong to the Athabaskan language and culture family, and virtually all Athabaskans have female initiation rites. Like other Athabaskan cultures, the Mescaleros were originally from the far north, where Athabaskan cultures are still found today in what is Alaska and Canada. Their tradition of the Big Tipi is something that they brought with them in their migrations to the Southwest, and as such, it has an ancient lineage of at least hundreds, if not thousands, of years.

Another major traditional practice is that of the Mountain Spirits, which, according to all accounts, is a tradition that the Mescaleros began after migrating to the Southwest, and is most likely inspired by Pueblo practices of masked dancers, commonly known as "Kachinas." Their tradition of Mountain Spirits, which is also found among other

Apache cultures in the Southwest, is only superficially similar to Pueblo Kachina dancers, however. Among the Pueblo cultures, Kachinas are all characters with names, personalities, and often have various oral narratives and stories that serve to identify and classify the different kinds of Kachinas. When a dancer takes on the role of a Kachina, he has to learn his part and character, and properly play that role in a ceremonial context.

In contrast, the Apache Mountain Spirits are not characters and have no personalities. While there are various stories of the origins of different dance groups, the Mountain Spirits are not "characters" in these stories. They have no personal names, have no individual personalities, and are not narrative agents. In fact, they are far more abstract than that, and are more closely related to Mescalero metaphysics, sacred geography, and sense of sacred space.

Mescalero Mountain Spirit dance groups are all led by a "medicine man." I put that term in quotes, as leaders of these groups are generally referred to as "medicine men" by the Mescalero population, but they are not all necessarily "medicine men" in the sense that they are practitioners that someone might go to for personal healing, counseling, or ceremony. They "carry" the "medicine" of the dance group, but may or may not practice individually as medicine men. There are a number of medicine men and women among the Mescalero, and only some of the men carry dance groups. And several of the leaders of the dance groups do not practice as individual medicine men.

The dance group itself is made up of a core group of male singers and the dancers. Each dance group has four *Gaahe,* or Mountain Spirit dancers proper, and from one to three *Gaahelbaye,* or "Clowns." Men dance the Mountain Spirits; boys dance the Clowns. All of it is strictly men's business; women do not have any roles in the Mountain Spirit tradition, and their involvement is in fact considered taboo. All the dancers are painted and masked, with the regalia of the Mountain Spirits being far more detailed and elaborate than the Clowns. The Mountain Spirits are understood to be representative of, and embodiments of, the power of the Four

Directions of east, south, west, and north, in that order. The Clowns are more rogue elements and are not associated with any particular direction. Collectively, they perform highly structured dances that are understood to mobilize and actualize the power of the Four Directions to create blessings, healing, and to sanctify spaces, people, and events. They are routinely hired by Mescaleros to perform blessings for individuals, buildings, life changes, or large groups of people, such as the tribe itself. Everything that they do comes in sets of two and four, and symbolism that makes use of four repetitions dominates their look, attire, and actions. In many ways, I consider the Mountain Spirits to be a Mescalero take on the fractal nature of reality, as they give life to repeating forms that manifest across various levels simultaneously, much like fractal mathematics. Mountain Spirits embody fours within fours within fours within fours. As such, they are understood to embody the very power of life itself.

The group that was brought out to UCSC was known as the "Sun Clan" group, led by Sydney Baca. Sydney, in addition to being the leader of this particular dance group, was also a ceremonial singer for the Big Tipi, and a medicine man who could perform private and individual blessings and healings, so he pretty much spanned the spectrum of traditional Mescalero practice. He, like many of his fellow Sun Clan members, was also a Catholic. Despite the fact that the Mescalero tribe is relatively small, with around 2,500 members, at that time, there were something like twelve different Christian organizations that missionized their reservation, and most Mescaleros belonged to one church or another. Very few Mescaleros practiced Mescalero tradition exclusively.

Over the course of that weekend, I was introduced to Sydney, and other members of his group. Professor X's idea was that these introductions would pave the way for me to come out to Mescalero that summer and begin making connections and preparing the way for me to do more extended research. Much to my surprise, she told me that she wanted me to research the Mountain Spirits and make that the focus of my graduate work. As it was men's business, it was off limits to her as a researcher, and she had been waiting for a student to bring in to study the Mountain Spirits. Apparently, I was to be that student. It was an amazing opportunity, and not one that I was going to pass on. Though I hadn't come to grad school to study Apaches, the door was now open, and it was up to me to step through it. So, I did. Plans were made that I would travel with Professor X to Mescalero that summer and make my first visit to the reservation.

There was a time that virtually all ceremonies and traditional practices were outlawed by the federal government. In the Southwest, tribes were legally allowed one day a year to perform traditional ceremonies, and the ceremonies had to be held on a federally recognized U.S. holiday. Given their practice of holding Big Tipi ceremonies in the spring and summer, Mescaleros chose the 4th of July as their "feast" date, and to this day, this is the considered the prime date for a young woman to have her ceremony, though they do happen throughout the spring and summer. So, the original plan was for Professor X and I to meet at Mescalero in early July. This didn't actually happen, but we did eventually get out there a bit later in the summer.

When spring came around, I made a trip up to see Devon in Eugene during my break. He was living in a communal house, still attending the University of Oregon, and was with a new girlfriend, Minda, who was to eventually become his wife (and later, ex-wife), though their relationship was still relatively new at the time of this visit. The highlight of this visit was to be my first session with mushrooms since the experience of the eagle eating the mushrooms and my rainbow self telling me that if I wanted to visit with the eagle, I needed to eat the mushrooms. I had no specific expectations of what I thought was going to happen, but I was eager to experience mushrooms again, and anticipated that it might be something big.

I was correct.

In my first book that was specifically about entheogens, *Mushroom Wisdom*, I described this experience as being foundational for my spiritual outlook and as entering me into a new kind of relationship with mushrooms. It was by far the strongest, most profound, and also the longest, mushroom experience I had yet encountered, and it was to be many years before I was able to fully grasp the significance of what occurred on that day in Eugene. Looking back now, I recognize that it was my ego that prevented me from really accepting the profundity of what occurred, though the seeds were sown in that experience in what was to fully flower many years later after moving to Ashland, Oregon. This was a very significant beginning, however, and initiated me into what Timothy White, editor of *Shaman's Drum* magazine was to describe, in his review of *Mushroom Wisdom,* as my mystical-shamanic approach to spirituality. I'd put the emphasis on the mystical side of that description, because it wasn't shamanism in the traditional sense of working with spirits or traveling into the so-called "spirit world." It was more a revelation and gnosis of the nature of the self, the instructive nature of mushrooms, and the power of self-reflection and awareness.

Prior to this trip, I had read everything I could find on entheogens and shamanism, and also was heavily steeped in popular books on physics and quantum theory, in addition to all my studies of religion and philosophy. I'd been gathering everything I could that I felt addressed the big questions: what is real? What is knowledge? What is the nature of the mind? What is being? What do altered states of consciousness reveal about the world and the self? So I had a lot of intellectual material to work with, and had the inspiration that maybe, just maybe, I was going to get to the bottom, or the center, of some of these questions in this experience. And aside from that, I just wanted to take some mushrooms and see what would happen.

It wasn't long after consuming the mushrooms that it was clear that this was going to be stronger than any previous experience I had had. In my own personal terminology, I tended to measure how strong a mushroom experience was going to be based on how quickly the "mystic lizards" showed up. This was my term for the inter-linked geometric images that appeared in carpets, similar to M.C. Escher drawings of interlaced forms. If the mystic lizards didn't show up, it was going to be a very mild mushroom experience with very little visual content or effect. If the mystic lizards showed up early, soon after consuming mushrooms, it was going to be strong. If they didn't show up for an hour or so, it was going to be a medium strength experience. This time, they showed up almost right way, and that's how I knew: this was going to be big.

Writing about entheogenic experiences cannot truly capture the profundity of the experience itself. There's a real difference between intellectual, language-based knowledge that is learned and shared through writing and speaking and the direct experience of something that reveals itself as tangible, immediate, and often overwhelming in its impact. Directly *feeling* and *experiencing* something is very different than *believing, thinking*, and "knowing" something *intellectually.* The visceral and immediate nature of the mushroom experience cannot be captured by the latter. To really *know it,* you must experience it.

For me, this was my moment of truly experiencing what had previously been more of an intellectual understanding of the nature of the self, reality, and being. It was now something that I could *feel* and *experience directly,* and it was obvious. There was no uncertainty here, no intellectual grasping at maybes and possibilities. It was just truth: clear, present, and beyond argument or doubt. It was profound in ways that I was not able to adequately describe to anyone after the event, and it provided a major shift in my sense of self and my relationship with mushrooms.

The strength of the mushrooms was such that the only reasonable thing for me to do was completely surrender and let them unfold however they would, with no attempt to control the experience. It felt to me that they were simply taking over my being, and for the duration of this event, I was to be under their tutelage. I learned that I could simply trust and let go, and let my body, mind, and heart be a vehicle for this overwhelming power. It felt like "Martin" was disappearing, and in his place was this kind of "mushroom man." Rather than the mushroom being something that "I" was experiencing as "Martin," it was more a shift into a different state of being where "I" was this pure witness, and "Martin" was merely this character that was living out his life in the form of this body, here, from which I experienced a personal perspective. It was the Witness that was the true observer and true identity, not this "Martin" fellow, with all his fears, insecurities, ambitions, and plans. The Witness was the real deal, and from this perspective, I could appreciate the flow of self and reality in an entirely new way. I was completely dispassionate about myself as "Martin," though also simultaneously deeply sympathetic, yet personally detached. Reality itself was a nexus of personal choice as manifested from an individual perspective that was shaped and formed by ongoing and endless patterns of transformation and change, some of which were open to personal manipulation and alteration, and others that simply needed to be accepted. At the heart of it all was this universal consciousness and heart that was deeply invested in parading as "individuals," yet was also unconditionally universal and without attachment to any one individual, myself as "Martin" included.

In short, I was the universe observing and experiencing myself as the person known as "Martin," so I was simultaneously "Martin" and "Not Martin." Somewhere within this paradox was the "real me," whoever or whatever that was. Under the influence of mushrooms, all these aspects of myself were being revealed to me, and I knew that there was absolutely nothing within the mushroom experience that was not a reflection and expression of the larger, universal self as experienced from my personal perspective. Everything that arose within the experience was related to me. It wasn't some spirit world, or some archetypal and collective unconscious – it was I. It was a reflection of my thoughts, my choices, my patterns, my ways of thinking, believing, and acting. It was all me, and there was no one and nothing else there. There was no "other" there, for it was all a reflection of the self. I later labeled this process "looking into the Spiritual Mirror." "Martin" was a product of the self, but it was not, in any way, the limits of the self. It was an expression of something far larger, far more universal, and far more profound than I had ever imagined.

My ego struggled with these revelations, for it sounded fairly solipsistic, and perhaps grandiose. The conclusion seemed clear: the Self was *everything*. To put it in other terms, the logical conclusion was that everyone and everything is, despite appearances, actually only one universal being and consciousness – everything was God, including me. My ego was definitely not ready to go this far at that time, however, so I held that final conclusion at bay. However, I was fairly confident in my conclusion that everything that arose within the mushroom experience was a reflection of the self, and if you paid attention, observed carefully, and centered yourself in your heart, as opposed to the intellect of the mind, then you could use mushrooms to learn about yourself and how you were making choices that were impacting your experience of reality and being. Some things merely needed to be accepted, and many others were open to choice and free will.

All of this was expressed through the unfolding of patterns of energy that manifested both as, and in, space and time. I was later to understand that these are what can be called fractal patterns, though at the time, fractals weren't really on my personal radar and I hadn't understood their centrality to the process of reality. So, I just called them patterns of manifestation that were complex and geometric in nature that structured our experience of reality from the smallest to the largest. Reality itself was a vast, undulating and interconnected network of these patterns, all mutually informing and giving rise to each other. It was all information, encoded in geometric patterns of reality formation.

At the personal level, it meant that we, as individuals, were the results of patterns of formation and expression. As individuals, we chose patterns of how we wanted to appear, think, and act. We didn't choose these patterns very consciously, however, and most we adopted for reasons that were not clear to us. Some of these patterns developed harmful habits within our sense of being and expression. When these choices were inauthentic for our genuine nature, poor mental, physical, and emotion health would be the result. The responsibility for this process fell strictly and exclusively on the individual. It was up to each person to make choices for him or herself, and the individual was responsible for the results. We weren't at the whim of spirits, entities, and deities – we were the authors of our own reality and being. It was all about the self. And by carefully observing the self, we could make more authentic choices for ourselves and therefore change the patterns of our being, and enter into a new experience of reality. It was all about choice, and awareness.

Much of what is revealed in a mushroom experience can be challenging and uncomfortable for an individual, but this is all a necessary part of the self-examination process. If there is a truth that you are hiding from yourself, mushrooms can help expose it. In short, I saw mushrooms as the premier route to the true contents of one's heart – not the bullshit rationales and justifications that we construct within our minds, but the true reality of what we actually feel and experience in our hearts. And beneath our sense of individuality, within our hearts was a universal heart that doesn't take anything or anyone personally. Our personal reactions and choices are our responsibility, and no one else's. Each person is fully responsible for him or herself and the state of one's heart and wellbeing. In being willing to confront ourselves and face ourselves fully, we can liberate ourselves from our false thinking, our attachments, and our destructive habits and choices. But it takes willingness and perseverance, for the mind can always intrude into the experience and start "tripping out" and making up a bunch of crap that would only serve to confuse and confound the individual. To truly learn from mushrooms takes work, unwavering attention, and willingness set the ego aside and allow the experience to unfold without interference. And, it is all about *right here* and *right now.* Everything that makes one an individual with free will is available to observation and exploration in the present moment. There is no need to travel back in time, or forward into the future, for everything that is needed is present in the immediate reality. The key is willingness to face the truth. Taking mushrooms isn't at all about entering into some other reality – it is all about getting clear on the reality that is happening right here and now, in one's being and sense of self. It is a mirror – nothing more, and nothing less, and what it reveals is so much more than the personal ego of who one thinks one is or has constructed over the course of one's life. The true self is so much bigger than the individual characters that we play through our social and personal lives.

From that time on, I knew that I could trust the mushrooms completely and without reservation, for they only showed me myself, and I was not afraid of myself. I knew that there was nothing to fear within the experience, no matter how challenging or difficult it might become, and that as long as I stayed present and focused, and set my ego and personal concerns and desires aside, I could trust that I would show myself whatever it was I needed to know, when I needed to know it, and that there was nothing else for me to worry about. For me, mushrooms became the ultimate reality check, and served as a way for me to move beyond my personal perspective and into something that was far more universal and profound.

Thus a new phase of my relationship with mushrooms had been initiated. I knew from then on that any time I needed clarity on something, or needed to go beneath the surface of things to experience the inner connections and significance of what I was experiencing, all I needed to do was take mushrooms and let reality unfold in its immense and immediate clarity. I found that I could easily know the truth of my heart, or anyone else, as truth just became obvious and it was something that I felt directly, rather than intellectualized.

It was also at this point that I intentionally stopped talking when taking mushrooms. My practice was to be completely silent when experiencing mushrooms unless there was something I felt directly inspired to say. I didn't necessarily understand it this way at the time, but it was a way of keeping my ego out of the picture. Rather than taking mushrooms and attempting to engage in any kind of normal social interaction or discourse, I would set all such concerns aside for the duration of any mushroom journey and would stay completely quiet unless inspired (compelled is a bit more accurate) to do otherwise. It also started the practice of either staying perfectly still, or moving, only to then move or stop moving when it felt that it was necessary – another way of keeping my ego in check. In other words, I set all my normal behavior patterns aside in order to be completely open to the inspirations that arose within the mushroom experience. And furthermore, I started to look at taking mushrooms as a form of "work," and not just a curious exploration of psychedelic states of consciousness.

From that point on, whenever I took mushrooms, it seemed to "Martin" that the mushrooms just took over and the work began. I started working with others, to help guide them through the experience and reveal aspects of themselves and their patterns. Whenever I took mushrooms, it was as though I could look directly into each person's heart and see the "real" being beneath the mask. All "normal" social interaction appeared to me as people playing characters and as wearing carefully constructed and maintained "masks" of particular identities, none of which were truly genuine, for they were all artificial constructs of who we thought we were or should be. Part of my role in working with others was to help reveal this artificiality to others and the choices they were making in constructing their sense of self. At times, it was very challenging for those I worked with, and not everyone was appreciative or comfortable with the process.

After this amazing experience, I was walking on air for weeks. It had been so profound, so revelatory, that I had difficulty speaking about it or adequately sharing what I had been through. Even if I couldn't understand everything that I had revealed to myself in that experience, there were things that I now knew without any doubt that had only been intellectual constructs previously. My entire outlook and self-understanding had shifted in ways I could not have imagined or anticipated. It felt like a new me.

I didn't have a label for my new state of being. From what I had read of shamanism, my experience and new understanding didn't quite fit, though there were similarities. Sure, there *seemed* to be some "otherness" about my experience, but I understood that whatever appeared as "other" was in truth just an aspect of myself that I didn't understand or recognize as myself. In contrast to Terence McKenna's obsession with the "otherness" and "alien nature" of the mushroom experience, complete with UFO's and intergalactic mushroom spores, this felt like coming home – something so profoundly intimate that there was no sense of alienation or otherworldliness. Though I didn't quite grasp the language at the time, my own perspective was more along the nondual side of things, whereas much of shamanic practice and culture is thoroughly dualistic in the sense that the shaman works with spiritual "others" and "other realms" and such. From my perspective, it was all the self, and therefore, there was no "other," and any spirits or entities were just misrecognized manifestations of the fundamental self. It was all, after all, just a spiritual mirror into which I was gazing. There wasn't anyone or anything else "there." I didn't quite understand it as such at the time, but I was becoming a "mystic," not a "shaman," and the difference was more significant that I might have imagined.

Shamanism also tends to be highly ritualistic, and here, there was no ritual. Furthermore, contrary to what I had read, there was no "spirit guide" that came to instruct me, or initiate me. There was no "power animal," despite the earlier "vision" of the eagle and the mushrooms. The "eagle" was the experience itself, not some being *within* the experience. And as that vision had shown me, the eagle was actually I, so there was nothing "other" about it.

But mysticism didn't seem a good fit either, for everything I'd read and learned about mysticism said that you needed to spend a lifetime (or many lifetimes, if you were Buddhist or Hindu) meditating, practicing good ethics, praying, clarifying and purifying consciousness and the body, ridding yourself of karma, devoting yourself to God, etc. I had spent a few years meditating, but it wasn't like I was a monk or some profoundly spiritual person. I was just me – some guy who wanted to know what was really going on here, and to claim that I had experienced a mystical revelation sounded grandiose and self-inflated to my ego, so I steered away from it. From everything that I had read, very few people ever had mystical experiences or awakenings, and they were far more rare than other kinds of "spiritual" experiences. Many people who spent their entire lives devoted to some kind of enlightenment and awakening never got there, even with dedicated and deeply devoted practice. So how could I have had an experience like that?

It was after this that people like Terence McKenna started making less and less sense for me, regardless of how I wanted to label or identify my own experience. All of Terence's talk of machine elves, hyperspace, aliens, UFO's, and the like seemed to be completely missing the point. If entheogens were a "spiritual mirror" that revealed the self to the individual, then by all appearances, Terence seemed to be observing himself in a distorted fun-house mirror, more suited to a carnival than any kind of serious spiritual work of introspection. I held open the possibility that this difference might be due to his use of DMT, something that was still many years into my future before I was to have any personal experience of, but even his descriptions of mushrooms seemed off the mark to me. There was something deeply wrong about how he was writing about mushrooms as revealing the "alien other." What was this alien other? Wasn't it just the Self? Overall, Terence seemed to be radically disconnected from himself and too tightly trapped in his personal narrative of "Terence the Psychonaut and Explorer of the Psychedelic Landscape." Rather than being a profound explorer, to me, he seemed more and more like a lost ego, unable to recognize himself in the mirror of reality, refusing to acknowledge his own projections and illusions. It seemed to me that his approach was completely backwards, and most of his conclusions highly suspect. Was I missing something, or was Terence simply a peddler of psychobabble nonsense? I suspected the latter. Whatever the case, I returned to Santa Barbara with a new perspective, and a new sense of self. For the first time in my life, I felt that I truly knew something about the nature of reality, being, and the entheogenic experience – not because I had developed an intellectual understanding, but rather had explored these truths through direct and unmediated experience. Things were never to be the same.

Phoebe's mother had died earlier in the school year, finally succumbing to the breast cancer. We were present for her death, with Phoebe administering her mother's final dose of morphine. The day before her death, she had gotten up out of bed for the first time in weeks. She got up, brushed her teeth, and then went to look out of her bedroom window, commenting on how the crows were gathering outside – crows no one else could see. The next day, she peacefully died in her bed. Phoebe worried that it was the morphine that had done it, taking her mother beyond the point of no return, and thus had some guilt about the matter. It was just her time to let go, however, and as far as I saw it, the morphine just eased the transition.

Phoebe's father was feeling very lonely, so at the start of that summer, after my first year of grad school, he decided to take us on a driving trip of the western states and Canada. It was the most extensive trip I had yet been on, and we got to see many beautiful sites, including the Grand Tetons, Glacier National Park, Yellowstone, Banff, the Olympic Peninsula, and much more.

It was toward the end of this trip that I encountered my first personal taste of the ways that Professor X could cause problems for her students. Our plan was to meet out at Mescalero for their big 4th of July feast and ceremony, and to accomplish this, I needed to fly out of Seattle, leaving Phoebe and her father to complete the road trip by themselves. I had purchased a plane ticket and was ready to go. It was almost impossible for me to get in touch with Professor X to confirm our trip, and it was then that I learned that she almost never answered her phone, and even more rarely called people back. This was also true of the still-nascent mode of communication, email, which she apparently never read, and never answered. I finally got a phone call from Professor X with her telling me that something had come up and we'd drive out to Mescalero later that summer together, rather than fly. When I told her that I'd already spent several hundred dollars on a plane ticket, which for me, at that time, was a significant chunk of money, being an only occasionally-employed student, she casually said that I could get a refund from the airline, which wasn't true. That was my first personal experience of being frustrated by my professor, but it wasn't to be the last. I was beginning to understand what I had been warned about.

We did eventually make it out to Mescalero some weeks after Phoebe and I returned to Santa Barbara. Rather than fly, we drove, taking my car. As a side note, I drove the entire way, with Professor X telling me that she couldn't drive a stick shift, so the full driving duty was left to me (which I didn't really mind). Some years later, there was a time that someone, probably another student, offered to let Professor X borrow a car. I blurted out that Professor X couldn't borrow it because she couldn't drive a stick shift. Professor X looked at me critically and said, "Of course I can drive a stick shift," as though I had just insulted her. She obviously didn't recall our driving arrangement on that first trip out to Mescalero and the lie she had told me in order to manipulate me into doing all the driving.

It took us a few days to get out to Mescalero. It was during this time that I started to notice certain aspects of my experience that had perhaps been around before, but not noticed, or possibly were just starting to manifest and thus were only then becoming apparent to me. With all the time we were spending together, Professor X and I shared many conversations, several of which were about my personal spiritual practices and experiences. It was then that I first noticed that, when we would have these conversations, especially if it was in the evening, after we'd stopped driving for the day and I had slipped away to smoke a little herb, I would tend to shake and vibrate when the subject matter got "deep." I attributed this to getting "the chills" when having such conversations, though I had no idea why. I also noticed that I would experience periods of needing to gag, sometimes even with a small amount of vomit. Once I noticed these features of gagging and vibrating, I found that they were fairly regular in my experience, especially if I was in some altered state of consciousness, like smoking herb or taking mushrooms. I couldn't figure it out. Was I reacting to something I was eating? Was I just getting cold and reacting to that? What was this all about? I didn't spend too much time trying to get to the bottom of it, but it was something that I was noticing more and more, and it seemed to be related to my spiritual experiences, though in a way I couldn't understand.

Many years later, I now understand this as part of my process of opening up and processing energy, but at the time, it was just a mystery. I had virtually no personal understanding of energy, how it worked, or how it related to the body and mind as an integrated system of energetic processing.

Mescalero was like something out of time for me. Professor X and I rented a room at the Apache Motel in Tularosa, just beyond the borders of the Mescalero Reservation. We were attending a ceremony that was taking place out in the forested hills of Mescalero, which Professor X assured me was better than the feast on the 4th of July, which was held at the Mescalero fair and rodeo grounds, and was overrun with tourists and visitors. This, in contrast, was a private feast, and well off the beaten path. As far as I could tell, I was the only non-Native at this particular event, as was to be true for many of my ceremonial experiences at Mescalero over the years to come.

To get to the ceremonial grounds, we drove along a dirt and gravel road through the forest. I was completely surprised by the environment. It was far more lush and green than I was expecting. Knowing that we were headed into southern New Mexico, I had expected the reservation to be more of what we were encountering along our drive – desert, cacti, and shrubs. My expectations were completely off the mark. I had been to New Mexico once before, as a child, before my parents got divorced. Our family had flown out to New Mexico with my grandfather one winter so that he could take us to some of the Pueblos and go see some traditional dances, as well as connect with old friends that my grandfather had grown up with when he had lived with the Navajo as a young man. That was in and around the Santa Fe area, which has a very different environment than Mescalero. The Mescalero reservation itself, located up in the mountains, is extremely different from the desert lowlands and canyons of the Rio Grande just beyond the reservation.

Here, in the heart of the Mescalero reservation, everything was green, with tall pine and spruce trees, green fields of grasses and wildflowers. Summer is also "monsoon" season at Mescalero, so the blue sky was regularly populated by late afternoon and evening clouds that would alternately rain and produce thunder and lightning. The ceremonial grounds were an open field, surrounded by tall, dark pine groves. In the middle of the field was the ceremonial structure of the Big Tipi and adjacent cooking arbors, attached to which were private tipis for the girls going through their initiations. In the center of the ceremonial space was an area for a bonfire. Numerous tipis surrounded the grounds, and a bit further out, along the edges of the field, were a couple different tipis that were for the various Mountain Spirit dance groups that were to be dancing for this ceremony. Aside from the numerous trucks and cars that were present, the scene seemed timeless to me. I couldn't believe my good fortune at being able to share in this experience.

A note about tipis: Mescaleros are the only culture in the Southwest to use tipis, where they are called, in Mescalero, *kuugha*. Traditionally, the Mescaleros had their home base in the mountains of southern New Mexico, and would venture east onto the southern plains to hunt bison. They are therefore something of a bridge culture between the peoples of the Southwest and the cultures of the Great Plains. Once, some years later, I was attending the annual American Academy of Religion conference, where there was a sub-group called SSNART, the Society for the Study of Native American Religious Traditions. In this group, there was a woman who claimed to have Mescalero ancestry. She gave a presentation on something Apache related. At the end of her presentation, I made a comment about how Mescaleros used tipis for their ceremonies. This woman corrected me, saying that, "Apaches lived in *wikiups* – they never used tipis!" It was an interesting exchange, as no one in the room believed me that Mescaleros used tipis, despite the fact that I had studied out at Mescalero for many years, at that point. Somewhat naively, I hadn't understood the racial politics of being a white man studying Native religions. What I was learning was that as a white man, no one listened to me, and "Native scholars" were prepared to dismiss anything I might say if there was a "Native" who could disagree, no matter how ignorant and uneducated that person might be. Personally, I wondered if this woman, who claimed to be Mescalero, actually knew anything at all about Mescalero culture. Only someone who had never been to Mescalero could erroneously claim that they didn't use tipis.

Sydney Baca, the medicine man I originally met in Santa Cruz that spring, was serving as both a signer for one of the girls having her initiation and as the leader for his Mountain Spirit dance group that was to dance for the girl. Though the two traditions are distinct, it is standard practice for a girl's family to hire a Mountain Spirit dance group for her ceremony, so the two traditions have become integrated in this instance. At these ceremonies, the Mountain Spirits serve both a blessing and entertainment function. On the first and last nights of the ceremony (it lasts for four nights), the Mountain Spirits perform a private blessing for the girl, her family, and entourage prior to her time spent in the Big Tipi dancing to the songs of the medicine men through the night. After this private blessing, the Mountain Spirits dance around the central bonfire that is located to the east of the opening of the Big Tipi, and while this is still a ceremonial practice, it is considered to be done mainly for the entertainment of those attending the girl's ceremony. When there is more than one dance group at a ceremony, their singers take turns singing sets of songs. All dance groups can dance at the same time, though their order around the fire is the same order that their singers will take turns singing. When they dance, women can dance around the outer edge of the dance circle, though they are expected to wear a shawl and their hair down if they choose to do so.

There was apparently some controversy over Sydney singing for both the Mountain Spirits and the Big Tipi. In Mescalero culture, these are distinct roles, and it isn't considered proper for someone to be "carrying" both "medicines" simultaneously. Sydney had been looking for someone to take over as the one carrying the Mountain Spirit group, but it was a huge responsibility, and he hadn't found a replacement yet. It also required someone to know a large corpus of songs, and thus far, no one had been up to the challenge.

I was invited to go with the other men into the Sun Clan Mountain Spirit tipi and join them in their preparations. Each dance group has its own tipi that they use for their ceremonies. In the old days, these tipis would be set up far away from the main ceremonial grounds. In the past, dancers would never been seen in public with their masks off, so supposedly, no one knew who the dancers were. Dancers are not considered to be "themselves" when they are masked and dancing – they are embodiments and representatives of their designated direction of east, south, west, or north. These days, everyone knows who the dancers are, and they tend to put up their tipis relatively close to the main ceremonial grounds, though still removed at a short distance. It was also the case that people were forbidden to attempt to talk to a dancer, or call him by name, as this was calling on their individual identities and not the power they were meant to represent and embody. I never saw these restrictions enforced, though all the old-timers insisted that this was the way it *should* be.

I was the only non-Mescalero in the tipi, as was to be true over many different ceremonies that I attended in my years as a grad student. I felt awkward, but the men did what they could to make me feel comfortable and include me in their conversations. I was even called upon to help paint and dress the dancers. I was struck by the playfulness and joviality of the men. In contrast to my expectations, the scene was anything but serious. There were ongoing bouts of joking and good-natured teasing, and lots of laughing. I later was told that this was considered to be an integral part of ceremonial preparation. One of my teachers, Willeto, said that it was important for the success of any ceremony for people to be in a good mood, and joking was a way of making people "be of one mind." It was this sense of unity that made ceremony effective for the Mescalero.

The mood changed instantly, however, when the time came. The transition was marked by Sydney rolling a traditional cigarette and then quietly saying some prayers that were echoed by the other men in the tipi. Even before then, there was proper etiquette in the tipi: no hats, and always move about the tipi in a sunwise (clockwise) direction. Now, however, all the joking stopped, and for the first time, the dancers started making their ceremonial noises in response to

Sydney's prayers. Whenever he mentioned them, the dancers would raise the ceremonial wands and feathers they held in their hands, and made a reverberating cooing sound, kind of like a dove or turkey, and then turn around in place. After the prayers were said, the men got out their ceremonial water drums (the same kind of drums that are now used in the Native American Church – another indication of the Mescalero influence on the religion), and began singing their "we're coming out soon" songs. This was the transition between the preparation stage and actual beginning of ceremonial practice. From this point on, things were serious and solemn.

That night I alternated between going inside the Big Tipi to listen to the singers and watch the girls do their standing-in-place dancing and shuffling from side to side, and standing around the bonfire, watching the Mountain Spirits dance. It was an amazing experience, and one that I was to repeat for the duration of this visit, and in many visits to Mescalero in the future. Everyone was welcoming and friendly and I felt right at home, despite being the only obvious outsider.

It was on this first trip to Mescalero that I met Willeto Antonio. Willeto had been working with Professor X for some 20-25 years at that time, and was her main source of information on the Big Tipi. He was completely different than anything I might have expected, having heard from Professor X that he was the most prominent and respected medicine man on the reservation. He lived in a dilapidated home in the town of Mescalero, the only town on the reservation and the location for most of the residences on the reservation, though there are a few other smaller communities scattered about, more out in the mountains. In Mescalero proper, there are the fair and rodeo grounds, the tribal government center, the tribal school, the courthouse, hospital, tribal services buildings, tribal store, post office, and Catholic Church. Willeto lived up the hill from the tribal center in an area called "Gallerito Flats," an area of oak trees, pinion, and juniper.

Willeto was in a wheelchair. It was years later that I heard the full story of what had put him there. When he was young, he had been singled out by the tribal elders as being an individual who would become a repository of tribal tradition and knowledge. When he was only nine, a tribal-wide ceremony was held for him where he was given four ceremonial arrows, all representing different forms of knowledge and practice that he was expected to learn. He was told that while he didn't need to become a medicine man, it was expected of him to learn everything that he could about medicine, ceremony, stories, and songs.

Despite the fact that Willeto did not consider himself a medicine man, everyone else did. In some respects, what makes a medicine man or woman is not his or her learning, but how other people regard and treat the person in question. According to everyone else, Willeto most certainly *was* a medicine man.

He began his traditional practices dancing as a Clown with a Mountain Spirit dance group; a role that he cherished and enjoyed to its fullest. According to Willeto, these days, Clowns were timid and didn't know how to properly perform their roles, mostly just following after the Mountain Spirit dancers. Willeto relished the fact that Clowns were actually free agents, in a sense, and could dance out of line, could make fun of people, could behave crudely and thoroughly inappropriately, if they wanted, and could be all-around troublemakers. "The boys who dance as Clowns these days don't know anything!" he would often complain to me.

Willeto had considered undergoing the apprenticeship required to become a medicine man proper, but ultimately had other plans. "I wanted to drink and run around chasing women," he confided in me, "and being a medicine man is more strict with more rules. I didn't want to do that, so I didn't." He did go on to become a singer in the Big Tipi, but that's as far as he wanted to go. It was his view that the spirits had punished him for his lack of commitment to becoming a full medicine man, and it was this choice that he believed put him in the wheelchair.

He was still a young man when it happened. He had been home, drinking and watching football on TV one Christmas when a relative came over and opened the front door to find him almost passed out on the floor. The large relative picked Willeto up and threw him over this shoulder, exclaiming, "Get up, you lazy guy!" He threw too hard, however, and Willeto went all the way over, coming down directly on his head, breaking his neck. He'd been in a wheelchair ever since.

And that's how Willeto was when we first met. Had I not known, I never would have looked at him and said, "There's a highly respected medicine man!" He had absolutely no interest in "dressing the part," and there was nothing about him that spoke to his role within his culture. He wore black slacks from Walmart, which he always wore with the zipper down so that he could easily get to his urinal when the unexpected urge to pee would suddenly come upon him. Above that, he wore an old t-shirt with holes in it with some food and drink stains. On his head, he wore a NY Yankees ball cap, underneath which was his military-style crew cut hair. There was a can of beer in his lap and a pack of Marlboros in his shirt pocket. He had a stubbly little mustache and goatee that would come and go as he occasionally shaved (Apaches tend to have very little facial hair in general). He kept a trashcan nearby that he could frequently spit into, and a pile of napkins on his lap to catch anything that didn't make it into the can.

Willeto seemed to me to be a wonderful contradiction, and I liked him right away, despite the fact that I felt intimidated and awkward when I was around him. Whatever he was, he wasn't a bullshitter, and despite any misperceptions to the contrary, he was definitely the real deal. In my time at Mescalero, I met a lot of younger "medicine men" who went to great effort to "look the part" of being a medicine person with beads, feathers, leather clothing, sashes, and other items of ceremonial regalia (much like New Agers who get into "indigenous spirituality"). Willeto didn't give a shit about these kinds of things, and felt zero need to project an image of himself to others. "They're just wannabes," he would tell me, in reference to the more flamboyant and decorative medicine people. Willeto was the real deal. He knew it. Everyone else knew it. There was no need for him to play the part.

In fact, he didn't even want to be a medicine man. It was only with reluctance that he operated in this fashion, and in many respects, he did his best to chase people away or direct them elsewhere. He wasn't trying to make a name for himself, or have a regular flow of clients. Really, he just wanted to drink beer, watch TV, and be left alone. However, part of his initiation as a young child was that he was told he was to do anything he could to help and instruct anyone who might come to him, and that there would be spiritual consequences if he failed to do so. Thus, if he couldn't chase someone off, or convince visitors to leave and go find someone else, he always did everything within his power to help them. In some respects, I fit into this category, and Willeto and I were to eventually develop a close and mutually rewarding relationship.

Professor X was terribly protective, and possessive, of Willeto, however, and my relationship with Willeto was to prove to be the crucial factor in my later struggles with Professor X. But that was still to come, and was several years away.

On this first trip out to Mescalero, I also met Meredith Begay, a medicine woman who was to become one of my primary teachers out at Mescalero. She was a contemporary of Willeto's. Over their many years of practicing as medicine people, Willeto and Meredith had often worked in tandem. When a girl goes through her Big Tipi ceremony, she has to hire both a medicine woman, or "sponsor," and a medicine man, or ceremonial singer. For most of their lives, Willeto and Meredith fulfilled these roles together for countless girls going through their ceremonies. By the time I met her, Meredith was mostly "retired," like Willeto, and her daughter, Zelda, was beginning to follow in her mother's footsteps as a regular sponsor and medicine woman for girls having their ceremonies. Meredith had lived a number of years in San Francisco, with her Navajo husband, Keith, where Keith had worked for NASA. When they moved back to Mescalero, Meredith had gone on to become a medicine woman, but Keith was unable to get work at the nearby Holloman Air Force Base or White Sands Missile Range for jobs that he was well qualified. The local racism insured that he was overlooked. He thus turned to drinking, and had effectively lived as a drunk for many years.

As a side note, White Sands Missile Range is the largest military installation in the United States, and sits squarely within Mescalero traditional territory. There are a number of mountains in the missile range that are considered to be sacred and medicinal mountains by the Mescaleros, including Oscura Peak, the location of Trinity Site, the exact spot where the very first atomic bomb was detonated, just beyond the borders of the Mescalero reservation. The sacred sites in the missile range are effectively off-limits to the Mescalero, only having been allowed to visit them once within recent tribal memory, and that was under the escort of armed military personnel. The sacred mountains can be seen from many places on the reservation, and prayers are still directed toward them, despite their off-limit status. Several of them are connected to the Mountain Spirit tradition and are understood to be homes of the Mountain Spirits, and there are stories that you can hear the songs of the spirits when you visit those mountains. White Sands is also now a park and national monument, so everything that is found within the park is considered to be protected. There's a form of sage that grows only in the white sands, so on occasion, Mescaleros sneak in to harvest the sage that is necessary for their ceremonies. The sands themselves come from the local mountains, which are actually fossilized coral reefs, as millions of years ago, the entire area was a shallow ocean.

Meredith, like many Native men and women, was overweight and suffered from diabetes, needing to be hooked up to dialysis machines in her home several times a week. She was always chipper, however, and I found her to be a warm and inviting presence. When I first met her, she was living in a house just down the hill from Willeto's in what was called "Old Ladies' Town," an area where a number of retired women lived in tribal housing. The day we met, Meredith was outside with a couple other women, chewing on deer hides, softening them up and stretching them out for their planned used as a feast dress for a girl who was to have her ceremony later that summer. It was a hot day, sitting out there in the sun, so

Professor X didn't want to stay long – just long enough to say hi and get me introduced to Meredith.

As it turned out, Meredith was one of the few people I felt I could talk to openly about entheogens at Mescalero. She even sent me out on a vision quest, some years later, and told me that I could take some peyote with me, if I wanted. Of course, I had no personal access to peyote, so it was a moot point, but I appreciated her openness on this. Unlike Willeto, she thought that peyote was good medicine. This was due, in part, to her having Lipan ancestry, and according to Meredith, the Lipan had a peyote ceremony that dated back to before the advent of the Native American Church. She therefore saw nothing incompatible between Apache tradition and use of peyote. She had also converted to Baha'i when she lived in San Francisco, so she tended to be open and supportive of all religions and spiritualities. The only one she wasn't too hot on was the Christian church that was just down the street from her house, which regularly preached against indigenous Mescalero tradition, sometimes through a bullhorn, with hellfire and damnation echoing about the neighborhood. She was happy when she moved out to the country a few years later with no immediate neighbors and no annoying preaching coming from down the street.

Professor X and I returned home. The course of my graduate studies now seemed clear: I was going to study the Mescalero Apache Mountain Spirit tradition. For a time, I continued my focus on Buddhism, but after a year of taking courses in Sanskrit while simultaneously teaching myself Navajo (A closely related language to Mescalero Apache. Since there were no materials available to learn Mescalero, I chose to focus on Navajo as a matter of practicality. And since there were no professors who could teach me Navajo, I had to learn it on my own), I decided to drop the Sanskrit and give up on officially pursuing my Buddhist studies. So, I spent the summer dreaming of all the things I was hoping to learn at Mescalero and plotting out my future studies.

I also spent the summer learning to play the didjeridu. Toward the end of my first year as a graduate student, I saw a flier posted in the religious studies department office for a band called "Dreamtime Continuum" that would be performing at the Santa Barbara Yoga Center, and featured various grad students in the religious studies program. I got high before I went to the show. The players were sitting in meditation on cushions before a similarly seated crowd, the scene lit by only a few spare candles with nag champa incense burning. The show started with the bandleader, Sudama Mark Kennedy, playing a didjeridu with copious amounts of reverb and echo. It was my first exposure to the didjeridu, and it blew me wide open. By this time, I had relaxed into my "flashback" experiences, and one started to come on immediately when I heard the didj. It was clearly something that I resonated with, and I knew right away that I wanted to learn how to play that thing myself. I had never encountered a didjeridu player before, and was eager to connect with Sudama and see if he would teach me the secrets of circular breathing.

I officially introduced myself to Sudama the next week back at school, and he was happy to oblige and offered to meet me in Isla Vista for my first lesson. Sudama was an older student, and had led an interesting life. He picked up the name Sudama in an Ashram in India. His father was a diplomat, and had been one of the hostages in Iran as depicted in the recent film, *Argo.* He wasn't one of the lucky ones to escape, as depicted in the film, and had been held hostage for 444 days, along with the majority of the embassy staff. Sudama was interested in "mythopoetics" and "personal mythology." Though he was a few years ahead of me in his program, he never completed his Ph.D. and went on to become a healer in the local Santa Barbara New Age scene, where he still practices today.

He gave me my first lesson on the didj, and then put me in touch with another local fellow who was selling didjeridus that he was making from PVC piping. I got my first didj, and struggled to learn the fine art of circular breathing. I had the basic idea, but like most people learning to play the didj, I tried much too hard, and was lightheaded and felt as though I could never get enough air, and was constantly on the verge of passing out.

Things shifted when I had a dream. In the dream, I was playing the didjeridu and my circular breathing was perfect. It was a very vivid dream, and I could feel my lungs, my breath, the shape and vibration of my lips, the placement of my tongue, and the movement of my diaphragm. I didn't remember the dream upon waking, but it did pop back into my mind a few days later when I was walking through my apartment and caught a glimpse of my didj, standing in the corner. The dream suddenly flooded back into conscious awareness with all the vivid detail. I picked up the didj and started to play. That was about three months after my first lesson, and circular breathing has never been a problem since.

I loved the didjeridu, and used to spend hours playing it and experimenting with rhythms, drones, and barking and yelling into the hollow tube. I especially liked smoking some herb and then playing. It felt like a powerful tool of consciousness alteration, and I even incorporated it into my regular meditation routine, along with some shamanic drumming. It became one more tool in my spiritual toolkit, as well as a regular feature of my musical life. After a time, I became the official didjeridu player for Dreamtime Continuum, quickly surpassing Sudama in my didj playing ability.

The next school year I focused on my Master's thesis, completing it by the end of the year. I concentrated on Lakota culture for the thesis, attempting to present their spiritual practices and symbol systems in a way that respected their own categories and metaphysics rather than translating everything into academic categories. The thesis itself was titled, *Walking the Space Between Earth and Sky: an Exploration of Lakota Thought and Practice.* I mention this as, years later, I discovered that Professor X had published a paper where she used the same title, but changed it to Mescalero Apache, rather than Lakota. I guess she liked the title.

That year Phoebe started to bring up the topic of marriage. It seemed like the thing to do, despite the fact that I was rather unhappy in the relationship. Our sex life had dwindled to having intercourse maybe once a month, maybe once every two months. I tried talking to Phoebe about our difficulties, but every attempt got her so worked up that she would end up curled into a ball, hiding in a corner somewhere in our apartment. For my part, I wasn't very skilled at expressing and communicating my emotions either concerning this tender subject. I suggested therapy, but she didn't want to take that route. I still thought that I was somehow responsible for this and that it was all part of my spiritual development and commitment to non-attachment and transcendence of the pleasures of the flesh. I never talked to anyone about it, except for Devon. To everyone else, we appeared as the "perfect couple," never arguing, living in domestic tranquility. We had moved into a new apartment, living above a family's garage in Santa Barbara, and Phoebe had gotten a job teaching in the Goleta Union School district. We were financially secure, had plans for ourselves and our future, and to all appearances, things should have been great.

This was part of my own difficulty with our relationship. I kept telling myself that I didn't have much to complain about. Even if our sex life was lacking and there was very little intimacy between us, I *should* be grateful for all the good things in our life together. It wasn't like my parents' relationship where they were fighting and yelling at each other and filled with deep resentment that boiled over into passionate conflicts. I was just being selfish in wanting more, and wallowing in self-pity. I *should* be happy and accept our relationship, however lack-luster it might be.

And no one knew. Our families had no idea that we were radically disconnected from each other. None of our friends knew. No one at the university knew. It was our own private suffering, and something that we rarely talked about or even acknowledged. For me, it was the elephant in the room, but I had no idea what to do about it. What I wanted to do was end our relationship and move on, but I had no idea how to do that, for I certainly didn't have the courage and conviction within myself to do so, continually telling myself that it would be selfish. We also seemed too far along to me. Phoebe had come to Santa Barbara to be with me, and our relationship was five years old by the end of that second year of grad school. I was financially dependent on Phoebe by this time, as she was the main wage earner, with me making a paltry salary first as a worker at the Isla Vista Food Co-Op, and then as a teaching and research assistant at the university. I didn't make enough money to pay for myself or pay my own way, so leaving Phoebe would drastically change my life, and fear of that held me back. So, rather than end the relationship, we got married. Part of me hoped that getting married might help Phoebe feel better, and might actually improve our relationship. I could hope, couldn't I?

The marriage happened late in the summer before starting my third year of grad school and beginning work on my Ph.D. We were married in Walnut Creek, and the wedding was officiated by Nori, my Zen instructor from Occidental, making us formally married in the Pure Land Buddhist Church (which was a great surprise to my Mormon grandmother!). Before the wedding took place, I was wandering around the grounds, down by a creek, and found two owl feathers. I took this as a sign that our union was approved of by the universe, reflecting back on our first kiss with the owl on top of Mt. Fiji at Occidental. Like many self-deluded spiritual people, I thought that signs and things encountered in the world indicated the rightness of one's actions. I know now that it's all just a game, and a terribly delusional game, at that, for it is a way of abdicating responsibility for one's choices and actions, instead attributing it to outside agencies and forces beyond one's control, like karma, fate, or the will of the spirits or the universe. It's a way of creating a false narrative for one's self that tends to victimize the individual as being at the whim of others. If I was consistent in my appreciation for signs (most people tend to pick and choose what they feel best fits their desired invented narrative), I might have noted that there was a massive blackout during our wedding that affected most of the Bay Area.

Anyway, we were married, sealed with a peck rather than a real kiss. Phoebe looked beautiful in her dress, and everyone was happy. However, my ever-observant father was worried. Sometime before the wedding, he asked me if this was really what I wanted. Despite the fact that I hadn't said anything to him about my unhappiness, he could see it. He thought I was making a mistake. In my denial, I dismissed his concerns and went ahead anyway. As was to be expected, the marriage didn't change anything between us, and things went on much as they had before.

It was some days later that the marriage was actually consummated. For our honeymoon, we went directly from the wedding to the San Francisco airport, where things were a little haywire due to the blackout. No food was available and we were hungry, as well as tired and hot. Eventually, we got on a plane and were on our way to Costa Rica.

Though we didn't have much of an intimate connection, Phoebe and I were certainly friends, and enjoyed spending time together out in nature. We spent much of our free time hiking, exploring, and camping, and we were both excited to be going to Costa Rica and getting the opportunity to spend time in the real jungle and rainforest and encounter the wildlife there. It wasn't as though things were awful between us – there was just no passion, no intimacy, and no deep and profound connection – something that showed. Other people we met on our honeymoon had a difficult time believing that we were newlyweds, because we certainly didn't seem like it. "Oh, we've been together for five years," I would tell people, as though that excused our lack of intimacy and passion. Really, we were just two friends going on a trip together who happened to be married.

I think we had sex twice on that trip, which was pretty good, considering that we were only having sex once a month at best, and virtually all of my advances toward Phoebe sexually were met with "not now," or "not today" on her part. Sexually, I was developing major insecurities and feelings of almost universal rejection. But I just stuffed it all inside and shoved it down in there where I wouldn't have to look at it or deal with it. I carried on.

In other regards, Costa Rica was great. We visited a variety of different regions in the small Central American country and saw a great diversity of wildlife. My birding self was more than satiated, with hundreds of new species of birds I had never seen before. And there were monkeys, and sloths, and caimans, and gators, and lizards, and snakes, and crabs, and bats, and scorpions, and frogs, and various forest animals of all shapes and sizes. It was great.

As a musician, and as someone interested in the musical expressions of other cultures, Costa Rica was disappointing, however. All the music on the radio or playing in shops and hotels was American pop music – the same damn stuff that was playing on the radio back home. We never came across anything that seemed even remotely like "Costa Rican" music. We also never encountered any of the indigenous cultures of Costa Rica, which would have required our traveling further south than we planned on miles of dirt and gravel roads to get to where the few reservations were, and besides, we had no real business going there anyway, so any hopes I had of getting any "real" culture in Costa Rica went unfulfilled.

I spent the next two years of school preparing for the monumental task of researching and writing my Ph.D. dissertation. To fulfill my language requirements, I took translation exams in both French and Navajo. I also arranged my dissertation committee and areas for my exams. Though only three professors were required for exams, I decided to work with four, mainly because there was a new addition to the faculty at UCSB, B. Alan Wallace, whose areas were Tibetan Buddhism and the philosophy of science and religion. If Alan had come on at UCSB earlier in my time as a student, there's a good chance that my overall direction at school would have been very different, for he embodied all the original interests that had first brought me to grad school. He had been living as a Buddhist monk in India, under the instruction of the Dalai Lama. There came a point, however, when he decided that he wanted to go back to school. With the Dalai Lama's approval, he renounced his monk vows and went on to get a degree in physics from Stanford University. His mind seemed like a highly focused laser to me, and I was eager to work with him. So, I chose Alan for an exam on the History and Philosophy of Science and Religion, another professor, Bill Powel, for an exam on Sacred Space, Ritual, and the Body (which were his areas of study, in addition to a focus on Taoism), Dwight Reynolds on Oral Traditions, Myths, and Narratives, and of course, Professor X, for Native American Religions.

For each professor, I had to come up with a reading list from which they would construct exam questions at the end of my studies. My reading list for all four exams combined ended up being massive, with 40-60 books for each exam. Though I had been an avid and persistent reader as a student, nothing quite compared to this reading marathon. I read, highlighted, and took notes for months on end, with many days reading nonstop from early morning to late at night. I actually rather enjoyed it as it fed my insatiable appetite for knowledge and information, and I just gobbled those books up. Overall, I really liked being a student, and in many ways, it was what I knew how to do best.

All of the exams went well, except, surprise, surprise, my exam with Professor X, which was to be my last. On the day of my scheduled exam, Professor X showed up an hour late with no exam questions written, lamely telling me, "I sprained my ankle – I mean wrist – yesterday, and couldn't write your exam questions." The department chair knew that I was supposed to have started my exam over an hour ago, so he gave Professor X a stern talking to, and urged me to be patient. She eventually came down the hall with a few hand-written questions, none of which seemed to reflect the vast amount of reading I had done for her in preparation for the exam. It felt like an absurd joke. But I answered them, passed, and was done with it. Quite mistakenly, I thought that I was moving closer to not needing to rely on Professor X, which I obviously couldn't, and soon would be heading out to work on my own at Mescalero where her total lack of responsibility would no longer be a barrier to my making progress in my work. Oh, how wrong I was!

The next part of the process was my dissertation prospectus, which is something of a contract between the student and his or her dissertation committee. The idea is for the student to come up with an outline of what is going to be researched, what materials and methods are going to be used, what the relevant literature is, and what the student hopes to show or demonstrate in the dissertation. The dissertation committee reviews the prospectus, advises on changes, and eventually, literally signs off on the document with their signatures, thereby finalizing what the dissertation will be about, and it gets filed away as an official document of the university. Any changes to the plan need to be approved of by the dissertation committee, and no one member of the committee can demand unilateral changes once it has been signed off on. So, guess what happened?

In order to get to the punch line of this particular story, I'll need to back up a bit. In the several years that had passed since my first visit to Mescalero with Professor X, we had gone back together a variety of times as she continued her own research on the Big Tipi, and I paved the way for my own upcoming extended fieldwork by making connections within the tribe and firming up commitments from those who would serve as my teachers and mentors in my study of the Mountain Spirits. It had been both Professor X's and my hope that Sydney would be my primary mentor at Mescalero, and it seemed promising from that first visit to Mescalero. However, the more we went out to Mescalero, the more distant and unavailable Sydney became. When it came time for me to really solidify things, I found that I couldn't get him to come to the door, and whenever I went to his house, no one would answer, despite the sounds of people inside. To put it mildly, things weren't looking good, as far as a relationship with Sydney was going. I was perplexed, because he had seemed so agreeable previously, but now, I couldn't even catch him to say hello. The thought of having him as primary mentor seemed totally unreasonable and my hope was quickly waning.

However, there were other, quite interesting developments. One was that I found Meredith to be tremendously friendly and open to working with me. In one of my later trips to Mescalero, I had shared with her a dream that I had had, and her interpretation of it had buoyed me up and inspired her to take on a mentoring role with me. In the dream, I was in the back of my mom and step-dad's Jeep, and they were driving. We were going through the forest and I was busy looking out the rear window, gazing up into the sky and trees of the forest we were passing through. I saw a golden eagle flying above us, which seemed to notice me observing it. When it did, it dove down to the Jeep, pulling in its wings tightly and gaining speed. At the very last moment, it expanded its wings to their full breadth. In a flash of iridescent blue light, it crashed directly into the rear window. Suddenly, the back of the Jeep was littered with eagle parts – feathers, talons, beak. The eagle was utterly destroyed. In the dream, I felt terrible, for I was under the impression that the eagle had come down because I had called it to me, and in doing so, had killed it. I buried my face in my hands and cried, sitting there in the back of the Jeep. When I took my hands down from my face, I was amazed to find that the disconnected eagle parts had somehow transformed into various items. There was a yellow cloth, and on the cloth was an abalone shell, a turquoise stone, a piece of obsidian, and a red mescal bean, just like the medicine people at Mescalero were fond of.

And that was the dream. Meredith just smiled when I told her this. "You're a medicine man," she told me, "and that's a medicine dream. You gotta collect all those things you saw in your dream, and that's what you'll use for healing and ceremony. That's your medicine." She thought it was amusing that this hadn't occurred to me and that I hadn't immediately gone out and collected the items as I saw them in my dream. To help get me started, she went into her freezer and pulled out an eagle tail. She removed one small feather and gave it to me, saying, "If anyone ever hassles you for having this, just tell them you're a medicine man and you have a right to it."

It actually wasn't my first eagle feather. At one trip to Mescalero, Sydney had sent his wife after Professor X and myself just as we were getting ready to leave. They had gifts that they wanted us to have. For me, there was a beautiful black and white young golden eagle feather – what tends to be the most prized kind of feather in Native American cultures. I took this as a sign of Sydney's commitment to working with me, but perhaps it was a consolation prize, as nothing ever seemed to come of it. It was confusing, the say the least.

Meredith, on the other hand, appeared more than willing to take me under her wing and show me the ropes of medicine practice, so that was a very positive development. And while she was a woman, and therefore supposedly ignorant of the inner workings of the Mountain Spirit tradition (it's all men's business, as the reader may recall), she was deeply knowledgeable about the tradition and would be a great asset. Besides, what I really wanted to learn was medicine practice, as this was my personal, as opposed to professional/academic, interest.

Because things weren't really going anywhere with Sydney, I had also discussed things with Willeto, and shared another dream I had with him. In the dream, I was driving Willeto through the forest and the car broke down. So, in order to get him to wherever he was going, I had to get him out. For a while, I was able to push him down the path in his wheelchair, but we eventually came to a river. I needed to get him to the other side. So, we set the chair aside and I picked him up and waded into the water. The river wasn't deep and only came up to my waist. In the riverbed, I could see what looked like gold glittering in the diffuse light of the forest. It was beautiful and I marveled at it. However, by the time I got to the other side of the river, Willeto had died in my arms. In desperation, I went running through the forest until I found Sydney, crying that he had to help Willeto. Sydney just looked at me, dumbfounded, and said that he couldn't help. End of dream.

I was hesitant to tell Willeto this dream, given that he died in it, and I was worried that he'd take it as a bad sign. Much to my surprise, it was the complete opposite. He listened to me tell it with eyes closed, as though he were picturing the events I was describing to him in his mind. When I was done, he lit a cigarette and handed me one as well (he always had us smoke tobacco whenever we discussed things that were "sacred"). There was a look of disbelief on his face and he shook his head slightly. "That's a medicine dream," he finally proclaimed. "It's about the knowledge that you're going to learn from me. When you're taking me through that water, that's when everything is clear to you and you understand, that's what that gold in the water is about. It's also showing you that you'll learn more from me than Sydney, and that he doesn't know as much as you think he does. That's quite a dream. A powerful dream."

Thus Willeto agreed that he would do whatever he could to help me with my research. He would be my teacher, and he would take it upon himself to introduce me to as many people as he could, and would get me into ceremonies that no other outsiders would be able to attend.

I was elated. It was perfect. Even though Sydney didn't seem to want anything to do with me, Willeto and Meredith were stepping up, and I was able to share intimate details of my own inner workings with them, and they accepted me and were encouraging. Problem solved.

At the time, I had shared all this with Professor X, and we discussed how I would be working, at least initially, primarily with Willeto and Meredith, with the hopes that they could introduce me to others and help me gain access more broadly within the culture. It was a start, and certainly enough for me to begin my research in real earnest.

So, to return to the dissertation prospectus, after everyone, including Professor X, had signed off on the document and I had officially dated and filed it with the religious studies department and university, Professor X called me into her office. In that meeting, she told me that she no longer thought I should do my dissertation research at Mescalero, and wanted to put me in touch with some White Mountain Apaches in Arizona, and I could go there for my research. Nevermind that I had spent the past four years developing contacts at Mescalero; nevermind that I had received commitments from Meredith and Willeto; nevermind that I had even been awarded a grant to go do this work at Mescalero; and nevermind that my entire dissertation committee had signed off on my prospectus, herself included. Professor X now wanted to me to change everything about my dissertation and basically start over.

I couldn't believe what I was hearing. Was this woman serious? Was she out of her mind? How could she be doing this, now, just weeks before I was planning to move out to Mescalero and begin my research? This was unbelievable.

In her favor, Professor X argued that I hadn't been able to secure Sydney's commitment, so I didn't have anyone at Mescalero to work with anyway. It was then that I reminded her that both Meredith and Willeto were planning to help me, and that we had all discussed this together in our most recent trip to Mescalero. Incredulously, Professor X denied any knowledge of this, despite the fact that she and Willeto and I had all sat down together and talked about my working with him. What in the hell was going on here?

"Well, I don't want you bothering Willeto," she said, at last. "He's frail and not well, and he doesn't need a young guy like you coming around and bothering him." She said that she wanted me to ask her permission any time I might want to go visit Willeto or talk with him, begrudgingly accepting that I was not going to suddenly change my dissertation research plans simply because she was telling me to in the eleventh hour. It seemed like a rather specious request from someone who never answered her phone or responded to email. Just how, exactly, was I supposed to check with her about visiting Willeto, and why would I honor this micro-managing request anyway? Having to rely on Professor X for anything was absurd, let alone acquiescing to her wanting to have control over my actions on a reservation over a thousand miles away. It all felt like a bizarre farce, and was something that I was looking forward to putting behind me and simply doing the necessary work to get my dissertation project researched and completed. So, that's how we left things when I finally departed Santa Barbara for my time at Mescalero. Of course, this wasn't the end of it, and things were only to become more difficult between us.

CHAPTER FOUR

LIFE AMONG THE MESCALEROS

It was the beginning of the summer of 1998, and I was ready to head out to Mescalero. I had secured a small grant to begin my research, and had some future grants that I was planning on applying for after getting out to Mescalero. The plan was that I was going to stay out there through the next year, and hopefully through the following summer, as well. I would return to Santa Barbara and Phoebe for holidays and when she had time off from her work as a teacher, but otherwise, we were to be separated for the duration of my fieldwork. It was something I was looking forward to, and there was no heartache on my part about leaving Phoebe behind and getting away from our relationship. Realistically, I couldn't wait to go be free and not have to deal with this constant source of frustration and dissatisfaction.

To prepare for my time at Mescalero, I traded in my Mazda sedan for an Isuzu Trooper, a big white boxy vehicle with the all-important four-wheel drive. When Willeto and I arranged that we would be working together, he had insisted that I needed a four-wheel drive so that we could get to all the places he wanted to take me and have me visit, and my little Mazda just wasn't going to cut it. The Trooper was by far the beefiest vehicle I'd ever owned, and clashed somewhat with my environmental attitudes about gas consumption, but it was necessary for the work I wanted to do, and the truth was, I enjoyed driving it. So I loaded it up, said goodbye to Phoebe, and hit the road for Mescalero. I felt free, excited, and filled with anticipation about what would come of my time as a free agent in the Southwest.

In my last visit to New Mexico, I had made arrangements with the owner of The Apache Motel in Tularosa to rent a room on a monthly basis for fairly cheap. It was a small room with a kitchenette, a bed, a small table, and TV with crappy reception. I also had a laptop computer, access to the still-nascent Internet and email, and had brought a few instruments and my 4-track recorder with me so I could continue to record and play music during my time in New Mexico. The post office was just down the street, and laundry and groceries were just up the street (Tularosa has only one main road). There was also a basketball court beyond the grocery store that I would frequent in the evening for a little exercise and entertainment. It wasn't much, but it was enough.

Willeto had insisted that I get in touch with him as soon as I got to New Mexico, a request that I was sure to honor, despite Professor X's misgivings and instructions that I was to always contact her first for her approval of any meeting between Willeto and myself. When we met, I was cautious to let him know that I didn't want to bother him, or take too much of his time, or be a burden on him – all of which he just looked at me strangely in response to. He'd already agreed that we'd be working together, so why was I making a fuss? After spending the day together and I was ready to go back down to my motel room, he said, "So you'll be here around 10 am tomorrow morning?" And that was that. From that moment on, Willeto's was my default go-to location, for he expected me to come by every day and spend as much time with him as possible.

Willeto's family was thrilled that I was spending time with "Grandpa Tony," and in many respects, I became his caretaker for the duration of my time at Mescalero. Though Willeto had been a chronic drinker for many years, he had consciously given up all drinking in anticipation of my arrival, something for which his family credited me. It was in my second meeting with Willeto, which happened in Santa Cruz in my second year of grad school, when Willeto learned that I wasn't a drinker. Professor X's daughter had arranged to bring Willeto, along with a group of White Mountain Apache Mountain Spirit dancers, to UCSC, as she had done with the Sun Clan Mountain Spirit dance group the year before. I had arranged for an apartment in the faculty housing at UCSC for Willeto and his sons for the weekend, using my father as a connection, and we had spent that weekend together. Willeto had been a little shocked when he asked me to get him some beer and sit and drink with him, and while I got him some beer, would not have any myself. I explained to him that I didn't like alcohol and just wasn't a drinker, so I wouldn't ever be joining him with a beer. Thus, in order to be more accommodating, he had quit drinking altogether. I was deeply appreciative, as I never enjoyed taking him to the tribal bar where all the drunks hung out, and didn't feel good about supplying him with the toxic drink. Now it was "pop" that he wanted, preferably root beer. That was a drink I was more than happy to share with him.

An average day with Willeto: arrive around 10 or 10:30 in the morning. Make Willeto coffee, "cowboy" style. Sit around for a couple hours drinking coffee, watch *The Price is Right, Family Feud*, and then the early news. Next, help Willeto get dressed and ready, and then head out. First, go to the post office and check the mail. Then, drive out to Ruidoso, the small tourist town over on the border of the other side of the reservation, and grab a hamburger and sit and eat while watching traffic (one of Willeto's favorite pastimes). Get money from the bank and then purchase money orders for any bills Willeto needed to pay. Then head back to the reservation and take a drive somewhere out in the mountains or into the rolling hills of the outskirts of the reservation, find a place that had a story that Willeto wanted to tell me about, and sit in the vehicle while smoking cigarettes and talking about the subject of the day. Then, return back to Willeto's in the evening and have dinner with the family. Usually I was back down to my place by 7 or 8 in the evening, when I would then spend a few hours writing notes on my laptop, followed by a little herb, some guitar, catching the late airing of *The Simpsons*, and then bed. That was pretty much an average day.

This regular routine was broken up by my visiting with other people, though Willeto always expected me at his place both before and after I met with anyone else, mostly so he could check on the accuracy of what I was learning from others. Willeto also had me drive him around so that he could introduce me to other people who he thought might be open to working with me and helping with my dissertation project – some of whom were agreeable, and others who didn't want anything to do with me.

One person he took me to was Nathaniel Chee, a medicine man and Mountain Spirit dance group leader who had a reputation for being open to working with "outsiders" such as myself. Nathaniel and Willeto weren't exactly friends, so Willeto didn't want to get out of the car when he directed me to Nathaniel's place on the other side of the reservation, instead just telling me to go knock on the door, no introductions. I did as instructed, and Nathaniel opened the door, greeting me warmly. I awkwardly explained myself (this was the first person Willeto didn't personally introduce me to, so I was all on my own for this one), and then waited. Nathaniel looked me up and down, considered things for a few moments, and then instructed that I was to bring him a piece of turquoise with buckskin tied through it and a cigarette. Once I got those items, I should come back and we'd get started. When I told Willeto this, he had a curious look on his face, as he understood what this meant, though I didn't.

The turquoise with a hole in it was easy enough to find. There was a Southwest art and gem shop for tourists across the street from my motel room, and they had various cuts of turquoise that I could choose from. Getting a cigarette was simple to procure. It was Meredith who supplied the buckskin, the final item that I needed. Once I had everything, I made my way back over to Nathaniel's. He came out of the house and started walking to my vehicle, saying, "OK – let's go!" and climbed in, waiting for me to drive him somewhere. He directed us onto one of the many dirt roads on the reservation, taking us out into the forested canyons on the south side of White Mountain, the main mountain on the reservation and a focus of much of the sacred lore of the tribe. We went to the spot where he had been initiated as a medicine man and tradition carrier as a young man, a place that Nathaniel considered to be "sacred ground." We got out of the Trooper and went to go stand at a spot that seemed nondescript to me, but was the exact right spot, according to Nathaniel. As was typical of the summer, monsoon storm clouds were gathering and a light rain was starting to sprinkle. Nathaniel requested the cigarette, which he took with one hand while holding the turquoise with the buckskin in the other. Lighting the cigarette, he began praying in typical Mescalero fashion, with gestures to the four directions, speaking in Apache. When he did so, thunder rolled through the canyon. Nathaniel smiled and looked at me, winking and saying, "This is going to be good."

He then explained to me what had just taken place. "I've initiated you into my medicine," he said. "From now on, anything that you want to know from me, just ask. I'll teach you about herbs, medicine, anything you want to know. You're always welcome in my tipi and you can come to our ceremonies, learn the songs, and I can even make you a dancer, if you want." I was astounded. When I came to Nathaniel, I had, of course, introduced myself as a student doing a research project on the Mountain Spirits who was looking for knowledgeable consultants and teachers. I had not asked him to initiate me into his medicine, and certainly had not expected it. "You'll be a powerful medicine man, one day," he exclaimed. "I think in about ten years, maybe a little more, you'll be very powerful."

Thus my work with Nathaniel began. Nathaniel had been practicing since he was 16, when he was first hired as a singer for the Big Tipi. The girl he sang for in that first ceremony later became his wife, and they had a number of children together. Nathaniel's three sons all sang and danced in his Mountain Spirit dance group, and they were all very welcoming of my presence in their tipi. Nathaniel liked to meet with me around once a week, and most of our visits together consisted of driving out to various locations where he would have me identify and gather different medicinal plants that he used in his practice as a medicine man, instructing me on their uses, the proper way of gathering them with prayer, pollen, and small rituals. I also had an open invitation to any ceremony that his dance group was involved in, and the door to their tipi was always open – an invitation that I was sure to always take advantage of and never missed an opportunity to sit with them. And though Nathaniel said on several occasions that he could teach me to be a Mountain Spirit dancer, that seemed to me to be a line I shouldn't cross, for even though Nathaniel insisted that it was his group to do with as he pleased, it was clear that other members of the tribe would find this a serious breech of decorum, and that was more controversy than I personally desired to be embroiled in. So, I declined.

A personal difficulty that I had with Nathaniel was that he routinely spoke to me about God. Like most Mescaleros, he was also Christian, and his talks with me were always peppered with references to God, usually with Nathaniel pointing upwards to the sky. "You need to always put God first, in all things," he would tell me, "and as long as you do that, everything you do will be good. Trust God and put Him first." At this time, like many alternative/countercultural folks, I just wasn't comfortable with the word "God." Personally, I didn't believe in an all-powerful and omniscient deity that was the creator and sustainer of the universe. I didn't want anything to do with Christianity, or other theistic traditions, and such references only called to mind Christian fundamentalism, denial of science and evolution, superstition, mythical thinking, and other irrationalities – not to mention the fact that Christians had been responsible for devastating Native communities and cultures and done everything they could to convert Natives from their indigenous traditions and lifeways. In other words, I had my own biases – some perhaps more justified than others – but they were still biases. I never shared any of this with Nathaniel, and just nodded along, privately waiting for when he'd get to "the good stuff" that I really wanted to know, but like it or not, belief in God as a powerful and loving deity was a big part of Nathaniel's understanding of the universe, and if I was going to work with him, then it was something that I'd have to deal with.

Pretty much everyone at Mescalero believed in God, in some form or another. In indigenous Mescalero tradition, respect was given to "The One From Whom Life Comes," or a bit more succinctly, "Life-Giver," though there were no prayers or ceremonies to honor "The Creator." In their tradition, Life-Giver was seen as a distant deity that was largely unapproachable. While they believed in this deity, it was the Mountain Spirits that were the main intermediary between humans and the power of the Creator and the power of "heaven," the source of infinite energy that gives shape, form, and life to all things. The Creator had given the Mescaleros the Mountain Spirits as a form of ritual and spiritual technology so that they could harness the power of heaven for themselves, for their own aims and purposes. This spiritual energy was directed and manipulated by the Mountain Spirits, and it was the vehicle through which the Mescaleros prayed, along with the Four Directions in general. Furthermore, the Mescaleros had the Big Tipi, which was also understood to have originated as a gift from The Creator to provide the Mescalero with a path to meaningful existence and knowledge of the sacred.

In indigenous Mescalero tradition, the sacred technologies of the rituals are intended for leading a good, full, healthy, and happy life. There is no focus on an afterlife, or any kind of reward or punishment from a universal judge. As humans, they are responsible for living in balance with themselves and their environment, and any punishment would come in the form of lack of rain, game, or plants that were necessary for life. Mescalero prayers focus on the four directions as being the source of the seasons and yearly cycle of growth, maturation, and decay. By focusing their minds in ceremony and prayer, they can direct and enhance the power of life that flows through all things, and help make the land and environment more conducive to life for everyone, plants and animals included. In this sense, if there were a drought, the Mescaleros would interpret it as indicating that they needed to pray more and perform more ceremonies. With global warming, and the near disappearance of snow from the once-year-round snowy peak of White Mountain (the feature for which the mountain originally received its name – "Green Mountain" would be more appropriate these days), Mescaleros were of the view that humans were not fulfilling their proper duties with prayer and ritual and needed to enthusiastically return to following tradition.

According to Willeto, someone who saw himself as a strict traditionalist and had no involvement with any of the many Christian churches or traditions found on the reservation, "The Creator" was actually created by people, and not the other way around. Willeto explained that "heaven" was not a "place," but an energy that made reality possible, somewhat like a well or spring that fed and nurtured life and reality. The power of heaven just existed and wasn't controlled by any kind of omnipotent deity or agency. "It was the minds of people that created The Creator," Willeto explained. "They put their minds together, and they created The Creator in heaven through their prayers. They needed something that they could communicate with, and this is what they created. Then, after people created The Creator, The Creator could do things for people, like give them the Big Tipi and the Mountain Spirits – these things that we live by."

In contrast, Nathaniel's view of God seemed far more Christian to me than Mescalero, and I was never comfortable with it. In my somewhat biased view, he seemed "contaminated" by Christian teachings and therefore less authentic. However, I just needed to accept that, of all the people I met and worked with at Mescalero, only Willeto held Christianity at bay, and proudly so, and everyone else had been influenced by Christianity, in one way or another. It was just the reality of the situation, and no amount of wishing things were otherwise on my part could have any positive effect on the matter.

Early on in my time at Mescalero, representatives of the tribal government came by Willeto's place to hire him for some ceremonial work they wanted done that summer. In an unprecedented move, the tribal government was out to hire virtually every medicine person and every dance group on the reservation for a series of ceremonies to bless and revitalize the tribe collectively. I strongly suspect that it was due to my presence that Willeto agreed to participate. He wasn't a fan of the tribal government, or their attempts to influence the affairs of medicine people and singers. This attitude of Willeto's traced back to his younger days when he was regularly singing in the Big Tipi. At some point, he was approached by the tribal president, Wendell Chino, who had a plan: Willeto would go and sing in the Big Tipi and all the songs would be tape recorded. These recordings would then be passed around to the younger men who were in training as singers. As Willeto was considered the foremost authority on the tradition, it would ultimately be up to him to insure that the up-and-coming young singers were properly trained.

Willeto wanted nothing to do with it. "Tribal government has no place in ceremony!" Willeto told me, "And not even the president can tell me what to do!" Wendell Chino was prepared for such a response, however, and countered with his own challenge, telling Willeto that if he wanted his relatives to keep their tribal jobs and tribal housing, and not spend the week in jail, he would do as Wendell insisted.

Not wanting to cause problems for his family, Willeto agreed, though only with his own agenda secretly in mind. An anthropologist named Claire Farrer had previously written a book about Mescalero and her work with one medicine man in particular, Bernard. In her book, she quotes Bernard as lamenting how Willeto was "changing the songs" and "not doing it right." What Bernard, and everyone else, was unaware of, was that Willeto made the decision to intentionally sing the songs incorrectly as his own personal response to being coerced into singing by Wendell. So, the songs were all recorded, and passed out among the young singers, but Willeto had introduced changes into all the songs as a form of protest. "That's no way to keep tradition alive," he insisted. "You can't make people do things. It has to be their choice."

So, Willeto was reluctant to get involved with the tribal government again, especially as Wendell Chino was still president, and Willeto didn't have any love for the man. In fact, the tribe had recently gone through a contentious and controversial issue that was spearheaded by Wendell. In the late 90s, the U.S. federal government was actively searching for sites to store radioactive nuclear waste. All the states were essentially refusing at that point, with no American communities desiring thousands-of-years-toxic waste in their proverbial backyards, and thus the federal government had turned to Native American reservations. When it suits them and their purposes, the federal government and its agencies treat Native American reservations as sovereign territories that are fundamentally distinct and separate from the United States of America. Thus, in such a case, if the Mescaleros agreed to bury radioactive waste on their reservation, the state of New Mexico would have no authority to tell them otherwise, no matter how much the citizens of New Mexico might protest. The feds were promising millions of dollars in payment for any tribe that might agree, and had selected the Three Rivers site on the Mescalero reservation as an ideal location for a waste dump. Wendell was supportive of the idea, and pushed through two votes on the matter recently in the tribe, much to the opposition and disagreement of virtually all the medicine people on the reservation. The project ultimately never went through, but there were numerous accusations of vote manipulation, corruption, and bribery.

But what was different for Willeto at this point was that he had me around, and he was enjoying being my cultural ambassador. He also enjoyed being a troublemaker. Thus he agreed to be involved with this government-sponsored series of ceremonies on one condition: "That guy over there gets to come with me, and no one can say anything about it." The tribal government officials weren't thrilled with this condition, but they acquiesced out of their strong desire to have Willeto on-board, and lend his credibility to the entire affair. The condition that the tribal government put on the arrangement was that I was to agree not to write about any of these ceremonies, either in my dissertation, or in any later publications. So, mum's the word on all of that. I'll just say that through Willeto, I ended up at a variety of ceremonies that I otherwise would have been immediately and forcefully chased off from, without question.

This development, however, seemed to play into the narrative that Professor X was constructing for herself of what she thought of my work out at Mescalero. As the summer moved on and my work progressed, communication with Professor X had been nearly non-existent and was rife with excessive game playing. I tried emailing her, letting her know what was going on, but there was never any response there. I would also call her, but of course, she never answered the phone, so I never reached her there. I would specifically leave messages about when I would be home and available by phone, and without fail, she returned my phone calls at precisely the times I told her I wouldn't be in my rented motel room and available to talk. It was starting to get absurd, especially as I had grant applications due for which I needed her signature and approval, yet it was impossible to get in touch with her. Things came to a head when the due dates came and I turned in the grant applications without her signature. The granting agencies themselves contacted Professor X, and she was apparently refusing to sign the documents attesting to the fact that she was my dissertation advisor.

Right at this time several of the different groups of people I was working with on the reservation independently pulled me aside to tell me that they had received phone calls from Professor X, asking them how I was "abusing" Willeto. This came as a shock to everyone, as in their eyes, I was the best thing that had happened to Willeto in many years. He had quit drinking, was healthier than ever, and had come out of his semi-retirement and was performing ceremonies again. If this was "abuse," then perhaps Willeto could use more of it, not less. For people at Mescalero, I was the best caretaker Willeto had ever known, and my presence in his life was a blessing. It was at this point I decided that Willeto and I needed to sit down and talk about all this directly and openly.

"She doesn't control me and can't tell me who I talk to or who I spend my time with," was Willeto's response to my telling him about Professor X's condition that I not talk to him or see him without her approval, and her impression that I was somehow "abusing" him. I hadn't wanted to have such a conversation with Willeto, for he and Professor X had been working together for years, and it wasn't my desire to sow any kind of discord between them. I respected their relationship and didn't see it as needing to conflict with our relationship. However, things were getting out of hand, and something needed to be done. Willeto insisted that the relationship between the two of us was our business, and no one else's, and he made it clear that he expected me to keep coming around as usual and not change anything about my behavior. I was happy to hear this, but something needed to be done about Professor X.

I got in touch with the chair of the religious studies department, explaining that Professor X was refusing to sign a document for a grant acknowledging that she was my dissertation advisor, and that she was actively attempting to undermine my credibility on the reservation through phone calls and accusations. It was after this that Professor X finally called me at a time that I said I would be home, and we spoke for the first time in several months.

Professor X's position was that she had "no idea" what I was doing on the reservation, what my research plan was, or even what I was working on. Was I hearing her correctly? Did she *really* just say that? She said that she had refused to sign the grant docs for precisely this reason. I reminded her that I had written an extensive dissertation prospectus that detailed my plans for my time at Mescalero, and to the best of my ability, I was simply following the outline that I had created. From my perspective, it seemed absurd for her to claim that she had "no idea" what my research was, unless, of course, which is probably the case, she never actually read the dissertation prospectus in the first place – something that I strongly suspected. Of course, by this point, her signature on the grant docs was a moot point – the deadline had already come and gone, and she had already effectively undermined me there. We tentatively worked things out on the phone, and she assured me that it wouldn't happen again.

What I learned from that conversation with Professor X was that, aside from simply being protective and possessive of Willeto, Professor X was probably also concerned about what I was learning from the older medicine man. She had been working on her book on the Big Tipi tradition for some 25 years or more, by this time, and didn't show any signs of being close to publishing. She asked me many questions about what Willeto and I would talk about and what kinds of information he was sharing with me. Though she didn't say it directly, it was clear that she was worried that I was learning all the same information that she wanted to have in her book. In other words, she didn't want me to be able to publish these materials before her. She had decided to see me not as her up-and-coming student, but as direct competition, and a threat. I had been transferred to her enemy list, and she had taken to thinking of me as someone she couldn't influence, manipulate, or control, and this frightened her. She hadn't been able to keep me from Mescalero, she couldn't keep me away from Willeto, and despite her best efforts, my work at Mescalero was going well and I would soon have enough material to write my dissertation. It was more than she could handle, and she was starting to lash out in her fear of loss of control and competition. However, it was never my intention to compete with her, and while I was learning about the Big Tipi, it was for context – to understand the relationship between the two traditions of the Big Tipi and the Mountain Spirits and how they were situated within Mescalero culture. I certainly was not looking to focus my research on the Big Tipi, and was only using that as a backdrop for my specific research on the Mountain Spirits. We were past the point of no return by now, however, and I had effectively lost her support for my research and work at Mescalero.

Ultimately, it was thanks to my grandfather that I was able to continue my studies at Mescalero, as he provided me with funds to see me through the next year. I was grateful, as was Willeto, who decided that in my grandfather's honor, we should travel up north and go see all the places my grandfather had frequented when he was young and living with the Navajo. Besides, Willeto had relatives he wanted to visit up there at Navajo, and at some of the Pueblos, so it would be a multipurpose trip. And, there were some sacred mountains up there he wanted to take me to, as well.

In my time at Mescalero, Willeto and I traveled around almost the entire state of New Mexico, and even took some trips down into Texas. I kept a map on which I highlighted all the various roads we took on our trips, and aside from the northeast corner of the state, we pretty much had everything covered in yellow highlighter. Part of Willeto's teaching methodology was that we should actually visit anywhere he had a story, either personal or traditional, that he wanted to tell me. Thus, instead of just telling me about the different sacred mountains in New Mexico and their connections to Mescalero traditions or the Mountain Spirits, we went and visited all of them. Sometimes, it would require us to follow particular routes across the landscape, as "First the dancers stopped here," and then later, "they stopped here," and then "they crossed over these mountains here," and so on. This echoed Willeto's own instruction as a youth, when his grandfathers had taken him by horseback on a year-long trip throughout what they considered to be Mescalero territory, instructing Willeto all along the way.

In November of that year, 1998, shockwaves rippled through the Mescalero community with the death of Wendell Chino from a heart attack at a health facility in Santa Monica, California. The tribal vice-president under Wendell had been medicine man and ceremonial singer, Paul Ortega, who then ascended to president. I had started working with Paul, who I actually first read about in a copy of *Shaman's Drum* magazine, that summer, and had gotten to know him some. We had semi-regular meetings at his place in Mescalero. This change also meant that another artist and singer I had gotten to know, Oliver Enjady, moved up from his position on the tribal council to become vice-president.

Wendell's death brought out many of the contradictions in his role as president of the Mescalero Apache tribe. He was widely hailed as a Native American hero by non-Mescaleros, as he had spent his life fighting for Native American rights and sovereignty, but at Mescalero, his legacy was much more mixed. When I took Willeto to view his casket and pay his respects, we were informed that Willeto was the first medicine person to show up and offer a prayer. After, the tribal government soon showed up at Willeto's house to hire him to help perform a cleansing ceremony on the tribal government office buildings to pave the way for new leadership. For many at Mescalero, Wendell had been something of a corrupt semi-dictator and possible embezzler. He had served some 17 terms as president of the tribe, and many considered this a result of vote rigging, though nothing was ever specifically proven on the matter. Regardless of the status of his legacy, it was the end of an era.

Paul Ortega didn't last long as tribal president. When people started looking at the tribal books after Wendell's death, millions of dollars were found to be missing. Paul was painted as the person responsible for this financial mismanagement, though many people privately told me they thought Paul had nothing to do with it, and that the money had been stolen by Wendell and was probably hidden away in secret accounts. For the short time that Paul was president, he had me work on various projects for the tribe, such as creating a "feast-givers' guide" on proper ceremonial etiquette, and a report on the state of the Mescalero Apache language and its methods of instruction in the Mescalero school system. I enjoyed being able to do this work for Paul and the tribe, though most likely it was all lost in the transition to a new president. Rightly or wrongly, Paul became the focus for the money scandal, and he was impeached by the tribe, right around the same time that Bill Clinton was being impeached by the U.S. Congress for his affair, and subsequent cover-up, with Monica Lewinsky. Paul was always viewed with some suspicion by other tribal members, as he was deemed to be a "city Indian" in that he had been educated off the reservation, and also held workshops and talks for non-Natives, such as I had seen advertised in *Shaman's Drum.* According to some, he was a "red apple: Indian on the outside, white on the inside." Personally, I found him to be an interesting fellow with a curious way of speaking, and I liked him. He was also a musician, and his music can still be found on the internet. After his impeachment, he spent less time on the reservation, and was harder to track down to work with, so our regular meetings gradually fizzled out.

It was also from Paul that I first learned that Professor X's claim of being of Mescalero ancestry was something that was debated on the reservation, and that some people were highly offended by this. "She's from Las Cruces," Paul told me. "Her family's not from here. She's Mexican, not Mescalero." I was surprised to hear this, and found this view echoed by other voices across the reservation. As in many Native American cultures, identity was a big issue on the Mescalero reservation, and claims of lineage were not taken lightly. On the reservation there were divides not only among Mountain Spirit dance groups and their collective identities, but also divides along Mescalero and Chiricahua lines, mixed Pueblo heritage, Navajo, people with "Spanish" blood, and people with Mexican blood. Then there were the "full Mescaleros," like Willeto, who claimed allegiance with only Mescalero tradition, and those who also practiced Christianity. Beyond that, there were "city Indians" and "res Indians." There were also "real" medicine people and singers and those who were considered by others to be "wannabes." No one's identity was taken for granted, and virtually everyone had their authenticity and identity challenged by others at some point. Overall, there was very little sense of unity or shared identity, despite the overarching umbrella identity of being a member of the Mescalero Apache Tribe, and everyone was vying for power and influence culturally, spiritually, politically, economically, and religiously. Apparently, Professor X's identity was just as contested as everyone else's on the reservation, and for many, she was considered far more of an "outsider" (like myself) than I had originally believed.

Another medicine man and ceremonial singer that I spent some time with was Sherman Blake, who also happened to be a member of the Native American Church. We had various conversations about our experiences with entheogens; me with mushrooms, him with peyote. He expressed his displeasure with the fact that it was something he didn't feel he could be very open about at Mescalero, given local attitudes toward peyote, but he was glad that he could travel to the Navajo reservation to work with the medicine, as it was only a day's drive away and therefore still accessible. On occasion,

Sherman and I would get together simply to play guitar. He lived just up the hill from Willeto, and I was also giving guitar lessons to one of Willeto's grandsons, Scotty, so I had my guitar with me on occasion and would head up to Sherman's for a little jamming.

When I wasn't visiting people or hanging out or traveling with Willeto, I was at ceremony. Unlike the Big Tipi ceremony, Mountain Spirit dancers could do their work year-round, though ceremonies were rare in the winter, given the cold and snow. They could be "brought out" whenever the necessity arose, however, so potentially their season was year-round. There were six different groups of Mountain Spirit dancers on the reservation, and I spent many, many hours carefully observing all of them. While they all had similarities in their dress and dance styles, there were also many subtle differences. Dances also varied according to the style of song being sung, its placement in the overall ceremony, and the kind of ceremony being performed. For the uninformed, it all pretty much looked the same. But the more I observed, the more subtle differences I noticed, and I kept track of all of them. I also had an on-going project of drawing all the various features of their ceremonial regalia and symbolism, a task that took quite some time as they only danced at night around a bonfire, and thus it took a great deal of careful attention to detail to really get things right. Eventually, I had a number of "plates" of the Mountain Spirit dancers that I started taking around to my teachers, asking for their feedback on their accuracy. Everyone wanted to know where I got them, and upon learning that I had made them myself, all wanted copies for themselves.

As my fieldwork progressed, Nathaniel's health started to decline. First, he started to go blind in one eye, and then he began having seizures. This was the beginning of a series of tragedies for the Chee family. During my fieldwork, a relative committed suicide by hanging himself in his garage. Not long after I completed my fieldwork, Nathaniel died. Then, shortly after this, one of his sons, Abraham, who was my age, had been run over by his wife when she was backing out of their driveway, putting Abraham on life support, and then dying some years later. Sadly, these were the kinds of stories that many families shared on the reservation. There was more than enough tragedy and suffering to go around.

Meredith's health was also in decline. I helped her move out of "Old Ladies Town" to a more remote location on the reservation, spending many hours organizing and stacking all the boxes of fluids and equipment for her regular dialysis in her diabetes treatment. One of her feet became gangrenous and had to be amputated, and like Willeto, she ended up in a wheelchair. That didn't stop her from working with me, however, and she would always make sure that I was coming by whenever a client was coming to work with her, so I could observe her medicine practice in action, and then she could give me instructions for myself afterwards. It was a wonderful relationship, and one that I will always treasure. She died at age 68 in 2006.

Willeto died at 74 in 2010. I last saw him in the summer of 2008.

Toward the end of my time at Mescalero in the summer of 1999, my good friend, Devon, flew out to El Paso from Oregon to come pay me a visit and spend some time with me at Mescalero for that year's 4th of July festivities. The main significance of Devon's trip was that it was the first time I had ever heard about Burning Man. Devon had been the year before with his wife, Minda, and was planning on returning again that year. I must admit that I had a hard time picturing just what in the world Devon was talking about – playa, art cars, theme camps, naked people, a big man made out of wood and neon lights that would burst into flames to the wild cheers of thousands of partiers at the end of the week, costumes, art installations, radical self-reliance, participation, dust storms and whiteouts, MOOP ("matter out-of-place – Burner lingo for trash) – it all seemed like some fantastical world of psychedelic strangeness. Devon was obviously enamored with the event, and was looking forward to returning. "You've got to go." He told me. "You'd love it."

Despite all of Devon's praise for Burning Man, at that point, it seemed to me that it was something I'd never realistically be able to attend. For many schools, Burning Man is held during the first week of the fall term. I thoroughly expected that after I completed my dissertation, I would get a job as a professor somewhere, and that would be that. No Burning Man for me! I'd forever and always be busy teaching. I was wrong, of course, but I didn't know that then.

My official fieldwork at Mescalero came to a close at the end of the summer. Tribal politics had shifted after Paul's impeachment and the rise of a new tribal council and administration. One medicine man, Joey Padilla, called me over to his house one afternoon and told me that there had been discussions about me during a tribal council meeting, and some people wanted to see me chased off the reservation. Joey expressed concern that they might try and confiscate my research materials and urged me to head for home. I spent a great deal of time discussing the matter with my grandfather, who thought it was all just noise that really didn't matter for me or my research, but when I really thought about it, it was probably time for me to go. I was out of money, for one. Furthermore, I had more than enough materials to write my dissertation. By this point I literally had several thousand pages of notes typed on my computer. If I didn't have enough information to write a dissertation by then, I probably never would.

So I decided to leave. The only thing that was keeping me at Mescalero was the fact that I was thoroughly enjoying myself and had fallen in love with the people there and my relationships with them. I loved hanging out with Willeto, and we had become fast friends and companions. The hardest thing was telling Willeto that I would be going home. Though he was never one to show much emotion, he was clearly greatly saddened by this, and I shared his feelings. I also knew that once I left, he'd probably never see the kind of care and attention I had given him again for the rest of his life. It had been a very special time for both of us, and it would be something that neither one of us would ever be able to recreate again.

Originally, the plan had been for Phoebe to visit me out at Mescalero at the end of the summer, and I would return later to Santa Barbara, probably in the winter, after the main ceremonial season had come to a close. We shifted our plans, however, so that Phoebe flew out, and we drove back to Santa Barbra together, making a stop at the Grand Canyon on the way back. It was her one and only trip out to Mescalero, and I was sure to take her around to meet everyone I had worked with over the past year and several months. She was happy to be getting me back, though the feeling wasn't very mutual. I had actually quite enjoyed my time away from Phoebe, but now I was to return to the reality of our relationship together, something I had been able to just forget about out at Mescalero, as it hadn't been something that I was forced to face on a daily basis. At least in returning home, I had plenty of work to keep me busy. I had to sort through thousands of pages of notes and write a dissertation, after all, and then I would be on to looking for a job. My time at Mescalero was now at an end.

CHAPTER FIVE

FROM THE ABYSS TO BURNING MAN

The next few years were to be the most frustrating period of my life, and a time when I needed to make some radical adjustments to who I thought I was and what I thought I was doing with my life. While there were positive developments that came from this period, the frustration and disappointment were extreme and tended to overshadow most everything else, with the exception of Burning Man.

Upon returning to Santa Barbara, it was now time for me to write my dissertation and begin the arduous task of looking for relevant job openings and submitting applications. The university had a system set up to keep letters of recommendation on file for students that could be sent out for any job application. These letters were to be kept confidential, and though the student could send them out whenever necessary, they were not available for review. The standard practice was to get letters from professors and put them on file, starting early in the job application process, and the letters could be updated as the student got closer to completion of the dissertation. It was expected that professors would likely have to rewrite their letters a couple times in order to keep them up-to-date and relevant for the student. Some jobs required letters be written specifically for that job and these on-file letters were not accepted.

So, one of the first things I did was get the proper forms for the letters to pass out among my dissertation committee so that I had some materials ready as job openings came around. As should be no surprise, I had no trouble getting letters from all of my professors, except for Professor X. She finally did submit a letter, after missing deadlines for jobs for which I was applying (I turned in my applications anyway, though there was no possibility of me getting an interview without a letter from my dissertation advisor), and as it turned out, it was a joke of a letter. At some point, in one of my many trips to the graduate division in the school administration buildings, a worker left my file out as she went to see if a new letter had come in. On the top of the open file was Professor X's letter. It consisted of one sentence. "Though I have not yet seen Martin's dissertation, he has proven himself to be a competent writer," she had written. That was it. That was her letter of recommendation. Like much of the reset of my relationship and interaction with Professor X, this was a complete joke. There was no way I'd ever get an interview with a letter like that, so I never had it sent out in my job applications and I urged search committees to contact Professor X directly for a letter.

One might think that I was jumping the gun in asking for a letter before my dissertation was even written, but in some respects, my case as a student was exceptional. The majority of students who worked with Professor X were themselves Native, and every last one of them had teaching positions lined up at universities *before* they had even completed the research for their dissertations, let alone written them. Some of her students had been teaching for several years already while they continued to work on writing their dissertations. Demand for *Native* students teaching Native American religions was that high. Not so for a white guy like myself.

Not having any recourse, I pushed ahead anyway. I spent a couple months sorting through my notes from Mescalero, and by the end of December, had written a 600-

page dissertation. I turned it in to my dissertation committee, much to their astonishment. It was the professor of oral traditions, Dwight Reynolds, who called me into his office and told me that for one, the dissertation was much too long – it should be closer to 200 pages rather than the 600 it was now. It also needed to have a "literature review" – something I hadn't included, and, as he saw it, it had far too much of me in it, as I had written much of it in a manner that was similar to how I've written about my time at Mescalero here in this book – from a personal perspective, describing in detail my personal interactions with people at Mescalero. As such, it didn't seem academic enough, and Dwight wanted the tone of the entire document to shift into something that was more neutral and less focused on my experiences.

I appreciated the feedback, and immediately went about making the kinds of changes he suggested, and within another month, I had a completely new version of my dissertation that was more in line with what Dwight had requested and was under 300 pages, so still a little long, but far more manageable than the original 600 pages. Dwight provided more feedback on the new version, I made some more changes, and then had what became the final version within another month. He also told me then (and this was news to me), that standard practice was to write a dissertation one chapter at a time, and get directed feedback from the dissertation advisor all throughout its progress. Apparently, my sitting down and just writing the thing wasn't proper form.

Over the next couple months, I had the approval of three of the four members of my dissertation committee. The exception, of course, was Professor X. By all reasonable accounts, I should have completed my time as a grad student by the end of winter term, 2000, and at the very latest, at the end of spring term. As it turned out, I didn't complete my program, due to Professor X, until the end of the summer of 2000 in late August. In the meantime, I had even taken a couple more trips out to Mescalero to share the dissertation with those who had been my teachers and get their feedback on what I had written. Everyone but Professor X had read it, approved it, and was ready for it to be done.

Getting Professor X to read the dissertation was nearly impossible, and truth be told, I think it was impossible; I don't believe that she ever read anything that I gave her. By this time, I was exasperated and was having regular meetings with the dean of graduate studies as well as the chair of the religious studies department regarding both my dissertation and my need for a current and up-to-date letter of recommendation by Professor X. The best advice that came from the dean of graduate studies, knowing full well of Professor X's reputation, but also understanding that as a tenured professor, a woman, and a person of color, there really wasn't anything they could do, was that I should choose a different topic, find a new dissertation advisor, and essentially start again. Here I was at what was supposed to be the very tail end of my time as a graduate student, and the best anyone could offer me was the advice that I begin anew. It was maddening and beyond frustrating.

In order to officially graduate at the end of the summer, and not have to pay for another useless and unnecessary term as a graduate student with nothing to do, I needed to have my dissertation turned in to the UCSB Library by 12 noon on a Friday. Under "orders" from the chair and the dean, Professor X had been instructed that she was to read the damn thing and sign off on it. True to form, it was 5 pm on Thursday afternoon, the evening before the dissertation was due the very next day, that Professor X met me in her office and gave me "notes" on my dissertation. I was appalled. The "notes" were several hand written sentences on a piece of yellow paper with page number references to the *first* version of my dissertation, the massive 600 page document that I had immediately changed after Dwight's critique, and not on either of the two subsequent versions I had made available to my professors. In other words, her "notes" were completely useless and totally irrelevant, as they were not in any way applicable to the document as it now existed. I walked out of her office, crumpled the paper into a ball, deposited it in the nearest recycling bin, and rushed to the print shop to get everything ready to turn in the next morning.

A few days later was my graduation ceremony, and nothing in my life had ever felt more of a sham than that event. Even my relationship and marriage with Phoebe felt more genuine and authentic than this. When you complete your Ph.D., you are "hooded" at graduation by your dissertation advisor. When it was my time to be hooded, Professor X put the hood on me backwards and inside out. She also "blessed" me with an eagle feather, much to the astonishment of the audience, who seemed to feel that it was something truly special. I just wanted to cry. I was miserable.

To top it all off, Professor X had just recently ensured that I wasn't going to get a job at a nearby university in San Louis Obispo. The chair of their ethnic studies department was retiring, and I applied for the open position. After several phone calls and much anticipation, they said that they wanted to offer me the job, but all that was missing was – you guessed it – a letter of recommendation from my advisor. In response to my pleadings, Professor X had called the university and essentially slandered me to the hiring committee, telling them that I had committed "abuses" at Mescalero, had received poor reviews as a teaching assistant at UCSB (my reviews were actually in the top percentile of all grad student teaching assistants at the university), and whatever else she may have told them, and thus the job offer never came through.

It wasn't until 2002, two years *after* completing my program, and three years since I had first requested it, that the dean of graduate studies informed me that Professor X had finally submitted a decent letter of recommendation for me that was now on file. By that point, I had applied to over 30 jobs without any recommendation by my dissertation advisor – a fruitless and hopeless adventure.

Thus, there I was, at the end of the summer of 2000 – a 27 year old man who had been in school his entire life, up to that point, who had always assumed he'd continue with school, going on to become a university professor, with very little work experience outside of teaching, and absolutely no hope of getting a job in his chosen field of study.

It was devastating, and I had no idea what to do with myself. One response I had was simply to read. It had been many years since I had read something purely for pleasure – certainly not since I had been an undergrad some six years earlier. In high school, I had been fond of Herman Hesse and Anne Rice, but I had read all of their books. I had also read Frank Herbert's book, *Dune*, and knowing that there were more books in the series, decided to re-read *Dune,* and then all the rest of the Dune books, including ones that were being written by his son, Brian Herbert, and Kevin J. Anderson. That was one pleasure of not having an academic job: I could actually read for pleasure, and could read novels, as opposed to exclusively reading things that were relevant to my specific academic work.

I also started doing more music, at this point. As a grad student, I had performed for a few years with Dreamtime Continuum, and would continue to do so for the next few years, but recording my own music was something that was left for breaks in the school year. Over winter and spring breaks, I would get a bag of mushrooms and eat them over several days, interspersed with recording songs on my 4-track recorder. Now that I didn't have to study all the time, I could record music any time I liked, so I did.

My friend Kevin, whom I had played with in college, also got in touch with me at this time. He was living down in Santa Monica, and had just recorded an album on his new digital recording software, ProTools, and invited me to come down and add some mandolin, harmonica, flute, and percussion to diversify the sound of his album. I spent the weekend down in Santa Monica, recording on my own while Kevin was out at work and soon learned the advantages of digital recording. I downloaded the free version of ProTools when I returned home, and started using that instead of my 4-track. This same time was also the birth of MP3.com, and I started uploading my music on the Internet, which was a long, slow process, as all that was available at that time was snail-paced dial-up.

In order to have images that went with my music online, I also started using Photoshop and digital image editing software. In many ways, this period was a revolution in my use of the personal computer and my relationship to digital technology. Prior to then, I had really only used the computer to write papers, send a few emails, and occasionally make use of the Internet. Now I was actively posting materials online, sharing art and music, and making all of it on the computer. It was great, and I spent many hours in front of the computer screen in artistic pursuits, looking to build an online audience for my creativity.

As for work, right after graduating, I visited Sudama up at his place in the hills in Santa Barbara and lamented over my situation. It was then that he suggested I try getting a job at a school downtown where he worked teaching English to international students. At first I just laughed – I had no qualifications or experience in this area, so why would I be able to get a job there? Sudama pointed out that I had studied many languages – some Sanskrit, a little Tibetan, Navajo, Apache, and French, and that I had taken many classes in linguistics – so I was probably more qualified than I realized.

What sealed the deal when I went in for an interview was the fact that the academic advisor at the school was a former partner of another student who had worked with Professor X at UCSB. She was very perplexed when I came to her looking for work, but all that I needed to say was that I had had troubles with Professor X, and as a result, had been unable to get a job. She hired me on the spot, and I was to begin teaching the next day.

Thus began my involvement with teaching English to international students. Compared to the rigorous academic work that I was accustomed to, the job was an absolute breeze. The pay wasn't so great, but at least it was work, and at least I was teaching – something I enjoyed doing, even if it wasn't in my area of study. I soon also took on the job of leading the internship program at the school as well as arranging a weekly lecture series. Compared to Phoebe's pay as a kindergarten teacher in the Goleta Unified School District, I was making very little money, but at least I was finally doing something to contribute to our financial wellbeing.

The work was fairly simplistic, especially when I was teaching the lower-level classes, which is where new teachers started out. Here I was with my Ph.D. in religious studies teaching students to ask, "Where is the beach?" It was definitely a knock down from any high expectations I might have had about an academic career and sharing my knowledge of religion, philosophy, and culture with eager young minds. The up side was that the job itself didn't come home with me, didn't require any research or study on my part, and it was interesting to be working with students from all over the world and getting to know their cultures and their impressions of Americans and the United States. It wasn't glamorous or prestigious, but at least it could be fun, and it gave me a reason to get out of bed in the morning other than just wallowing in pity that my life wasn't at all what I had hoped or expected it would be.

When summer came around in 2001 and it was still painfully apparent that I wasn't going to be getting an academic job and going off to teach at a university, I started making plans with Devon to join him at Burning Man. Devon's marriage to Minda dissolved that spring, and though we were originally planning to all attend Burning Man together, it was just to be Devon and myself. Phoebe wouldn't be going, as the week of Burning Man was, for her, the first week of school, and she'd be at work. Thus began the tension that long-existed between Phoebe and myself regarding Burning Man. As our main source of income, Phoebe was thoroughly displeased that I would be spending "our" money on a vacation that didn't include her – and that I was saving up my earned days off from teaching English to take this trip with Devon. The English school was year-round, and unlike Phoebe's job, didn't have any automatic time off like winter, spring, or summer breaks. As a teacher, I earned time off based on how many hours worked per month, and they accrued slowly. Also, my pay was so low that the idea of "saving" any of it was a joke, as everything went to paying off student loans and our basic living expenses like rent and groceries. This also began Devon's habit of essentially paying my way to Burning Man, as I couldn't afford it on my own, and certainly didn't have Phoebe's approval to spend what was really her money on my private vacation. The tension over the situation only got worse over the years as I continued to attend Burning Man, and it increasingly became the focus of my own happiness and sense of purpose and personal expression of freedom and creativity. Phoebe was never happy with it, and as she was to routinely let me know, "I hate Burning Man, I hate that you go to Burning Man, and I hate that you love Burning Man."

Regardless of how Phoebe felt about it, I made up my mind to go. Things hadn't been so great for me lately, and the thought of going on a wild vacation with my best friend was by far the most appealing thing that had come my way in a while. I wasn't about to pass it up after all the enthusiastic praise Devon had made of the Burn. I wanted something fun in my life to look forward to, and this beat out all the other options by a long shot – especially when contrasted with the idea of going on vacation somewhere with Phoebe. There was no comparison in terms of which idea got me excited and feeling positive about life.

Thus began my 11-year love affair with Burning Man, first attending in 2001, and then returning every year through 2011. My life has now changed so dramatically that Burning Man no longer serves as the release valve that it once was for me, and while I still desire to go, I don't feel the need to go the way I once did.

At the time of that first trip to Burning Man, however, it was like a beacon of hope in my life. It was to be Devon's third trip, and his first without Minda. We spent many hours on the phone and communicating online in epic preparation for the Burn. I read everything I could on the Burn and how to prepare and what to bring. Still, I had no idea what I was really in for, and that was part of the joy.

We arrived at the Burn on the opening day of Monday, along with a long line of cars. We had met in northern California at our parents' houses in Chico, me coming up from Santa Barbara, Devon coming down from Eugene. We loaded up a van Devon had rented for the adventure with all our gear, our PVC pipes for a new style of dome Devon wanted to make that he had previously seen on the Playa, food, and crappy Playa bikes, and headed over the mountains of the Sierra Nevadas and made the trip out to Black Rock City, USA.

We could hardly contain our excitement, especially after we got off the main highway after Reno and started heading out on the highway that would take us to the open playa beyond Gerlach. It felt as though we were on some profound pilgrimage, along with the other obvious Burners on the road. You could just sense everyone's excitement and anticipation. I marveled at the crazy arrangements of packing on other vehicles and the strange and marvelous art cars that were being towed in. All the vehicles looked dangerously over-loaded, bloated with gear, supplies, and strange odds and ends that were to become decorations, art projects, and party materials. Clearly this event did not involve camping light or sparingly. I had no idea just how outrageous the place truly was, and could only imagine while looking at the other cars along the road.

We arrived late in the afternoon and made it into Black Rock City without having to wait in line with other cars – only a short delay at the greeters' station and then on to the city proper. In that first year, I think there was something like 20,000 people at the Burn. In my last year, 2011, there were almost three times that many people present, and the lines for getting in and out of the event have become astronomically worse, with multiple-hour-long waits on the short drive in and out of the city.

After looking around for some time, we settled on a spot somewhere between 3:00 and 4:00, and made camp on the corner of the street. There weren't any major theme camps near us, as at that time, the big theme camps were all located along the Esplanade and center of the city. Here on the outskirts, it was all open camping, and theme camps hadn't yet been moved out on the radial streets. In addition to our personal tents, we put up a PVC dome, which we covered with a parachute. The weather was near-perfect at that year's Burn, so wind and dust was mostly at a minimum, with the exception of one big dust storm late in the week that was followed by a refreshing rain and light thunder storm as the sun set. It was the first time I had ever been anywhere that people applauded the weather, with people cheering for the thunder and ooing and awing at the stunning sunset.

Across the street from us were two young women who had bikes decorated with paper maché and rendered as Willie E. Coyote and the Roadrunner. The bike I had purchased for the event blew a tire on my first ride on the first day, so the women across the street were kind enough to let us borrow their Looney Tunes bikes on occasion, which always got a good response from others, watching me as Coyote chasing after Devon as the Roadrunner, but otherwise we just enjoyed walking about the playa during my first Burn. Also, one of the women across the street was a stripper by profession, and part of her daily hygiene routine was to squat out front of their camp, right along the road, in a kiddie pool, while she shaved her vagina. She'd be over there, waving at Devon and myself while we sat in the shade and drank our morning coffee, just marveling that a place like Black Rock City existed where a sight like this was just a regular part of the day and nothing special.

I absolutely loved Burning Man. That first night we went out and wandered the playa. I had never seen, nor even imagined, anything like it. All kinds of stuff was burning, there were lasers and art cars everywhere, people were all dressed up in crazy outfits and blinking lights, and everywhere I looked there was another wild thing, the likes of which I had never seen. It was just one marvel after another. I took a drum and a didj out with me and got into several jams, at one point playing didj for people who were dancing around a flaming art piece. It was just too cool. I was in heaven! I LOVED Burning Man!

Like so many other Burners, I felt happy and free at Burning Man. I'd never been anywhere that had so many happy and creative people. Though I had been to various festivals and music events, I didn't think I'd ever been anywhere that if you asked people, "If you only had one week left to live, what would you do?" they would most likely answer that they were in the process of doing it. Everyone was just so filled with joy and enthusiasm. It was profoundly beautiful. And the night that the Man burned, I'd never been so passionately thrilled in my life. I screamed and yelled and jumped up and down and gloried in the destruction of the faceless man who was sacrificing himself so that we all might party like there was no tomorrow. In all, Burning Man repeatedly brought tears to my eyes and made my heart feel like bursting with joy. Whatever else was going on in my life, I knew that this was where I wanted to be, and this was what I wanted to be doing. I was hooked.

It was also at that Burn that I experienced *Salvia divinorum* for the first time. In college I had gotten into reading the *L.A. Times,* a habit I continued through grad school and beyond. That spring, I had read an article about this guy, Daniel Siebert, who was selling salvia over the internet in southern California, and the article even came complete with his web address. I looked it up, and sure enough, there was *Salvia divinorum* for sale, right there on the Internet! With great enthusiasm, I ordered a small package of enhanced leaf salvia from Daniel and stashed it away as a special treat for Burning Man.

Devon and I waited well into the event before trying the salvia. Everything we read about it indicated that Burning Man might not be the best environment for the radical and brief action of salvia, so we waited one night until our local neighborhood was quiet, with everyone having gone out for the evening. We set ourselves up in our dome, lit a candle, and got out the pipe and the salvia. From what I had read, you only needed a little bit of the enhanced leaf salvia, so I packed a relatively small bowl of the leafy green herb. I took a hit, held it in, and waited. Nothing happened. Devon did the same, taking a tentative hit to no result. I cleared out the bowl, packed about twice as much in, and took a big, throat-searing hit.

And that did it. Within seconds, I had blurted out, "It's here!" To which Devon replied, "What's here?" "I'm shrooming – no – I'm saging!" I proclaimed. As I was later to describe it, the action of the sage hit me like a psychedelic tsunami, seemingly welling up out of nowhere, and then breaking over my being in a torrent of psychedelic experience. The only comparable experience that I could think of was experimenting with nitrous oxide with my cousin Tim when I was a teenager. Like nitrous, this came on fast, but nitrous is just expansive and dreamy, whereas this was fully psychedelic, and very strange.

I was elated. I absolutely loved it. I've since learned that salvia tends to scare the shit out of most people who try it, especially if they're working with enhanced leaf, but my own reaction couldn't have been more opposite of that. I thought it was probably the most fantastic herb I'd ever experienced. It was radical, profound, terribly powerful, and fast. It was a psychedelic explosion in my consciousness and sense of being. Though it moved quickly, there was a strange "stickiness" to it, almost as though it was stretching things out like the taffy I used to watch being made in the windows of the saltwater taffy shop on the Santa Cruz Beach Boardwalk. It seemed multi-dimensional, fractal, and strangely segmented into conveyor-belt-like-bands of moving energy. After I recovered from the initial wave, which sent me bowing down to the ground before the overwhelming power of the sage, I rushed out into the street, bellowing ecstatically, "Now I understand!" For his part, Devon took another good hit, and the sage bowled him over, with him barely making it to his tent where he crashed on his sleeping pad and didn't get up the rest of the night.

After that first encounter with salvia, I began working with it regularly, and enthusiastically shared it with anyone who wanted to give it a try. I took notes on most of my salvia experiences, and for several years kept an ongoing salvia journal, which eventually turned into a book, though that was several years away from that first experience. One of the things that I really liked about salvia, aside from its being very strong (in its enhanced leaf form), was that it was fast-acting and I didn't need to devote a whole day for the experience. In the years since the time Phoebe and I first shared mushrooms together, she had been open to taking them with me a few more times, but not more than once a year. So that meant that if I wanted to work with mushrooms, it was basically on my own time, and Phoebe didn't want that competing with her time with me. Thus I confined my mushroom experiences to days that I had off when Phoebe was at work (when I was a grad student, our vacation times often didn't overlap), or when I would go up to visit Devon in Eugene, or when we met in the giant redwoods in California to go camping in the spring. Salvia, however, I could do just about anytime, and it was easy for me to find time to work with it before Phoebe came home from work. I also experimented with sage tincture, which is held under the tongue (and is extremely painful), and grew several salvia plants of my own for chewing and smoking. Essentially, I became a salvia enthusiast.

There were many differences between salvia and mushrooms, and I tended to use them in ways that were quite different. Salvia, being so fast-acting and brief in duration, I found, was best for meditation, prayer, and energetic expression, whereas mushrooms were best for working with others, deep contemplation, and psychological and emotional healing and exploration. From my time and experiences at Mescalero, I had developed my "medicine bag," as seen in the dream and encouraged by Meredith, and I always used this to start any entheogenic session or meditation, setting up my little altar and praying to the four directions with cattail pollen, as I had learned form my Mescalero teachers. I would always bless any medicine before taking it, putting it in the abalone shell in my medicine bag and sprinkling it with pollen. By this time, I had also taken to wearing a small medicine bag around my neck and underneath my shirt which contained a turquoise stone, a piece of obsidian, a red mescal bean, some pollen, and some fragments of mushrooms. Before spending time at Mescalero, I never prayed or performed rituals, but these were now regular features of my medicine and spiritual practice.

With salvia, I found that the expressive qualities of prayer were greatly amplified with the use of the sage, and it always felt more authentic to me, helping me to really tap into what I felt and thought and express it verbally. As a grad student, I had also started experimenting with throat and overtone signing, but it was something that I had struggled with and didn't quite do correctly until I started working with salvia, when suddenly, and much to my surprise, all these bizarre tones and sounds started coming out of me, usually accompanied by what felt like an energetic shift in my throat. At the time, it felt to me as though the salvia was teaching me how to throat sing (as a side note, I've found that it can help others learn how to throat sing as well). I would now reword that to say that I taught myself how to throat sing through the medium of the salvia. The distinction is important, as it relates to the question of duality versus nonduality. But at the time, it was much like mushrooms for me in that it felt like "something else" just took over and started expressing itself through me. Yet it strangely always left me feeling deeply empowered, centered, and present, and it wasn't clear how something acting through me could make me feel personally empowered and so *myself.* Whatever the case, salvia seemed the perfect tool for my ongoing shamanic and mystical explorations, and fit nicely with my mediation practice, musical expression, and work with mushrooms.

I often felt a little nervous before embarking on a sage experience. I'd get the feeling of, "Here we go!" as I held up the pipe, much like the sense of anticipation I would feel as a child on the Big Dipper roller coaster in Santa Cruz as it chugged its way up the initial incline to the first big drop. But afterwards, I was almost always thrilled that I had done it. There were a few times where I struggled with it, and it was through these times that I found such struggles were usually accompanied by sensations of heat and profuse sweating. Mostly, however, it just made me pop right open, and I loved it. It was so different from the long and sometimes disorienting build-up of mushrooms, and I really enjoyed the instantaneous quality of the herb. I also enjoyed the slower methods of sage consumption in terms of the overall experience, but I found eating sage to be too bitter for my tastes, and the tincture method always burnt my mouth, so I only did that on occasion, as I did not enjoy the lingering effect of feeling like I had drunk scalding coffee for a week after. So, mostly I smoked it, and my preference was definitely for enhanced leaf over regular leaf, of which one must smoke a great deal more to get a comparable effect. Basically, I liked the bang that salvia provided, and if I wanted something of longer duration to work with, I'd turn to mushrooms.

When it came time to leave Burning Man on that first adventure, I was sad, but happy to know that now I had something to look forward to every year. My life in the "default world," as Burners like to call the world outside of Burning Man, might not live up to my hopes and dreams, but there was always Burning Man. At that point, I started dreaming about Burning Man almost every night. At first, the dreams were all, "I'm still at Burning Man!" kinds of dreams. Then, they would shift into "I'm at Burning Man, but something's wrong because it's not the right time of year." Next, they would shift into "I've got to get ready for Burning Man – there's so much to do!" and finally, "Yay! I'm back at Burning Man. But oh crap! I've forgotten X!" This pattern of dreaming continued for several years.

Phoebe soon found that the only thing I talked about or responded to with any enthusiasm was Burning Man, and she hated it. It was becoming more and more clear that I simply wasn't happy with my life, and Burning Man was fast becoming my lifesaver and the source and focus of my own happiness. This fact ate away at her, and it didn't help our relationship at all. But if given a choice, I'd choose Burning Man over Phoebe any day, so I didn't care. I'd rather be happy and have something to look forward to than remain miserable just to keep Phoebe from getting angry about Burning Man. From that very first visit to Burning Man, it was starting to work its magic to help drive Phoebe and me apart, though that was still to be many years down the road before reaching its completion.

The next year brought about several important developments in my life. The first was that Phoebe started to get the baby itch right around this time, and the second was that the University of California at Berkeley started to express interest in having me teach a couple classes in Native American studies on a temporary basis. The third was that I started to contemplate trying my hand a being a writer. As it turned out, all these threads came to fruition simultaneously.

The process of making a baby proved to be the most sex Phoebe and I had enjoyed in many years, though it was all rather business-like, formal, and completely devoid of any passion or connection. Thus the frequency had gone up dramatically, but other than that, our relationship still lacked the kind of heart-felt connection that I really desired.

Personally, I wasn't passionate about the idea of having a child, but it seemed like the next reasonable step in our relationship, and when Phoebe brought up the idea, I agreed, and thus we set about the task of conceiving a child.

It was about halfway through Phoebe's pregnancy that something amazing happened: she started actually *wanting and enjoying sex.* Much to my astonishment, I awoke in the middle of the night one night to find Phoebe fondling me – something she had not initiated in more years than I could remember. For the first time in what felt like ages, she was actually horny. I couldn't believe it. It was the best sex we had had in years, though Phoebe still refused any kind of kissing. I didn't complain, however, and relished the experience. For the next several months of her pregnancy, she continued to act on her newfound passions, and for a while, there was a pleasantness between us that had been missing for many years. However, as soon as her hormones subsided, so did the passion, and things eventually returned to exactly as they were before; frigid, passionless, and totally lacking in connection and shared desire.

Conversations with UC Berkeley started in the summer, and arrangements were made for me to teach there in the spring – the same time that Phoebe was due to give birth to our first child. It was a far from ideal time, but this was the first, and only, opportunity I'd received to actually teach in my chosen field of study, and it wasn't an opportunity I wanted to pass up, despite the inconvenient timing. It had already been over a year since completing my degree, and the longer one was out of the academic loop, the less likely any kind of job became, and thus I felt that it was something I needed to do. Phoebe wasn't thrilled about it, but she was understanding and knew that it wasn't a job that I could pass up.

By this time Phoebe's father, Winsor, had remarried and moved into a new house in Berkeley – coincidentally, on the same street my grandfather had lived on and where my mother grew up. My grandfather had died at age 87 in 2000, so there was no overlap with Phoebe's father on Alvarado Rd. in Berkeley. As it turned out, Winsor's next-door neighbor was looking to rent out an apartment on the bottom floor of their home, and arrangements were made for me to rent the apartment for my time teaching at UC Berkeley. It was relatively close to the university – a short bike ride away, and also had easy access to the freeway for my commutes back and forth between there and Santa Barbara, where Phoebe stayed to continue her work as an elementary teacher. My standard week was to drive up to Berkeley every Monday from Santa Barbara, teach on Tuesday and Thursday, and then get in the car on Thursday afternoon, usually around 2:30, and drive back down to Santa Barbara for the weekend. The drive was around 5 and a half hours, so it wasn't too bad. At least I wasn't attempting to drive the entire length of California.

I had two classes at UC Berkeley, both of which the university let me develop on my own. The first was "Languages, Landscapes and Philosophy in Native American Traditions" and the other was "Native American Visionary and Healing Traditions." I got into trouble almost immediately at Berkeley when I put a photo of myself with Willeto on the door of my office. Apparently, this photo had greatly offended the sensitivities of some of the Native American students. In the photo, I was standing next to Willeto, who was seated in his wheelchair, and the photo was taken near the peak of White Mountain, which was featured in the background. Personally, I thought it was the perfect photo representing my time at Mescalero – there was my good friend and teacher, Willeto, and there was White Mountain, home of the Mountain Spirits. However, according to the professor I shared my office with, Native students found it offensive, for here was some tall white guy towering over an invalid Native American, the photo capturing an imbalanced power relationship. I learned of this interpretation when I returned to my office after teaching a class and found the picture removed from my door and placed on my desk with a note that it was "too offensive" to put on public display.

Personally, I was shocked. When I looked at the picture, I saw the special relationship that I had with Willeto, a man I loved and respected. I didn't see anything that indicated an imbalanced power relationship – the fact was, I'm tall, and Willeto was in a wheelchair. It was just the way things were.

That students could get all worked up about what, to me, was an innocent picture from my time at Mescalero, astounded me. I'd always known that Native American students could be very sensitive, but I never expected something like this.

My classes were going well, and I had attracted a number of students to the courses who were outside of Native American studies, getting students from philosophy, anthropology, sociology, and other disciplines. Interestingly, when the classes were completed and my students had an opportunity to review me as a professor, I found that most of the reviews were very positive, especially from the non-Native students. However, some of the Native students had written on my evaluations that I was "too white" and complained that I included readings on philosophy, comparative religion, and neuroscience in my courses. On the other hand, these were some of the aspects of my courses that the non-Native students found most compelling and interesting. Clearly, there were two very different audiences at work here, and I was not pleasing both of them.

Near the end of my one term of teaching at Berkeley, I got called into the department chair's office to discuss what might come next. He informed me that they would be opening up two tenure-track positions in the ethnic studies department in the next year, and he sincerely hoped that I would apply. However, and I quote, he said, "We're really looking for Native scholars, so you won't get the job, but we really want you to apply."

Among other factors, what my academic career was really boiling down to was that I was the wrong race. Given my area of study, almost all of the job openings that were relevant said the same thing: preference is for Native scholars, who are strongly encouraged to apply. That, coupled with the fact that I had been struggling to get a letter of recommendation from Professor X, meant that I was virtually doomed to be overlooked for any serious job. It started to sink in that I had blown my academic career on the wrong focus.

Missives that were coming from the Society for the Study of Native American Religious Traditions, SSNART, right around the same time, exacerbated this view. For the upcoming American Academy of Religion Conference, the SSNART group was planning on having a pre-conference meeting for members of SSNART, but the meeting was explicitly *only open to Native members,* and non-Native scholars working in the field were not invited. Given that this was being paid for by the group – which was funded by the dues of all its members – this seemed highly questionable to me, ethically. I, and all other non-Native members, was expected to pay my dues so that the group could hold a meeting to which I was specifically not invited. I ended up emailing the chairman of the group, and we got into heated email exchange where I pointed out that the Supreme Court had decided in the Brown vs. Board of Education verdict of 1954, which brought about an end to segregation in the South, that "separate is inherently unequal." The chairman did not take kindly to this, and wrote back something along the lines of how "some of us do not see the Supreme Court as being legitimate."

I was also busy sending off my re-worked dissertation to various academic publishers at this time, attempting to get it published as a book – something that I thought would help my chances of landing an academic position somewhere. True to the rest of my experiences at this point, reviews of the manuscript came back with completely contradictory assessments. One reviewer would say that the manuscript was groundbreaking and excellent. Others came back, and I kid you not, questioning whether I had ever actually spent any time with the Mescalero Apaches, it clearly being written by a white person, and basically claiming that there was zero legitimacy to anything I had written. It wasn't hard for me to figure out which reviews had been written by Native scholars and which weren't. Everything in my experience was telling me that being a non-Native scholar was making it next to impossible for me to make any headway. I even got a personal letter of apology from one publisher for the reviewer's outrageous claims that I had clearly made up the content of my dissertation, informing me that she considered the review inappropriate and unprofessional, yet this couldn't change the fact that they were a peer-reviewed publishing house and would be unable to move forward with publication as a result of the review.

With all of the frustration and setbacks I had been experiencing over the last few years regarding developing an academic career for myself, these events proved to be my personal tipping point. I had applied for over 30 jobs, the only one of which that came to anything was my temporary position at UC Berkeley. Identity and racial politics were so deeply embedded in the academic study of Native American traditions that I just gave up. Academic programs and professional societies were set up more as support groups for Native identities than anything else, to my mind, and I, as a white guy, was not fitting in. Everywhere I turned, I was confronted with the issue of my race, and my legitimacy as a scholar and teacher was routinely questioned for that reason alone. I had had enough. So in defeat, I just gave up. I stopped looking for academic work and stopped applying for jobs. The entire process had left a bad taste in my mouth, and what with my personal struggles with Professor X, I just didn't want anything more to do with it all. What I had originally thought would be a perfect fit for me, given my personal and professional interests, turned out to not be at all what I had expected or hoped. It was a deep disillusionment, and I had a hard time seeing the positive side of the events that had unfolded in my life. I was clearly battling with myself and others, but I didn't know what I was battling for. Did I even want an academic position, given everything I'd learned about Native American studies and the troubles I'd had? Could I ever be what others wanted me to be in this area of study, or would I always be an outsider and troublemaker, and forever "that white guy"? Why was I putting myself through this? What did I want from it? If other scholars and students weren't going to take me seriously, what was I doing?

For her part, Phoebe was completely supportive of my decision to stop seeking any kind of academic employment. In fact, she had been urging me to do so over the past couple years. She was personally very happy with her job as a teacher in the Goleta Union School District, and had never liked the idea of us packing up and moving somewhere across the country for an academic job for me, and she had done her part to convince me that teaching English to international students in Santa Barbara could be enough for me. The problem, however, was that it wasn't enough, because it didn't require the full engagement of either my intellect or education. I was interested in big ideas and big questions, and teaching students how to ask where the beach was just wasn't ever going to satisfy me. When I finally made the decision, however, it seemed that this was precisely what I had to settle for, and thus it was best for me to just accept my fate. Whatever the rules were for getting ahead in the academic game, I felt that I was exceedingly poor at following them, either through my own obstinacy or ignorance.

In the midst of all this navel gazing, questioning, and reassessing, Phoebe and I were having a baby. It was a Thursday, and I had classes to teach that day at Berkeley. Phoebe called in the morning, saying that she thought something was happening, but wasn't sure enough to call me home just yet. By the time I got out of class, a little later that day, it was confirmed: the baby was on her way and it was high time for me to hit the road and get to Santa Barbara. I made the drive in record time, but it was still to be many hours before the baby arrived, with our daughter, Miranda, being born at 11:58 pm on the day of her projected due date of March 14th. Phoebe and I were now parents.

The birth had gone well without any major problems or difficulties. Phoebe had chosen to have an epidural and the birth took place at the hospital in Santa Barbara. When all was said and done, we had a beautiful baby girl to take home with us. Though Phoebe wasn't passionate about us (nor was I, for that matter), she was passionate about being a mother, and in many respects, set out to be the loving and devoted mother to Miranda that Phoebe's own mother had never been for her.

Miranda's birth had a big impact on me as well, and this change in my status to being a father had a huge influence on my compulsive creativity. Prior to her birth, and inspired by the release of the first of the trilogy of *Lord of the Rings* films, I had recently read most of Tolkien: *The Silmarillion, The Hobbit,* and *The Lord of the Rings.* I finished up LOTR not long after Miranda's birth, while completing my stint teaching at Berkeley. I had recently finished two epics of sci-fi and fantasy literature – the Dune Series by Frank Herbert, and now the works of Middle Earth by Tolkien. Having finished these epics, and not knowing what I should read next, the idea came to mind that perhaps I could write my own sci-fi fantasy epic. Why not? I thought. I was a creative fellow. Though I'd never attempted writing fiction before, it sounded like a fun idea, so why not give it a try? My academic career wasn't going anywhere, so it wasn't like I had tons of reading, research, and paper writing to do, so filling my time with writing a novel was an appealing idea. At the very least, it would give me something to do, and I just might enjoy it, too.

It was 10 pm on a Tuesday night that I put down LOTR, turned on my laptop, and started going about constructing an epic story. I began by simply starting to write, with no idea what I was really writing, what the plot would be, or where the whole thing was going as a story. But as I've learned, the most important step in writing any book is simply to start it, and the rest tends to take care of itself. The result was that I had started writing the book that would become *Orobai's Vision,* volume I of a four-volume series of books that I came to call *Tales of Aurduin.* To date, this is the most ambitious creative project I have ever embarked upon, and one that I am personally quite proud of, despite the fact that I never got the books published and they've only had a small handful of readers over the years I've made them available as self-published works. It was a complex tale that centered on the theme of a prophecy of an apocalypse that would forever change, and ultimately remake, the world of Aurduin. Though there ended up being numerous characters and several interweaving storylines and plots, the main story revolved around two characters in particular; Orobai, and his little "sister," Miraanni, and the people closest to them. The story begins with the ancient being, Orobai, discovering a unique jewel that transforms into a baby girl. He then sets off on a quest for a vision to discover her identity and purpose, as well as his own, and understand the nature of their relationship as it relates to both the past and the apocalypse to come.

After writing the first couple chapters, I got the main ideas settled in my head, and then skipped ahead to writing what ended up being the final chapter of the first book. Then, I went to writing a philosophical/metaphysical appendix (which I eventually excluded from the final book). And after that, now that I understood the parameters of the world I was working with and the overview of the plot, I filled in the book from the first couple chapters to the end.

Oh the sleepless nights! I was immediately struck by an extreme case of insomnia, and found that most nights I would just lie in bed, thinking over the story and what I needed to write next. This was compounded by the fact that I was creating several languages that were used by the different imaginary cultures that inhabited the world of Aurduin, and my training in linguistics had me obsessing over tiny details of the languages, words, syntax, and grammar. Basically, the story was backlogging in my head, and I couldn't write fast enough to keep up with its development in my mind.

I spent every spare moment that I had writing. I poured everything I had at my disposal into *Orobai's Vision* and the volumes that were to follow. Everything I had learned from my graduate studies made it into the books. Everything I had learned and been inspired by at Mescalero went in. Everything that had come from my mushroom and salvia experiences went into the books. Some chapters were dreams that I had had. Others came out of experiences and impressions at Burning Man. All of my interests in altered states of consciousness went in. My interest in music and sound went in there, including throat signing and didjeridu playing. Everything I knew about ritual went in. Everything I knew about mediation went in. Even everything I knew about quantum physics and string theory went in. All of my political interests and social concerns went into the books as well. Even 9-11 and terrorism made it in. In short, *Tales of Aurduin* became the repository of everything I thought about everything, and anything that I cared about or thought about was featured in those books, in one way or another.

I didn't finish up *Orobai's Vision* until sometime after my second trip to Burning Man, and I subsequently revised it several times. The first draft was very formal, with elaborate descriptions and almost obsessive attention to detail, almost as though I were writing a fictional dissertation where every cultural detail needed to be richly described and explored. It was when I wrote the second book, *The Fate of Miraanni,* after I had embraced abandoning any quest for an academic career, that I loosened up as a fiction writer and really got into the swing of writing fiction with characters, dialog, and twisting and interweaving plots.

After I finished *Orobai's Vision,* I was actually quite terrified of what I had started. I knew that the story was far from over and that there were many, many pages between the conclusion of that first book and the conclusion of the story as a whole. For many months, I felt paralyzed by the fear that I wasn't up to the task and wouldn't be able to figure out how to write the rest of the story. Ideas and plot fragments were building up in my mind, but I couldn't see the path that led through it all and bound it all together into one coherent narrative. It was like I was looking down at a jumble of puzzle pieces that I could distinctly see, but had no reference for how to put them together or what the final image should be – all I had was the pieces. Then, some six months or so after having finished *Orobai's Vision*, I woke up one Sunday morning and something had just clicked in my mind. I suddenly knew how all the pieces fit together, which characters were important and who the new characters were that I needed to successively introduce in the following books, and I was ready to begin. So, I got out of bed that morning, turned on the computer, and started writing volume II, *The Fate of Miraanni.*

From that point on, it was merely a matter of time and persistent work for me to finish the epic project. After *Miraanni* was finished, I went back and made a major edit to *Orobai,* making it far more readable as a novel, and also altering a few minor details here and there to make the first book square away with what I knew had to come in the following books. Then, after taking a couple months off, I wrote volume III, *The Alchemist and the Eagle,* and a few months after finishing that volume, I completed the series with *The Fifth Temple*, the longest and most complex volume of the series. In all, it took around three years for me to complete the whole thing, and then a bit longer to go back and edit all the volumes to make sure everything was consistent and correct.

By the time I started writing volume III, I had given up on trying to get the series published. I had sent out materials and queries to maybe 30 publishers when I was working on the first half of the series, but the response was pretty much always the same: "Thank you for your submission, but your work is not right for our publishing needs at this time. We wish you the best of luck in your writing." While I wanted to share the books, and had some hope that maybe instead of being an academic, I could make a career as a published author and novelist, I wanted to complete the series for myself. I had given myself the challenge of writing an epic sci-fi fantasy, and I wanted to see it through, no matter if anyone else would ever read it or cared that I had written it. It had become the medium through which I was exploring and expressing everything that mattered to me, and though fame and book sales would be nice, in reality, I was doing it for myself and it was a vital outlet for my own expression and compulsive need for creativity. And despite the chronic bouts of insomnia that accompanied the first few weeks of writing for each of the books, I loved the process and thoroughly enjoyed getting to know my characters, their cultures, their histories, and their fates. In that sense, it was a wonderful project that brought me tremendous amounts of personal satisfaction and pleasure. I was also happy to share the novels with friends and family, the bulk of my reading audience for those books. Quite tellingly, Phoebe was never interested in reading any of them, yet another huge part of my life that she had no personal interest in sharing or partaking in.

As for work, after completing my stint at UC Berkeley, lacking other clear options, I returned to teaching English to international students in Santa Barbara. From there, I applied for the position of academic director at a competing English language school in Santa Barbara, and was accepted in that position, where I was to work until leaving that job at the end of 2007. In many respects, I was actually quite fortunate to have gotten that job and not been reliant on being a teacher, for the international student trade just got worse and worse in the years following 9-11. It became harder for students to obtain visas, and numerous restrictions were put in place, so international student numbers were in serious decline across the country. Then, with the advent of Gulf War II, things got even worse, especially as the international esteem of the U.S. started to plummet under the unilateral leadership of George W. Bush. Many English language teachers were getting laid off, and those that weren't were having their hours cut back, so getting an administrative job at least proved to be consistent work with a reliable paycheck.

It was mostly easy work, however, and with declines in student numbers, it often meant that I had long periods during the day where I had very little to do as far as official duties. So, I filled my time by writing my novels, mostly when I was at work, sitting at my desk, looking so productive and busy. My immediate supervisor knew what I was up to, and was happy to encourage me along. As long as my duties as the academic director of the school were fulfilled, he didn't care how many books I wrote in my spare time.

I wasn't thrilled with the job, however. Being an administrator included vast amounts of data entry, scheduling, hiring, firing, training, placing and testing students, and also having to deal with upset students and parents when students didn't advance to the next level due to poor grades or failed tests. English language instruction is very different from standard academic teaching in that the students are there because their parents are paying for them to be there – they aren't there on any kind of academic or intellectual merits. There's often a strong sense of entitlement and ownership of the school on the part of students and parents, and making demands on the school was a common practice. I even had students try and bribe me to let them advance to the next level of instruction when they failed their exams, or would turn to their parents who'd send me angry messages about how they were paying for this, so they were entitled to what they wanted. And the situation only got worse when the school was bought out by a larger company as then there were even more demands coming down from on high from the corporate offices, and overall, as an academic director, I had very little autonomy and had to field complaints and commands from many different sources simultaneously. I wasn't terribly fond of it all, and mostly looked forward to the times when I could sit at my desk and peacefully write without interruption.

My third trip to Burning Man in 2003 proved to be a significant year. The theme that was announced for that year was "Beyond Belief," and based on that theme, I developed the idea of The God Box as a theme camp, which was to become my Burning Man focus for the next seven years. That year, the plan was for my good friend, Rod, to accompany Devon and myself to the Playa. Ever since Jerry Garcia's death, Rod had felt a bit displaced, having been a long-time deadhead, and he was curious about making Black Rock City his new home. We all wanted to make an official contribution to the culture and activities at the Burn for the week, and tossed around ideas for a theme camp. Inspired by the theme as articulated by Larry Harvey, I wondered what would happen if we told people we had God in a box and invited people to open it up and see what was inside. Of course, it was meant as an ironic joke because for one, I didn't "believe" in God – at least, certainly not some transcendent mythical creator that oversaw the workings of the universe and who cared about the fate of our souls – and secondly, if God did exist, he/she/it probably couldn't be contained in a box. It sounded like a fun idea, and we decided to run with it.

I went out searching for a box that could fill this role, and I had in mind trying to find something that looked "ark-ish" – old, ornate, and mysterious. Shopping in Santa Barbara, I couldn't find anything that fit my mental picture that wasn't many hundreds of dollars, and I didn't have that kind of cash for what was essentially a joke. However, as I searched, I got a brilliant idea. Phoebe's new stepmother had purchased what she thought were baby booties for our daughter, Miranda, that were in the form of foam lizard feet. She had been mistaken, and they weren't baby booties at all – they were intended to be put on the legs of a table or chair. I had stashed them away in my Burning Man gear, thinking that they might come in handy at some point. In my search for the perfect God Box, I had purchased a mailbox for our theme camp (we didn't want to be harassed by the Black Rock City postal service). One night, while sitting around thinking what to do about the God Box, I got the idea that I could use the mailbox, along with the strange green foam lizard feet, and create a kind of mythical creature out of it. I went to the local drug store and got some large foam balls, some googly eyes, some plastic jewels, and metallic pipe cleaners. I then proceeded to paint the mailbox green and affixed the various decorations about the box and finished it off with the feet. Thus was born the Mystic Toad.

I then created the basic structure of how our camp would work. The goal was for supplicants to venture alone into the "Lair of the Mystic Toad," wherein they could privately open the God Box, which was also the Mystic Toad/the mailbox. However, there would be a process that they would have to go through first in order to reach this inner sanctum. First, they would have to sign an oath, which I would deliver verbally, swearing that they would not reveal the contents of the God Box to anyone, under threat of "divine punishment" and "holy wrath." Next, they would have to write something in the Book of Confessions, revealing their innermost thoughts and preparing the way for their encounter with God. From there, supplicants would be taken for a private didjeridu cleansing, which, once completed, would allow them access to the Lair and the Mystic Toad.

My original thought was that we would randomly place different objects in the box, but after various debates about what we should put in there, I decided we should go with my original idea of a mirror. I thought this was a good idea as it could have a wide range of interpretations: God isn't real; God is just a projection of the self; God depends on what you believe; God is the self/the individual is God, etc.

What we found was that not only was running the God Box a tremendous amount of fun (and work!), but that people loved it. That first year, we could hardly believe the reactions we were getting. People were going through our process and coming out crying, profoundly moved by the experience. Many people told us it was the greatest thing they had ever experienced at Burning Man, and people gleefully left our camp to go and convince all of their friends and campmates to come and open the mysterious God Box. And furthermore, it brought the whole neighborhood together. Spontaneously, Rod and Devon had decided to echo various parts of the oath as I would read it out to new supplicants, saying "God Box," "Mystic Toad," and "Holy Wrath" in a profound chorus. Very quickly, all our neighbors picked up on this fun part of the game and soon these phrases could be heard echoing about the neighborhood for each recitation of the oath, much to the delight and surprise of fresh supplicants. Each year that we did the God Box, we found that neighbors were always eager to join in on the fun in this way, and it was a regular feature of the God Box experience.

The God Box thus became the hub around which our ongoing Burning Man experience revolved until I finally retired the God Box after the Burn of 2009, for reasons that I will get to later. Throughout it all, there was a shifting cast of characters involved with the camp, but Devon, Rod, and I remained the primary instigators of the game and were the core of the camp. It was a huge amount of work, however, with us generally being open three times a day – once in the morning, then in the afternoon, and again at night – so it kept us at our camp for most of the time, and as the years wore on, grumbles could be heard among the servants of the Mystic Toad about wanting to get out more and have less work to do.

I also started giving musical performances at Center Camp around this time, and that was always a highlight of my Burning Man experience. I can recall the first time I played a Native American flute up on stage. I had all of Center Camp enthralled, and aside from the sound of the flute, Center Camp was perfectly quiet, and perfectly still. Then when I ripped out a didjeridu jam, the place went crazy. It was the kind of thing I dreamed about – performing for a large and deeply appreciative audience. I loved it. Back in Santa Barbara, I never performed by myself out in public, so this was always very special for me. Apparently people also thought I was pretty witty with my between-songs banter, and it was common for people to ask me if I was a comedian. Post performances, I loved walking around Burning Man and having people come up to me and randomly tell me how much they enjoyed my musical performance. One time, as I was walking across the Playa by myself, a large, multi-storied art car passed by and someone way at the top yelled out, "Your performance in Center Camp rocked!" That really made my day. Also, when people recognized my campmates and myself as being from the God Box, we routinely received proclamations of "We love you, God Box!" all around the Playa. Truly, Burning Man was the one place in the world that I felt genuinely happy, free to be myself, and welcomed within a community of equally happy and joyous people. Burning Man was my heaven.

Around this time, my relationship with Phoebe underwent a period of minor improvement. When I had first met Phoebe back in college, she, like so many college students, had been a drinker. Not being a drinker myself, I had steered her toward marijuana – something that we could enjoy together. When she decided that she wanted to get pregnant, she quit smoking herb, and continued with her abstinence until after she was done breastfeeding Miranda.

The shift in our relationship came one night when Phoebe told me she was ready to get high, once again, and wanted to smoke a bowl. I gladly obliged and we spent a nice evening together after Miranda begrudgingly went to sleep. When we went to bed that night, I felt an energy between us that had only shown up during Phoebe's pregnancy – there was sexual energy present. Cautiously, I moved my hand between Phoebe's legs. Typically, she would have moved my hand away, not allowing me to touch her, but this time, rather than pushing me away, she opened up. What transpired was, at that time, the most unusual sexual experience I had ever had. I held my middle finger out, hovering just beyond her clitoris, not actually in physical contact. Energy seemed to be passing out of my finger, which strangely felt like a penis, and into her. Without ever actually physically touching her, Phoebe had an orgasm. I couldn't believe it. What was going on here?

From that, we learned that Phoebe was more open to sexual relations if she got high. She still wouldn't let me kiss her, but she did allow me to touch her now, something that hadn't been part of our interaction for many years by this point, and she now consented to sex once a week, or once every two weeks, which was far more frequent than the once every month or two as it had been for many years. It was nice. It still wasn't the connection or relationship that I desired and craved, but it was nice, and it afforded us at least a small connection and some degree of intimacy, even if it wasn't ideal. Unlike me, however, Phoebe only wanted to smoke on the weekends, so any other time of the week she was still basically off-limits to any advance I might make. At least it was better than nothing.

I finished up the *Tales of Aurduin* books after our third year of doing the God Box. In the default time in between Burns, Phoebe and I did a weekend of house sitting for one of Phoebe's fellow teachers in Santa Barbara, and as it turned out, there was a copy of Don Miguel Ruiz's book, *The Four Agreements* on the nightstand next to the side of the bed, so I picked it up and read it over the weekend. Personally, I didn't feel that there was anything I was getting from the book – I knew all of this stuff already – but what occurred to me then was that *I* could write a book like this, but base it on what I had learned from my ongoing work with psilocybin mushrooms. It also occurred to me that it would be very easy for me to write such a book as I had already written everything I had learned from mushrooms in the *Tales of Aurduin* books, and it would just be a matter of compiling all this information specifically into one place, one manuscript.

I secretly began writing another book. I didn't tell Phoebe I was working on it, as I was apprehensive about how she would react. Santa Barbara was a relatively small community, and if I were to put out a book like this, she might be concerned for her position as an elementary school teacher. I also didn't tell any of my friends or family. I was excited about it, however, and dove into the project, thinking that perhaps *this* would be the book that I could get published by a real publisher and get my work out there to the world, and perhaps from that, I could direct an audience to my novels and get new readers there.

The title I originally came up with for the project was *Mushroom Wisdom: Cultivating Spiritual Consciousness with Psilocybin Mushrooms,* and with the inspiration from *The Four*

Agreements, I wrote it as something of a self-help-style book. By the time Burning Man rolled around in 2005, I had completed the manuscript, sent it off to several publishers, and was eagerly awaiting a response to see if I could get any takers. I brought two photocopies of the manuscript with me to Burning Man to give as surprise gifts to Devon and Rod, though I ended up giving a copy to a woman I met at that year's Burn, Marianne.

We were once again doing the God Box for the Burn in 2005. I don't know how long Marianne had been sitting in our greeting dome before I noticed her, but it eventually came to my attention that this woman had been sitting in our dome for several hours with a big shit-eating grin on her face, clearly loving the proceedings and relishing simply being present for what was taking place in our camp. When things slowed down, I sat down next to her and started a conversation. One of the first things she said was, "So what's your energy practice?" I just looked at her quizzically. I didn't think of myself as having any kind of energy practice, and the phrase brought to mind things like Tai Chi or Tantra, neither of which I was practitioner of. I had done some experimenting with Tai Chi in college, and did have some spontaneous Tai Chi-like experiences while wandering about the Playa on mushrooms and feeling myself move about fluidly with gestures that were reminiscent of the little Tai Chi that I had been exposed to, but other than that, the idea of myself as being someone who had an "energy practice" was totally alien to me and her question caught me by surprise.

"Uh – nothing," I think was probably my answer.

"Oh yeah?" she responded skeptically. "Well, maybe you don't know you're doing it, but you are. Why do you think I'm over here? My camp is right across the street, and when you got started today, I saw this burst of white light come out of you and knew right away that I wanted to come over here and enjoy the energy work that you've been doing all day. You're really good at it."

That was all news to me. I was flattered, but I didn't quite know what to make of her comments. From my perspective, I was just doing something that I really enjoyed, and I had a way of really getting to people and bringing supplicants into a space where they'd be ready for their experience of opening the God Box – something that was still getting radically profound reactions from people, and my role in getting them ready for it was a crucial part of the process. I just saw it as the joy of service, and not as some kind of "energy practice." Marianne insisted that that was what I was doing, however, and suggested that I start to pay attention to what I was doing and how I was doing it. She found it a bit unbelievable that I wasn't even aware of what she insisted I was doing, and apparently had been doing, for the past several years now.

Thus began my friendship with Marianne. As there wasn't anything particular going on at her camp, Marianne and her two campmates ended up spending most of the Burn with us at the God Box, and wandering around the Playa at night, with all of us popping down mushroom-packed capsules Marianne had brought with her. As I was to learn, Marianne was an advanced magikal practitioner and Wiccan from Albuquerque, New Mexico, and the younger woman she had with her in camp was her apprentice and student. Over the week, Marianne and I spent most of our time together, and despite the fact that I had no similar official practice, we felt like compatriots. I opened up to her in a way that I hadn't with anyone else, except perhaps Devon, and poured out all my hopes, dreams, troubles, and frustrations. Other than Devon, it was the first time I had ever told anyone about my rocky relationship with Phoebe. In hearing all this, Marianne immediately launched into talking about her own divorce. The message was clear: you should divorce this woman, and the sooner you do it, the better off you'll be. To Marianne, it was obvious that this was what needed to happen, and she wasn't about to pass any pity my way, because it was my responsibility – it was my choice to stay in this unhappy relationship or have the balls to do something about it.

I appreciated her candor, and appreciated our budding friendship even more. It was nice to have someone to talk to and there was a profound connection between us that was unlike any relationship I had with anyone else. In addition to being friends, it was like we were colleagues and on equal footing. It was so nice! Over the years of being with Phoebe, my own spiritual quest and practices had become increasingly removed from anything that involved Phoebe, who didn't share my spiritual concerns or interests. Yet here, with Marianne, there was someone I could really talk to and share with, and she got what I was talking about, and always had her own experiences and insights to share in return.

Our conversation didn't end with the conclusion of that year's Burn. In fact, it only increased in intensity, much to the displeasure of Phoebe. After going home, Marianne read the draft of *Mushroom Wisdom,* and then requested copies of the *Tales of Aurduin,* which I eagerly sent her. Phoebe had never read anything I had written, nor had she ever expressed any interest in doing so, and here was someone who couldn't get enough of my writing, and was responding with detailed comments and reactions, issuing out a running commentary on where she was in the books, what it brought to her mind, what she liked, and suggestions for various changes and edits here and there. No one had ever shown such an interest before, and I loved it. It might be an audience of just one, but at least it was an audience. That's the thing about being a writer, musician, or artist – you create because you feel that you have to or that your life is incomplete if you don't, so much of it is done for self-gratification, but beyond that, you want to share it with others, and ideally, have them enjoy it and appreciate it. Being creative for oneself is only half of the deal. Every creative person desires an audience, even if it is very small. Phoebe had never been an audience for my creativity. She didn't want to come to musical performances I was involved in with Dreamtime Continuum, complained when I spent time recording music, which she never wanted to listen to, always fought with me over money if I wanted to buy new gear or a new instrument, never read anything I wrote, and routinely complained about my spending hours in front of the computer when I was working on a book. In sum, Phoebe was not only not supportive of my creativity, she also had no interest in the products of my creativity, so it was always a battle with her. Yet here was Marianne, passionately exploring all that I had to offer as a creative individual. It was the kind of affirmation I had longed for, and no matter how angry and jealous Phoebe would get that I had this ongoing conversation with this woman in New Mexico taking place over the computer, I didn't care. Marianne was making me feel valued in a way that Phoebe never had, and I wasn't going to give that up for her sake. I'd given up too much already, and this was something that I was going to do for myself.

Marianne also took it upon herself to push me further along the path of my spiritual interests. That year at Burning Man, I had randomly picked a card from a supplicant at the God Box that had "accept your own divinity" written on it, along with a picture of woman meditating in a patch of luminescent mushrooms. In virtually every email that Marianne wrote me, she concluded with the question: have you accepted your divinity yet? My answer was always no.,

Despite Phoebe's fears, there was nothing sexual or romantic about my relationship with Marianne. She was a colleague and friend, and I was more than happy with that. One of Phoebe's greatest fears about Burning Man was that I would find some "spiritual hippie woman" there and have an affair. Devon had repeatedly encouraged me to hook up with women at Burning Man, and there were certainly opportunities to do so – "What happens at Burning Man stays at Burning Man," Devon would tell me – but I stayed true to Phoebe and just appreciated the occasional attention I would get from women at Burning Man, never taking any steps to take it further than that. In many ways, I had created an "I'm not available" barrier around myself, so it wasn't that difficult for me not to get into something with a woman at Burning Man. Of course, since Marianne was encouraging me to divorce Phoebe, there were grounds for Phoebe to be concerned, though she didn't know that. But Marianne's encouragement was not for me to leave Phoebe so that she and I could be together – she was encouraging it simply for my own happiness and wellbeing, recognizing that I was fairly miserable in this relationship.

It was sometime between Burns that I received a letter from Ronin Books that they were interested in publishing

Mushroom Wisdom. It was the most exciting news I'd gotten in years, and I was ecstatic. "This is it!" I thought. This was the break I had been waiting for, and just might bring about a shift in my years of frustration and feelings of failure. I was going to have a book published, at last, and that would allow me to start a new career as a writer.

However, the publication was not going to take place without some edits. The publisher felt that there was too much of my own experiences written into the book and she wanted it to be more neutral and less personal, telling me to take out any personal stories that weren't necessary to the points I wanted to make. "No one is going to want to read about you," she told me. She also didn't like the subtitle I had chosen of "cultivating spiritual consciousness with psilocybin mushrooms," as the word "mushroom" was in both the title and subtitle, and she felt it was redundant. Her suggestion was to put the word "shaman" somewhere in the title to give it more market appeal, and also encouraged me to use the word shaman more frequently in the text. I hadn't really intended the book as being about shamanism per se, but it was easy enough for me to include the word scattered about the book. The subtitle that I suggested was "The Shaman's Path to Spiritual Consciousness," but she wanted "How Shamans Cultivate Spiritual Consciousness," and as the publisher, she had the final say on the matter.

After a few months of back and forth edits and reworkings and formattings, the project was complete, and eventually, a box containing 25 copies of *Mushroom Wisdom* appeared on my doorstep. With great anticipation and excitement I opened up the box, pulled out a copy of the little yellow book, and thumbed through it. To my amazement, I immediately saw errors. Most were not major, though there were enough there to be of concern. On the cover, there were periods where there should have been commas, and commas where there should have been periods in the Ph.D. part of my name. Also, in the back of the book, my name was written as Martin Bell. Worse still, there were places in the book where the publisher had inserted artwork that obscured some of the writing, thereby rendering several sentences into fragments.

Trying to be professional about it, I wrote to the publisher thanking her for working with me on this project and how excited I was to have received copies of the book, and, if the opportunity were to arise for a second printing, perhaps these errors could be corrected, and at the very least, could they please be corrected for the eBook version, and furthermore, I apologized if I was personally responsible for any of those errors as I had not caught them in the proof version she had sent to me for my final review and OK.

I did not expect the response I got from the publisher. She was livid. She lashed out, saying that I was a "wannabe author" and informed me that I was not to contact her again, as she wanted nothing more to do with me and my amateurish critiques for minor issues that "no one will ever notice."

I couldn't believe it. Was this for real? Not knowing how to respond, I didn't.

My joy at having found a publisher who was interested in my work, and who might be open to publishing further books that I thought I might write, was thoroughly dashed on that day, making the publication of *Mushroom Wisdom* something of a bittersweet victory and unsatisfying personal triumph. At least the book was out there, even with those errors, and perhaps it would open future doors that I had not yet knocked on. At any rate, I had no intention of ever sending a manuscript to Ronin Books again.

Because the publisher had insisted that I include "shaman" in the book, I thought I'd take a chance and contact *Shaman's Drum* magazine and see if they might be interested in writing a review of the book. I felt that the book had some important ideas to share and that it was somewhat unique. Most of what was available about psilocybin mushrooms was of two kinds: anthropological literature about traditional uses of mushrooms by indigenous cultures, and the wild speculations and adventurism of people like Terence McKenna. There wasn't anything else out there that took a straight forward look at how mushrooms could be used by anyone for spiritual growth and maturation that was not involved with metaphysical speculations like McKenna or connected to a specific cultural tradition. Thus I thought that maybe

Shaman's Drum might find the book interesting and be willing to review it and help me get some publicity.

To my absolute astonishment, I got a message back from Timothy White, the editor of *Shaman's Drum*, that, not only was he interested in the book, but he also wanted to meet me for an interview for the magazine. I was ecstatic. The plan was that he would drive down from Williams, Oregon, and I would drive up from Buellton (Phoebe and I had moved out of Santa Barbara to the nearby commuters' community of Buellton, just up the coast and over the mountains), and we would meet at Peet's Coffee in Berkeley, after which we would go to a friend's house in Oakland where we'd conduct the interview. I was thrilled, and also a little nervous. While I was experienced with mushrooms, realistically, I wasn't *all that experienced*, and I felt self-conscious about how a veteran like Timothy White would take what I had to share. If anyone was going to see through any pretence in what I had written, I assumed it would be him. Yet I also felt confident that I did have something special to share, so despite my fears, I eagerly agreed to the plan.

I didn't sleep the night before leaving for Berkeley, and was so excited that I couldn't figure out why cars were flashing their lights at me on the freeway as I approached the Bay Area and it was getting dark. It wasn't until I pulled into the driveway of my friend's house that I discovered that in my last stop for gas, I had neglected to turn my headlights back on after filling up, and had been driving on the freeway without my lights on. All I could do was shake my head, recognizing that I indeed must be very excited about this for me to make a mistake like that.

I had never seen a picture of Timothy, so I didn't know what he looked like, yet we had no problem recognizing each other at Peet's. I was standing out front when a small red car pulled up with an older man with a white beard drove up and waved. We greeted each other warmly, got some coffee, and then made our way to Oakland for the interview. We set ourselves up in my friend's house, Timothy got out a recorder, and we started the interview. Six hours later, exhausted but elated, I had told Timothy everything I could about my experiences with mushrooms, what I had learned, and how I worked with them. "I knew you were one to keep my eye on," he commented when we were all done. It was great praise coming from a man who had spent his life working with entheogens and had long practiced with mushrooms, along with his work with peyote in the Native American church and ongoing experience with ayahuasca. When all was said and done, he said that he'd love for me to come out to Williams, Oregon, at some point, and come into the tipi and eat some peyote, and maybe meet some like-minded folks. At the time, it seemed like a fantasy that would most likely never come to fruition. Sometime later, the interview came out in *Shaman's Drum,* and Timothy had even decided to make a painting of me that was featured on the back cover of that edition. It was great, and very personally fulfilling.

In relating the developments around the publication of *Mushroom Wisdom,* I've gotten a little ahead of my story, and thus need to back up. The process of editing and actually getting a book published was a long process, and in telling about it here, I've skipped over one more Burning Man, as *Mushroom Wisdom* wasn't fully published until the fall of 2006. At this point, I need to return the story to the Burn of 2006, as this was the beginning of the end of my marriage to Phoebe, and what started there as a small ripple eventually turned into a tsunami that completely overturned everything in my life, bringing me to where I am today.

CHAPTER SIX

THE BLUE-EYED WOMAN

It's Burning Man, 2006. Our camp for that year consisted of Rod, Devon, and myself – the usual crew – and Marianne and her protégé, Jessica, also joined us. When we had met Marianne and Jessica the year before, Jessica had been partnered with a young man, Corbin. Devon, who had always been quite the Casanova at Burning Man, had set his sites on Jessica, and when Jessica and Corbin ended their relationship, Devon began to look forward to seeing her again at Burning Man. Devon had a long history of continually revolving relationships, by this point. When he was married to Minda, he had started working in Australia, where he lived part-time. He had a girlfriend there, and after his divorce from Minda, he kept this Australian girlfriend as well as at least two more in Eugene. Plus, he had several women he had met at Burning Man who would come by camp for special visits over the years, and there were others that served for one-night stands. This year, he wanted Jessica, and Jessica apparently wanted him as well, having developed eyes for him the year before when she was with Corbin.

We were set up along the 4:30 strip, which was now an official location for theme camps, and we were just up the street from the Heebee Jeebee Healers, which always provided interesting sonic entertainment, especially the monkey chanting, and were also next door to a gay bar with drag fashion shows and daily alcoholics anonymous meetings. As usual, it was another fantastic year at Burning Man, and despite large dust storms and lots of wind that year, everything was superb.

I first met Maya one afternoon early on in the week. I was sitting in our greeting dome, looking out at the flow of traffic. There was a fellow across the street who came out of his camp with a large didjeridu. I got up from my seat and crossed the street, intending to talk to him about his didj, but before I got there, he started doing a didjeridu healing on a woman in a red bikini. So, I walked up and stood off to the side, hoping that we'd get a chance to chat.

While I was standing there, a young woman came walking up the street in khakis and a floppy hat. She had blond hair and bright blue eyes, and much to my surprise, walked right up to me, also observing the didj player, and commented to me that it was a nice didj. "You know what that is?" I asked her, somewhat surprised. In my ten-plus years of playing the didjeridu, it was seldom that I found others who were familiar with the instrument, and when I played the didj, most people asked me what it was and how it worked. Interestingly, I'd found that men were more likely to know what it was than women, and this was one of the first women I'd run into who knew what the instrument was right off the bat.

We then struck up a conversation, of which I don't remember any specific details, other than that we exchanged some information about where we were camping, and I pointed over to the God Box across the street and recommended that she come back sometime when we were open and take a turn at opening the God Box and visiting with the Mystic Toad. Maya was intrigued, promising that she'd be back, and then floated on down the road.

It was maybe a day or two before she returned. After she had her turn opening the God Box, she came back into the greeting dome, all smiles and beaming. She, like many who opened the God Box, walked up to me and gave me a big hug, thanking me for the experience. She then took out a small vial of scented oil and handed it to me, asking me to rub some on her chest through her open blouse.

Talk about an awkward moment! I found her terribly attractive, and an invitation to touch her was a bit more than I could handle. I fumbled with the small vial, heart beating rapidly and hands trembling, eventually getting a tiny amount of oil on my fingers, which I then tentatively rubbed onto her chest. “Not like that,” she said, taking the vial from me. She then rubbed some of the oil into her palm, spread open my shirt, and proceeded to massage the oil all over my chest. “Do it like this,” she said with a warm smile and entrancing blue eyes, looking up at me as she moved in closer.

It was electric. I couldn’t remember feeling anything quite so intimately exciting in years. To put it simply, I felt touched, and touched in a way that had been missing from my relationship with Phoebe for over ten years. It was thrilling and intoxicating and I almost swooned. It was like something that had been dormant within me suddenly awoke, and it - I - wanted more.

Maya was soon off, however, flitting away to other attractions for the day. Of course, I had no intention of actually acting on my feelings, and certainly had no expectations, so I watched her go and sat down, letting the scent of the oil on my chest waft up to my nose, and just relished the lingering sensations of having been touched by a beautiful woman while simultaneously feeling a bit sorry for myself and the reality of my domestic situation. It was what it was, and I was happy for the brief moment of connection that Maya and I had shared.

A few days later we were all gathered in our purification dome, our most wind-and-dust-protected space, having a drum circle and waiting out the whiteout and dust storm that was raging across the Playa. Quite unexpectedly, the cover of our dome suddenly rose up, and in slipped Maya, this time topless, wearing only a yellow bandana and shorts. She jumped into our circle and started playing with various crystals that had been set out in the dome for decoration as we drummed. Seeing her love of crystals, Marianne got out some more crystals that she had brought with her that year and Maya promptly positioned them about her body and nestled a large one between her shoulder and cheek.

I did my best not to stare and just kept on drumming and playing music with the other people present. When the dust storm finally ended, she popped up, said good-bye, and was gone. It was already late in the week, and I doubted that I would see her again.

That year, for the actual burning of the man, we all took mushrooms and headed out onto the Playa. When we got to the man and my campmates sat down, positioning themselves for the spectacle, I felt uncomfortable and didn't want to sit. There was a real torrent of energy raging within me, and simply sitting there and waiting wasn't going to do it for me. I looked around and felt into my situation. When I caught sight of the Temple out in the distance beyond the Man, it felt right, and I quietly separated myself from my group and began to make my way down the lamp-lit street to the Temple.

By the time I got there, the mushrooms were flowing strong. Making my way along the street to the Temple had been like walking through a vaulted fractal hallway or great hall, and the closer I got to the Temple, the more my energy smoothed out and the better I felt. Everything was quiet at the Temple. There were a few people there, mostly by themselves, quietly crying or otherwise having introspective moments. It was perfect. I had no intention of being social or interactive – I was in my standard mushroom state of not talking or engaging others unless immediately inspired and moved to do so. So I walked around the Temple until I found a place that looked and felt right to me, and then stood, facing the Man and the wild gathering of people and art cars that had amassed to watch and celebrate the immanent conflagration of the iconic figure.

It was such a different perspective on the whole affair, and one that I found fascinating. Every previous year, I, along with my friends, had gotten as close as possible to the Man and the Burn, and this was my first time being at a distance. I found that I liked the solitude of observing from the Temple, and deeply appreciated how quiet and introspective it was out at this distance. Here, I was able to simply stand in mushroom-inspired silence and just observe and think.

I found that my mind was busy accepting the fact that this might be my last Burn. Things had gotten increasingly tense with Phoebe over my attendance at Burning Man, and she was pregnant again with our second child. It seemed unlikely to me that she would agree to my coming out to Burning Man the following year, and once she managed to keep me away for one year, then the momentum would have turned against me. So in my heart, I allowed myself let go of Burning Man, and I let go of the God Box. Maybe next year it would be Devon and Rod and Marianne and Jess. Or maybe it would cease to be altogether once my involvement with it ended, for I was the main person running the whole show and keeping the God Box flowing, despite the fact that Devon was mostly the money behind our yearly adventure. The God Box was an extension of me in a way that wasn't the same for either Rod or Devon. And as much as I wanted to continue with it, it seemed increasingly unlikely, so I knew that the best thing for me to do was to prepare for that reality by letting it go.

It was bittersweet, and memories and recollections of all the profound and wonderful times the God Box had provided flooded through me. It had been a beautiful and touching gift, and as much as I wanted to keep it, I let it go, accepting that it might have run its course, at least my connection to it, that is. My hope was that it would continue on, but for my part, I had to let it go.

The closer it got to the actual burning of the Man, the wider the circumference of the circle of the inevitable party became, getting closer and closer to the Temple. More people were showing up, but aside from one woman who approached me asking if I was a Temple guardian, no one attempted to make contact with me, which I appreciated. Then, at long last, the Man burst into radiant fireworks and the immolation began. I was amazed that even at this distance, I could distinctly feel the heat from the light of the fireworks on my exposed face. It was cold that night, and the warmth felt exquisite. Stunning fractal geometries flowed around the vision of the fireworks in my mushroom state and I just stood and took in all that beauty. By the time it was all finished, the party had officially reached the Temple and now introspective mourners were outnumbered by jubilant partiers, eager to get the celebratory events of the night underway.

Walking back to the Man was like passing through successive layers of energy and vibrations that were quite palpable. The crowd was starting to dissipate and wander off in every random direction by this point, and I felt there was little hope that I would encounter any of my friends. Nevertheless, I decided to walk all the way around the Man, just in case. As I settled into this pattern, the energy started to dissipate, and before long the mushrooms were bringing me back down to normal. When I got to the far side of the now-fallen and burnt Man, there were Devon and Jess, standing there in each other's arms, smiling broadly at having seen me. I walked up, embraced them, and together we made our way back to camp for the final opening of the God Box for that year – an opening that, at the time, I thought might be my last. Burn night openings of the God Box were always the best, and we had found that many people saved it for a final treat for themselves and it would generally mean that we'd be up late, tending to supplicants and getting every last person possible in to have some face time with the Mystic Toad and the God Box.

The next day, Sunday, it was time to pack up and go. Just as we were about to get in our vehicles and drive out, bringing our 2006 Burning Man adventure to a close, Maya showed up. She wore that same floppy hat as the first time I saw her, and she came around to the God Box crew, asking for us to all write something on her hat, and share email addresses. I wrote, "Thank you for your beautiful energy!" on her hat and gave her my email as well. And with that, she was gone once again.

It wasn't until Halloween that I heard from Maya, via email. She sent out a picture of herself in a Halloween costume to a group of friends, so it wasn't in any way a personal email. I responded, however, with a short note that she looked good and was surprised and excited when I got a message back with an enthusiastic, "Hey Mr. Magic Music Man!" We thus struck up a correspondence and also connected on Myspace, which was the social networking site of choice at the time. With the demise of MP3.com as a place for independent musicians, I had started using Myspace to promote my music. A feature that I had liked about MP3.com was that you could collect music into "stations" (playlists, actually), which was great for a musician like myself, for I didn't have one particular kind of musical style or identity. I could use the stations to parcel out my music according to style and genre, and pair it with other songs of similar styles, and as such, better reach a possibly interested audience. For Myspace, since they didn't have the playlist feature, I had created numerous different pages for my many styles, and thus I had a world fusion/shamanic page, an electronic page, a folk rock page, a goth/alternative page, an acoustic reggae page, and a roots reggae page. Before long, Maya and I were connected through all of the pages, and I promptly moved her into one of the "top friends" spots on each page.

We hadn't really talked at Burning Man and knew very little about each other, so we proceeded to share aspects of our lives through email. It was then that Maya learned that I was married, had a daughter, and had a son on the way. I learned about her family, which was Mormon (though she was most decidedly NOT Mormon herself – something she made very clear), that she had recently traveled to South America where she had tried ayahuasca for the first time – coincidentally, with someone who contacted me after reading *Mushroom Wisdom*, which was now out, and who was sending me documents about his own initiation into the practice of being an Ayahuasquero. We talked about music, art, crystals, entheogens, Burning Man, and as with Marianne, had a running conversation that extended over the months.

Since Burning Man, she had moved to the area around Eugene, Oregon, where she was working in a forestry program. She was from Colorado, but since returning from South America (which had been just before that most recent Burn), she had been looking for new work and a new place to live. So, she was up in central Oregon, for now, and didn't know where she'd end up next. Ideally, she wanted to save up some money and then do some more traveling – perhaps to South America again, or maybe Australia.

My son, Ethan, was born in the spring, two weeks after his big sister's birthday. We had decided on the name Ethan at Miranda's insistence. When we first learned that we were going to have a son, the first boy name that popped into my mind was Jaden. Phoebe refused to have that be his name, however, as she had recently had a student named Jaden who was "a real terror," as she described him, and that name inevitably reminded her of the student's poor behavior and attitude. Since we couldn't decide on a name that we both liked, we asked Miranda. At the time, she was friends with a boy in her school named Ethan, so that was her immediate choice, and his name was settled.

I shared all of this with Maya, but never mentioned any of the marital difficulties between Phoebe and myself, so as far as she knew, we were all a happy family. I could tell that she was disappointed by this impression, but I didn't do anything to correct it, as I didn't want to lead her on about anything, for I had no intention of doing anything about the feelings I had for her.

As Burning Man of 2007 started to approach, Phoebe had expressed her strong desire that I not attend that year, flat out telling me how much she hated Burning Man, and that she even hated me when I went to Burning Man. Having made my peace, in a sense, with possibly not returning to Burning Man in 2007 during my mushroom trip out at the Temple, I agreed not to go that year. I wasn't at all happy about it, however, and now that *Mushroom Wisdom* and my interview in *Shaman's Drum* were out, I knew that it would be a great year for me to maybe give a talk and presentation at Burning Man and see if I couldn't make some inroads with the psychedelic lecture circuit. I was willing to stay away, however, for Phoebe.

As much as Phoebe wanted me to be happy with not going to Burning Man, she knew that it just wasn't so. Much to my joy and surprise, she eventually relented, saying, "I guess you can go to Burning Man this year." It was the last thing that I had expected, and it came as wonderful news. Thus plans were set in motion for me to get back out on the Playa, and Devon helped to make sure that I had a ticket, as usual.

Meanwhile, Maya started writing to me about how she wanted to go to Burning Man again, but there were various things she didn't know – how she was going to get there, who'd she'd camp with, how she was going to get a ticket, and other related issues. At this time, Devon was working most of the year in Australia, but he was planning on returning to Eugene in the summer, as that's where all our Burning Man gear was, and he'd be leaving from Eugene just as he had every year previous. I told Maya this, and suggested that she could get a ride from Devon, and also mentioned that she'd be welcome to camp with us, if she wanted.

Personally, my intentions here were pretty clear to myself – I wanted the opportunity to spend more time with Maya. Beyond that, I had no specific intentions or fantasies. I was married to Phoebe with two kids, after all, and all I wanted was a little time with someone I felt attracted to so that I could maybe experience just a little more of what I had been missing in my relationship with Phoebe, but nothing beyond that.

I let Devon know that I had offered him up as a ride to the Burn for Maya. When I first brought this up, Devon had no recollection of Maya or of her various appearances at the God Box the year before. Devon, after all, had been busy with Jessica, and then another woman toward the end of the Burn (on the night of the burn, actually, after we had returned from the Man to open the God Box. This woman who had been coming around camp showed up then and Devon disappeared with her, leaving Jessica behind. Their brief relationship was thus over before we left the Playa the next day). So, to remind Devon of who Maya was, I directed him to her Myspace page.

I could hardly believe Devon's next message after having viewed Maya's Myspace page. He informed me that his spirit guides had told him that Maya was the woman for him, and he had had a vision of them being married and walking through the jungle with Maya carrying their baby. To make this a reality, Devon was breaking up with his girlfriend in Australia, and the several girlfriends he had back in the States, as he didn't want any competing ties to get in the way of this new and fulfilling relationship he was going to have with Maya.

For my part, I encouraged Devon. I certainly was of the opinion that she was a beautiful and fascinating woman and said that she'd be great for him. Though my own heart beat for Maya, I wasn't going to do anything about it anyway, so there was no reason for me to attempt to dissuade my best friend from this new fantasy he was developing for himself, and compared to some of the other women Devon had been with, Maya seemed to me to be a big improvement, so I encouraged it and supported him, never letting on to my true feelings on the matter.

Devon returned to the States, only having to immediately turn back around as his father had just died in the Philippines. After settling business there, he made his way back to Eugene. I was then informed by both Devon and Maya that they had met in a coffee shop in Eugene where Devon had proceeded to tell Maya that they would be married and have a child together. Maya's reaction was something along the lines of, "And just who in the fuck do you think you are?" Needless to say, it hadn't been the magical and mystical encounter that Devon had envisioned. I wasn't at all surprised, but I continued to encourage the now-disconsolate Devon, who rhetorically asked, "I ended my other relationships for this?" I said there was still time, and maybe Maya would come around.

Personally, my biggest concern was that now Devon had scared Maya off and she wouldn't be accepting a ride from Devon, and certainly wouldn't decide to camp with us. Much to my surprise, and delight, however, she said that she would take us up on the ride, and would decide later where she was going to camp. And to top it off, the ticket issue was resolved by Devon presenting her with a ticket. As she later told me, "He wasn't going to get anything from me, but if this joker wanted to give me a ticket, sure, I'd take that." And thus our plans were made: Devon and Maya would come down from Eugene, and Rod and I would drive up from Santa Barbara. We'd meet at one of Rod's friends' houses in Sacramento, and from there, we'd all caravan to the Burn. Despite all the apparent obstacles, it looked like I'd get a chance to spend at least a little more time with Maya after all, and I was happy.

We all met in Sacramento, as planned. Rod and I arrived first, with Devon and Maya pulling in with the rental van some time after. Maya jumped out and gave me a hug. It was all just friendly and casual. That night, there was limited sleeping space, and Maya and I ended up sharing a mattress together; evidently the two of us were enjoying being in close proximity. When morning arrived, it was decided that Devon and Rod would ride in the truck, and Maya and I would drive Rod's station wagon.

When we arrived at Black Rock City, the greeter who came to our car to ask what theme camp we were with exclaimed with great enthusiasm, upon learning that we were with the God Box, "You're the mushroom guy! I loved your book!" He was appropriately dressed in a shirt that was covered in images of psilocybin mushrooms.

Once we had located our designated camp area, it was time for Maya to decide where she was going to camp – either with us, or attempt to find the group she had camped with the year before. It wasn't until everything was unpacked that she decided that she would camp with us at the God Box. I was pleased – and so was Devon, who still held out hope that he might be able to get something started with Maya. He'd had a vision of their future relationship together, after all, and one thing Devon did not like being was wrong. If he could have his way, Maya would be his before the end of the week.

Once camp was set up, we found ourselves joined by a couple who had come in from Grass Valley, California. They had been driving about, looking for a place to camp, when, in driving by the God Box, Patrick and Jenny had spotted the large collection of didjeridus that I had set up in one of our domes. Patrick was a didj player and maker, as well as crystal seller, and both he and Jenny figured that our camp looked inviting to them, so they asked if they could join us, not knowing anything about the God Box. They ended up being a nice addition to the camp, and made their home on the Playa with us for the next few years. Marianne brought out her new partner with her, and they spent most of their time attempting to put together an art car that would pass the inspection at the DMV, but were never successful. Her partner wasn't thrilled by the Burning Man experience, and it was to prove to be Marianne's last year at the Burn.

It was all just another ordinary Burn (if such a thing exists!) up until Thursday, well into the week. The morning of that day, Devon, Maya, and myself were all sitting in our greeting dome, applying that day's first round of sunblock and standard Playa foot maintenance. Somehow, I'm not certain how, Maya and I ended up applying moisturizing cream to each other's feet while Devon sat off to the side. It was amazing. It was like having sex with our feet and our hands. It was the most erotic experience I'd had in years (and reminded me of the dialogue in *Pulp Fiction* that there's no such thing as *only* getting a foot rub). It was more than Devon could handle. He did his best to hide his crying behind his dark glasses, but as soon as his nose started spontaneously bleeding, suddenly everyone in camp was there trying to comfort and care for Devon, bringing our lovely mutual foot rubbing to a sudden conclusion.

Devon insisted that he had "no idea" what was wrong with him – typical to form. For the past several years at Burning Man, Devon had been having what he claimed were inexplicable crying fits where he would just start crying uncontrollably for what he said was no reason at all. Personally, I felt otherwise. Back when I had my big opening with mushrooms with Devon those years ago in Eugene, the experience had begun with my observations of Devon and what I saw as the patterns that he was using to define himself and his life. At that time, it had been obvious to me that there were many aspects about himself that Devon didn't like, but was unwilling to face or deal with honestly in a way that might bring about healing and transformation. Though that had been more than a decade ago, by this point, nothing had changed about Devon, and in fact, his negative patterns were more entrenched than ever.

Devon had established a pattern of letting all this boil over at Burning Man. A few years previously, he had expressed to me that he "wanted a turn" at healing at Burning Man, but it was ever-illusive. Inevitably, there would come a point in the Burn where Devon would end up curled in a fetal position on the floor in one of our domes, to be found either by me or by Rod, who would then come and find me, informing me that "Devon needs you." Each year, I did what I could to help move a little energy in Devon and help bring him to a more positive state, but the basic truth of healing is that the client must be open and willing to go through their darkness in order to reach the light on the other side of their troubles, and not only was Devon unwilling, he was also in denial, so really, nothing ever changed. As much as I wanted to help Devon, unless he opened up and was willing to surrender to the process that needed to unfold, there was nothing I, nor anyone else, could do for him. As a friend, however, I always made a show of helping him and did what I could to help him to feel loved and valued.

Despite his claims of having "no idea" why he was crying and bleeding from the nose now, it was obvious to me: he was upset over the connection that Maya and I had together and he simply couldn't take it. He had always been the successful ladies' man at Burning Man, and it was eating away at him that this woman who had rejected him was interested in me, rather than him. As much as he was trying to keep it all to himself, he couldn't, and the foot rub had pushed him over the edge with all of his frustration and hurt feelings pouring out his nose in a red torrent.

After that, Devon disappeared for the rest of the day, with no one knowing where he was.

Right around the same time, a small group of people came by the God Box looking for me, calling me away from the attention to Devon. They had read my interview in *Shaman's Drum* and were asking me about "doing ceremony" with me that evening. I tried my best to explain that we'd be opening the God Box that night, as that's what we did at our theme camp, but they'd be welcome to come back and visit with the Mystic Toad. I think that they thought I was attempting to speak in code or be subtle, or something, for they returned that evening with a larger group of friends, perhaps 9 or 11 people in all, and they all wanted to take mushrooms with me.

There was a whole variety of things wrong with this. For one, they apparently expected *me* to provide them with mushrooms. Second, I had never agreed to take mushrooms with them. Third, we were having dinner, and then planning on opening the God Box. Fourth, the whole thing just made me terribly uncomfortable. Just because I had written a book and given an interview didn't mean that I wanted to take mushrooms, which, for me, was always serious business, with a bunch of random people I knew nothing about. That wasn't at all what I was looking for, and I admit that I didn't know how to deal with these people – and neither did my campmates. Even though we all took turns explaining to them about the God Box, I think that up until the last moment, they all thought we were speaking in code and any moment we were going to bring out a big pile of mushrooms and feed it to them.

We eventually got the God Box open, and then it started to sink in among this group that we really did have a God Box and this really was what we were doing at our camp – not handing out mushrooms to anyone who asked. At that point, most of the group left, but a few stayed to open the God Box. One of the group members came up to me afterwards and thanked me warmly and sincerely. *He,* at least, got it, so there was some positive resolution to that awkward debacle.

I felt so relieved when they were finally gone that when Maya and I crossed paths, we just stood there embracing each other for a few moments as I thanked her for her assistance in helping to deal with this assuming crowd of mushroom seekers. Then Rod, Jenny, and Patrick showed up, and we all agreed that it was just about time to go out and enjoy the Playa for the night. No one had seen Devon since earlier that day, so we figured that the five of us would go out together and have some fun. Rod and I went to go eat some mushrooms, Patrick downed some peyote, and Maya and Jenny got dressed up for the evening.

We were all ready to go with the mushrooms just getting started when suddenly, there was Devon. True to form, he was balled up in a fetal position in our back dome. Everyone turned to me with a look of "what are you going to do about it?" "Fuck him," I proclaimed. Tending to Devon right now was the last thing I wanted. I'd just eaten mushrooms, was looking to blow off some steam from the tension of the assuming group of people who had spent several hours at our camp waiting for mushrooms, and to top it all off, this was to be the first night that Maya hadn't gone off dancing by herself, and thus it was our first evening together (in fact, it had probably been the appearance of the group of people and the awkward situation they had created that had kept Maya at camp into the evening rather than her usual habit of slipping away as soon as it was dark to go dancing).

This reaction on my part was not at all what Devon had been desiring, or expecting. I'm sure that he thought I'd drop everything, just like I normally did, and spend a few hours attempting to help him out of his debilitating funk. I wasn't about to pass up an opportunity to go out on the Playa with Maya, however, and thus my shocking verdict of "Fuck him." As no one else wanted the dubious honor of helping Devon, with that proclamation, we left camp and went out for a night on the town.

It was a great evening. Our first destination was the massive and towering 10-story oilrig, "Crude Awakening." It was a long wait in line, but by the time we got to the top, Maya was nestled into my arms as we looked out over Black Rock City together. It felt so wonderful just to hold her and be close and enjoy that special and undeniable connection we had with each other. Really, this is the only thing that really stands out for me of that night the five of us spent out on the Playa – just embracing each other atop the oilrig, watching the pretty lights and feeling the wind whip about us. Where we went and what we did after that is a total blur, though I imagine that we all wandered around the Playa some more for the next few hours.

Perhaps it was sometime around 2 in the morning that we returned to camp. None of us had watches, nor were we watching the clock, so it could have been any time. Rod and I were on the downside of the mushrooms, though they still had some life left in them. There were no lights on at camp, and no activity. Standing in front of our camp, we made plans that we would all go back to our respective tents and get some warmer clothes, and then meet up at Patrick and Jenny's for some bowl smoking and late-night snacks. Thus Patrick and Jenny went off in one direction, Maya in another, and Rod in yet another direction. The quickest path to my tent was through our front dome, so I headed out in that direction, thinking that I would rejoin my other friends for a pleasant night cap in just a few minutes. I couldn't have been more wrong.

Waiting for me, there in the pitch-dark front dome, was Devon. He was completely enshrouded in darkness, wearing a black cloak with a hood that his grandmother had made for him to bring as a costume to Burning Man that year. I didn't see him until he was standing directly in front of me, blocking my path to my tent. "Dude. We need to talk," he said, with undertones of utmost seriousness.

"OK," I said, inviting him to take a seat next to me.

We took our seats and stared off into the darkness for a few minutes. After this long silence, Devon launched into what he had to say.

"I know it's not fair," he began. "I've been trying to think my way out of this all day, and I just can't do it, so here it is: you and Maya have got to stop gushing over each other. It's ruining our friendship, it's ruining my Burning Man experience, and if you don't cut it out, you'll never go to Burning Man again. I know it's not fair, but you've got to stop it."

I doubt Devon knew the significance of what he was presenting me with here, but I knew instantly: this moment, right here, was about to define my future in very significant ways, no matter how I was to respond to his demands. No matter how this was going to resolve, it would prove to be a breaking point in my personal relationships, and there was not going to be a happy and easy resolution.

Suddenly, the mushrooms felt strong again. I had thought that the mushrooms were mostly over, but now they were surging through me once again in a torrent of energy and excitement. I sat there silently, as Devon looked in my direction, awaiting some kind of response. What he most likely was expecting was my capitulation to his demands, but I had no mind to give him any such reassurance. Clearly it was true when he said that this was ruining our friendship, and though perhaps slightly overblown, he had largely financially made my trips to Burning Man possible, so it wasn't too much of an overreach to claim that if I didn't do what he wanted, I wouldn't be returning to Burning Man. But I wasn't ready to simply give in and be the "good friend" that Devon wanted me to be right then. We had been friends for many years, and best friends since my senior year of high school. What Devon wasn't prepared for, however, was that I was willing to throw that away for a little more time with Maya.

After sitting there in silence for a number of minutes, I finally spoke. "Thank you for sharing what's in your heart," I said to Devon. "I need some time to think." And with that, I got up, walked out of the dome, and headed out to the deep Playa for an environment that was more suitable for the space and time I needed to process what was happening, and what I would eventually decide to do. I found a spot that felt reasonably in the middle of nowhere, with no large art structures anywhere nearby, turned off all my lights, and sat down, putting my face in my hands, and started mulling over my options.

Devon wanted me to push Maya away. As much as that seemed to be the safe option for me to choose, I couldn't find it within myself to do so. Pushing her away would be going against everything I felt. Realistically, all I really wanted was a few more days with the woman. It was now already Friday morning, and we'd be leaving on Sunday, after which time Maya would head north, I'd go south, and that would be that. The last thing I wanted was to brush off Maya for the next couple days, especially after the great night of connecting we'd just had. However, if I didn't, and just ignored Devon's demand, he was probably correct that it would be the end of our friendship, which, in and of itself, wasn't necessarily something that I lamented as I contemplated it then. If I had to choose Maya over Devon, Devon was going to lose. The only problem with that scenario was that then I'd have to explain to Phoebe that Devon and I were no longer friends, and being the intelligent and perceptive woman that she was, it wouldn't take her long to figure out that a woman had come between us – what else could break up a long-time friendship such as ours?

There really wasn't a plausible lie I could tell Phoebe, and then she'd learn about Maya. Of course, what I wanted was for Devon to chill out, let me have a few more days with Maya, and then maybe we could stay friends and continue to camp together at Burning Man in the future, allowing me another week of being with someone I felt I had a meaningful connection with, but I knew Devon too well to hope for this. He'd made up his mind, and if he didn't get his way, he'd make sure everyone knew of his displeasure. Devon had a great way of making his problems everyone else's problem, and the thought that this could be kept just between us was an impossible dream.

What was I supposed to do? No matter what I chose, there were serious consequences, and it would be impossible for me to just sweep this whole thing under the rug and go about life as it existed before. Whatever I decided to do, someone was going to get hurt; me, Maya, Devon, Phoebe, or all of us. So who meant the least to me in this equation? That was an easy answer: Devon. He'd bet that I'd choose him. That was not, however, the conclusion I was beginning to reach.

Still, I didn't know what to do, or how to do it. I needed to decide something, because I knew with absolute certainty that Devon was back there, waiting for me to return and tell him how sorry I was and how I'd kick Maya out of camp, and then everything would go back to normal, and how I'd do whatever I could to make sure that Devon had a good Burning Man experience. I was frozen in fear and indecision.

It was at this point of inner turmoil that I was approached by a woman wearing a big white furry coat who came to me with the intro of, "Nice view from out here."

"I'm not here for the view," I responded.

"So what are you doing?" she asked.

"I have to make a decision," I said, "but no matter what I choose, something is going to break, and I'm afraid."

She bent down, gave me a hug, and then shared this simple advice: "Just listen to your heart, and choose from there. It will be hard, but ten years from now, you'll know that you made the right decision."

I knew she was right. I resolved at that moment that I was going to share my heart with Devon and Maya, and accept any consequences that came from that. I wasn't going to tell Devon what he wanted to hear, and though I couldn't anticipate what would come from me being totally honest with both of them, at least I could live with that in my heart and feel true to myself. It might mean the end of my friendship with Devon, it might scare Maya away, and it might also mean the end of my marriage to Phoebe, but whatever the cost might be, I had to be true. It was the only way I could navigate my way through this and still feel that I could live with myself and my choices. It was either truth and full disclosure, or nothing. I wasn't going to play Devon's, or anyone else's, games any longer.

Having resolved that I needed to talk to both Devon and Maya together, I knew that going back to camp would be a poor choice right then, for surely Devon was still waiting for me to return to reassure him that I would do as he demanded. I didn't want to see him until I had a chance to talk to both him and Maya at the same time – the three of us needed to have it out collectively to bring everything out in the open. So, my only option was to stay out until morning, and maybe then I could catch them both before things got going in camp and we needed to open the God Box.

It was a long night of wandering from one burning art project to another, trying to stay warm. As it was beginning to lighten, I made my way to the temple, where I watched the sunrise on the Playa for the first time. My guess was that everyone back at camp was probably still asleep, and I could safely return then without having to be confronted by Devon immediately upon re-entering camp. Sure enough, everything was quiet at camp, so I slipped off my shoes, opened up my tent, and threw myself down on my air mattress with my feet hanging out the opening, closed my eyes to try and get a little rest, and waited.

Before long I started to hear people stirring about camp. I just lay there, listening, trying to hear Devon and Maya. I knew Maya was up when someone passed by my tent and tenderly reached down and pulled on one of my toes. There's Maya. A few minutes later, I could hear Devon in the front dome. It was time. They were both up, and as exhausted and ready for sleep as I was, this was my opportunity to grab them both, and force us all to have it out with one another, for good or bad.

My heart was pounding in my chest and I was shaking all over from anticipation. I grabbed a box of tissues, thinking they might come in handy, and walked into the front dome. Sure enough, there were Maya and Devon, sitting there, not interacting with each other, going about their morning routines. Without saying anything, I pointed to both of them and then gestured toward the back dome, inviting them to come with me. Together, we all walked in and sat down with Devon to my left and Maya to my right. Knowing that something was up, Maya reached out and took my right hand in hers and held onto a large crystal with her other hand.

I began: "There are some things that should have remained unsaid. All I wanted was a couple more days, but Devon, you chose to break the water on this baby, so now it's time for us to give birth to it.

"In your quest for Maya, I completely supported and encouraged you, Devon, but it didn't work out. I didn't say anything to discourage you or get in your way. But she didn't want you, and that's just the way things are.

"I can't speak for Maya, but I have a pretty good idea of what's in her heart. The truth is, I love Maya. She's lit a fire in my heart that I thought I would never see again – a fire that's been gone from my life for a very long time. And all I wanted was a couple more days with her – just a couple more days at Burning Man with this woman who's touched my heart.

"But now here we are, and we have got to work this shit out."

I felt an excited squeeze of my hand from Maya when I declared my love for her, and she made no attempt to pull away or distance herself from me. And it was completely true. I did love her. I had started loving her when we first met, just over a year ago, and over time it had only grown, especially with our week together at Burning Man. I had no idea what, if anything, could come of it, but I needed Devon to understand that I had absolutely no intention of pushing away this woman I loved simply because he was jealous and feeling sorry for himself. This connection between us had been growing long before Devon ever began his infatuation with Maya, and it wasn't going to go away simply because he wanted it to, or was demanding it to.

I can't recall exactly what Devon or Maya said right then – it was a bit of an emotional moment for me, but I do remember that Devon started spewing venom at Maya, refusing to look at or acknowledge me in any way, and instead focused all of his wrath on her. Instinctively, Maya held up the large crystal that had been in her right hand and grabbed it with both hands, keeping it in front of her, a barrier between Devon and herself. "You will not direct that kind of energy at me!" she said with an as-yet-unheard power and conviction in her voice. Almost instantly, the barrage of negative energy he had been shoving at Maya flipped around and Devon crumpled into tears. At that point, he ceased speaking and just sobbed and sobbed, opening the floodgates to his pain.

After some time of this, Maya went off to find Patrick and dig into his large collection of crystals, which she then brought back to Devon to try and help him release and transform his energy. Overall, he wasn't very responsive, and after about an hour, she gave up.

After Maya left, Devon suddenly came back around, wiping away the masses of snot and phlegm that had oozed out of his face, saying "Where am I? What's going on?" "You're facing yourself," I told him. Whether his disorientation was genuine or a dramatic act, I couldn't tell.

Devon and I spent the next couple of hours in the dome together. It was then that he confided in me his dark secret. When he was younger, he had apparently been responsible for a terrible event for which he felt extreme guilt. He had never found forgiveness or closure within himself over this transgression, and had essentially lived with it, buried deep within, his entire adult life. He had never mentioned anything of this to me previously, but it was clear that he was haunted by this and could not forgive himself for it, and as a result, lived with a profound lack of love and trust in his heart. Suddenly, so much of Devon's behavior over the years came into context and I was immediately reminded of seeing him while on mushrooms on that spring day back in Eugene. Devon hated himself and lived with that hate every moment of every day. And worse, he felt that he deserved this hate and lack of love, unwilling, and unable, to learn how to forgive himself and make peace with the tragic events for which he had been responsible.

Each of us has to face our own fears, our own lack of love, and our own sense of worth and forgiveness in our own ways, and it is different for each individual. If Devon had chosen for it to be so, this could have been the turning point in his life. This could have been the moment that he chose to fully face himself and his fears and his pain, and began the hard work of moving all the way through it and releasing it into love and forgiveness. It had all the makings of the "turn" at healing and transformation that Devon had told me he wanted for himself and his life. It could have been a new beginning for him, one that would eventually free him from his burdens and his choice of suffering and self-punishment. It could have, but it wasn't, and Devon didn't choose to use this opportunity to release and heal. Instead, he doubled down, shoved it all back in, and decided to carry on as usual, set in his well-established patterns and choices, unwilling to do the hard work of really confronting and transforming himself.

Our time alone in the back dome was finally brought to a conclusion when Rod poked his head in, informing me that people had arrived to open the God Box and it was time for us to get to work. With that, I went about getting the God Box ready and Devon disappeared. I didn't see him again until several hours later when we closed the God Box for the afternoon. Apparently, he had gone to the camp next door, found a young woman, and quickly bedded her. His satisfaction and sense of self and purpose regained, he came up to me and informed me that, "You can do whatever you want with Maya – I'm over it," as though I still needed his permission and approval. Indeed, Devon was back to normal, and the moment for opening and transformation had slipped away.

It was then that Maya and I finally had time to sit down and talk. By this point, I felt that I owed her an explanation. We sat down outside her tent in the slightly overcast afternoon light, and started talking. For the first time, I opened up to her with all the details of my life with Phoebe, my many years of unhappiness and dissatisfaction, and my feelings toward her. I also told her of how much I wanted to kiss her, but that I couldn't find it within myself to allow it to happen, though I truly wanted to. We talked for a long time, opening our hearts to each other, and eventually broke our little huddle when it started raining and then rainbows appeared in the sky. We made plans that we'd go out on the Playa together that night.

Before long, evening rolled around and it was now Friday night on the Playa – the big night before the Man was to burn on Saturday. By this point, I hadn't slept since Wednesday, but I was buoyed up by the new-found openness and honesty between us. We spent the night riding about on the Playa, dancing together, embracing, and finally, kissing. It took me most of the night to allow myself to kiss Maya, but when I finally did, we couldn't stop – or at least, only long enough for us to ride to our next destination, where the kissing would then recommence. It was electric and our tongues felt like open currents swirling around each other. It had been over a decade since Phoebe and I had shared a passionate kiss, and our kissing had never been anything like this. It was divine and intoxicating, and we both wanted more.

We got back to camp late – I have no idea what time it was. We were both thinking the same thing, and when Maya asked if she could spend the night in my tent, I wasn't about to oppose the idea. I had made it clear, however, that I wasn't open to the idea of having sex – that, to me, seemed to be pushing things too far, and I still held onto some idea of protecting my relationship with Phoebe. However, when Maya informed me that she wanted to go down on me, I couldn't bring myself to refuse.

After the sweet release, Maya curled up next to me and was asleep almost instantaneously. I, however, couldn't sleep, despite it now being two days since I had last slept, so I lay there in the few hours of darkness left and enjoyed feeling

Maya next to me while I wondered just what in the hell I was doing, and what was going to come of all this.

Saturday was a blur with our final openings of the God Box. I tried sleeping a bit during the afternoon, but to no avail. When night came, Maya and I went off alone together again to be with each other for the night's pyrotechnics.

I honestly don't remember anything of the man burning that night. I do, however, distinctly remember the burning of the massive oil platform, "Crude Awakening." It seemed perfectly apropos for everything I was going through right then. Maya and I watched from a distance, having located ourselves at the Temple, well away from the massive crowd of eager on-lookers. The art piece represented the unsustainable energy practices that had propped up the American Dream, and it was demolished in a massive mushroom cloud explosion after a band played a disturbing, minor key version of the national anthem. Maya and I were both very emotional at the time, struggling with the reality that when all this was done, we'd be going our separate ways – me back to my unhappy life with my wife, and her to somewhere in Oregon, alone once more. In many ways, I had been living the American Dream myself: a wife, decent job, middle-class lifestyle, two kids, two cars – everything we were supposed to want and aim for in life. Yet I had been miserable, and now the façade of that artificial life was crumbling and going up in flames, just as the massive oil platform was being engulfed in the raging flames of the mushroom cloud. It was all just too perfect. As a side note, it was also the coolest damn explosion I've ever seen, and nothing before or since has compared at Burning Man. Nothing quite like blowin' shit up in a really big way to make a Burner's day.

When all was said and done with the oilrig, we wandered the Playa more, finally coming to rest in the tantric love pods that were located way out in the deep Playa that year. We cuddled up in there and this time it was my turn to satisfy Maya. We still didn't make love, but we took care of each other otherwise. Maya napped for a short time in the pod, but when the sun came up, we wandered back to camp, and it was time to break everything down and head home.

Maya and I elected to drive the moving truck together so that we could get a few more hours alone. It ended up being many hours alone, as it took us six hours just to get to the main road and exit the Playa. It was the worst exodus I'd yet experienced at Burning Man and was a telling reflection of the event's growing popularity. We talked the whole six hours of slowly moving to the exit, and then, the exact moment we hit the pavement, I lost my voice. Thus when we stopped in Reno to get gas, I had the perfect excuse not to talk to Phoebe on the phone as she had been expecting me to. In my raspy, hardly present voice, I said, "Devon and I had some issues, and I'm still processing." Of course, Phoebe knew something was up, but she didn't press me for any details, as I couldn't really talk anyway.

We arrived in Sacramento late that night. For one last time, Maya and I shared our sleeping space, and when we woke up in the morning, it was time to say good-bye. She got in the truck with Devon and headed back to Oregon, and Rod and I got into his station wagon and began the drive back to Santa Barbara, the default world, and the life that I no longer wanted for myself.

CHAPTER SEVEN

AS EVERYTHING FALLS APART

The ride back to Santa Barbara with Rod that Labor Day Monday was one of the most profoundly emotional days of my life. I alternated between elation over my experience with Maya and absolute dread and despair to be returning to my life with Phoebe. One moment, I was filled with absolute joy, the next, crushing misery.

One thing I didn't feel was any guilt whatsoever at having cheated on Phoebe with Maya. Contrary to my expectations, I was thrilled to have explored my connection and attraction to Maya and felt nothing but profound gratitude. Back in high school, in the summer between my jr. and sr. years, I cheated on a girlfriend I had just started seeing before the summer began. With my family's usual stint in Santa Cruz for the summer, we had agreed that it would be OK for us to see other people over the intervening months that we would be apart. Toward the end of the summer, another friend from high school came out to Santa Cruz, where she would be going to college in the fall, and we ended up going out and having sex on the beach. I didn't tell my girlfriend about it and felt horribly guilty. Many months later, when she had heard rumors, she confronted me about it, insisting that she only wanted to know the truth. Despite her reassurances, I chose to lie to her and told her that nothing had happened. I felt horrible and was very unhappy with myself for first choosing to cheat, and second, for later lying about it. I had decided then to never fool around on anyone again, as the misery far outweighed the transient pleasure.

Yet this was not at all what I was experiencing. I had always assumed that if I cheated on Phoebe, I would feel awful about it. But I didn't. I didn't feel bad about it at all. I felt like I had been a starving man who, after years of suffering and deprivation, had finally received a decent meal and was satiated for the first time. Rather, my misery was generated by the knowledge that I could no longer realistically convince myself that I *should* be happy with Phoebe and our life together. I could no longer hide from the fact that our relationship left too much to be desired to be fulfilling for me in any way. Now that I had honestly opened up to the reality of my heart and my desires, reflecting on my life with Phoebe was just unbearable. For the first time in many years of frustration, I finally fully admitted to myself that I was miserable, profoundly disappointed with my life and relationship, and the truth was, I wanted out.

I shared all of this with Rod for the first time. It was strange to finally be revealing this to Rod, someone who had been a good friend since childhood, yet had never known of my unhappiness, for I had kept it a secret from just about everyone in my life with the exception of Devon, and more recently, Marianne. Rod responded by saying that he prayed for the stability of my family and for the healing of my relationship with Phoebe, but I was having my doubts that we would last through this. I didn't yet know what I wanted, or intended to do, but I knew that I couldn't hide this from Phoebe. I would have to tell her something about what had taken place at Burning Man, and I would have to be honest with her about my heart. Even though the path before me was unclear, I wasn't about to go back into hiding, repressing my feelings, and pretending that everything was OK when it clearly wasn't. I had to do *something*.

The fact that I had lost my voice bought me a little time. Phoebe knew that something was up, but since I couldn't really speak, she accepted that I would share with her later, after my voice returned and I was done "processing" what had taken place at Burning Man. All I had told her was that something had transpired between Devon and myself. So, I just went about unpacking and cleaning up my gear and getting ready to return to work the next day.

When Tuesday came around, Phoebe left for work early with Miranda, leaving me to take Ethan into daycare before heading into work. I had no idea how I'd be able to manage myself at work. I was still exhausted from the Burn, having slept only a little on Sunday night, and hardly at all on Monday night after getting back home – the Wednesday before was the last time I had really slept. I found myself crying in the car as I got on the freeway, heading into Santa Barbara with my 5-month-old son, Ethan, in the back seat. However, shortly after getting on the freeway, I discovered that there was a fire not far down the road, and getting into work would require me to backtrack and take another route around the mountains that was now highly congested with diverted traffic. I decided then that I'd call in sick for the day and just stay home.

Shortly after returning home, the phone rang. It was Devon. "I've never seen this girl so sad," he said, referring to Maya, who had apparently been crying since the night before. She had been listening to a CD of my music and it had affected her profoundly. Ever since my first trip to Burning Man in 2001, I had made gifts of my music in CD form, which I would pass out to people at the Burn. Maya had received my music both in 2006 and now again in 2007. Something that struck her was that the music on the 2007 CD sounded sadder to her than the music from the previous year, and this had set her off, emotionally, thinking that something must have changed for me over the intervening year. Perhaps it had, though my music has always expressed a wide range of emotions and textures, so I didn't necessarily see the music as any different. Whatever the case, it hit her hard, and she was lamenting my pain, and hers as well.

Devon wasn't sure Maya and I should speak, sensing the danger and potential of the moment, but I insisted. Maya got on the phone, and at first, we just cried together. Once we got all that out, our emotions turned to joy and we spoke on the phone for some time. It was nice just to connect and hear her voice. She and Devon were at Devon's mother's house in northern California, and they eventually had to get organized and start heading back to Oregon, so we got off the phone after an hour or so.

I hadn't made up my mind what I wanted to do about my relationship with Phoebe, or even what I was planning on telling her, so no promises were made to Maya, and we once again left our conversation with good-byes. After we hung up, I was shaking and unsteady, so I decided to take a shower and just feel into my situation with a little nurturing warm water falling over me as Ethan took a nap.

It was in the shower that the decision came over me. As I let the fullness of this truth wash over me, I almost passed out and collapsed right there: I had to leave Phoebe, and if I didn't do it now, then I might never have the courage to do it, or perhaps would only be brave enough to do it after the kids were grown and moved out, but by then I'd be a much older man and so much of my life would have passed me by. Now was the window of opportunity and the moment of truth.

Something that was clear to me in that shower revelation was that this was something I needed to do for myself, and while Maya was a factor, in some respects, it had nothing to do with her. The truth was that I had been compromising myself, hiding my heart, denying my true feelings, and in some as-yet-undefined way, had been holding myself back. I knew that in my relationship with Phoebe, I had been avoiding doing something with my life that I couldn't yet understand or conceptualize, but I knew it was true. In compromising myself for our relationship, I had not been true to myself, and only by setting myself free could I discover what it was that I had been avoiding and holding myself back from. There was something very important that I felt I needed to discover about myself and my life, and my time with Phoebe had mostly been a diversion from this and provided me with the excuse I needed to avoid whatever challenges were awaiting me in this process of discovery. Now that the truth of my heart was painfully apparent to me, it was the time to act.

It was something that I needed to do for myself and no one else. Yes, I hoped that if I left Phoebe, Maya and I would be able to be together, but that wasn't what this was really about. Truthfully, it was about me, my heart, my happiness, and my sense of fulfillment in life. Maya was a part of that, but she was not the reason for my needing to leave, or the ultimate goal of ending my relationship with Phoebe. Leaving Phoebe would be me making my own heart and life a priority for myself in way I never had.

As a "spiritual" person, I had always believed that living for others and serving them was the way to go. Anything else was selfish and ego-based, was it not? Truly being spiritual was about being willing to give and give, caring nothing for oneself, willing to sacrifice everything for the wellbeing of others. I had let this warped and spiritually muddled perspective shape my choices and actions, and the results had left me miserable. I had contracted the spiritual do-gooder's disease – the same disease that had infected Buddhism with the introduction of the *Bodhisattva,* shifting priority away from enlightenment to the compassionate saving of others. What was becoming clear to me was that neglecting my own heart and own sense of authenticity was no way to find happiness and fulfillment in my life. Through my sense of being responsible for others, I had neglected to take responsibility for myself. Furthermore, I had let my fears of how I would be perceived by others dictate my actions and choices. I *wanted* to be seen by others as selfless and compassionate and loving and kind and caring, for I was using this to assess my own state of self-worth and value as a spiritual being. It was all a self-generated bullshit narrative, however, for I certainly wasn't making Phoebe happy, and despite my enjoyment at being a father, it was beginning to dawn on me that there was no possible way I could teach my kids how to find happiness and authentic being in their own lives if I didn't take responsibility for myself in this regard. Sticking it out "for the kids" wouldn't serve anyone. Sticking it out "for Phoebe" wasn't serving her. Sticking it out for my reputation or esteem in the eyes of others wasn't serving me. So it was clear: it was time for me to go.

Up until this moment of revelation in the shower, I hadn't known what I was going to do, or what I was going to say to Phoebe. But now I knew. I was going to leave her. I didn't know what was going to come after that – a relationship with Maya or not – but I did know that if I wanted to claim some happiness in my life, and set about discovering what I had been holding myself back from, then this was something that I needed to do, and I needed to do it for myself and no one else. While I acknowledged that it felt selfish, for the first time, I didn't see that in a negative or judgmental light. What, after all, was wrong with loving and taking care of myself and being true to my heart? If loving myself meant that I had to disappoint and hurt some other people, then that's what it was going to take, and I was no longer going to make excuses for myself. If I didn't want to be a victim to my own self-imposed suffering, then I needed to do something about it, and only I had that responsibility. I couldn't look to anyone or anything else for this. It had to be me.

Secretly, I had been waiting for "fate" to change the circumstances of my life. There were times when Phoebe was late arriving home from work, and I'd get excited thinking that maybe she got into an accident and wouldn't be coming home, and I'd be free. That shows the level of my own cowardice and fear. I wanted out of the relationship so much, but was so unwilling to do anything about it, that I fantasized that Phoebe would just disappear out of my life by an act of God. It was pathetic, and I had been avoiding the hard truth that if I wanted something better for myself, I would have to take responsibility and do something about it myself, instead of waiting around for fate, or God, or karma, or the universe, or whatever to step in and do the dirty work for me. If I wanted to be happy, I needed to make different choices for myself, and accept the consequences that came with those choices.

So that was when I decided that I would leave Phoebe, and that it would be soon – just a matter of days. Now that I had made up my mind, I saw no point in delaying the inevitable, and the sooner I began to live my life, the better. I checked in with Rod, who said that it would be fine for me to move in with him in his condo in Goleta, and he could take me in as early as that coming weekend. Though I didn't know exactly when or how I'd do it, my plan was to talk to Phoebe over the weekend.

The talk came on Saturday morning. The kids were still in bed and I was sitting on the couch drinking coffee when Phoebe came up and said, "I know that you're still processing whatever it is that happened at Burning Man, but I get the feeling that you're going to leave me."

Knowing that the kids would be waking up soon, my response was, "Are you sure you want to talk about this now."

It hit Phoebe hard and she reeled back, collapsing onto the floor. "I always knew you were going to leave me," she cried. And it was true – she always did know. It was something that both of us had known for years, but had skillfully avoided through our marriage, buying a house, having kids, and going on as though there was a healthy and happy relationship between us, when we both knew that it was a lie and an illusion. But now the truth was out, and though Phoebe was taking it hard, I could only feel a sense of ever-expanding relief and optimism for my life that had heretofore only been activated by my yearly trips to Burning Man. For the first time in many years, I started to feel that I might actually be able to find happiness in my life.

Before long, the conversation turned to the inevitable: "Is there another woman?" My answer was that yes, there was, but that this decision wasn't really about her. This was about me and what I wanted for myself. I wasn't leaving Phoebe *for* Maya – I was leaving her for *me.* I don't know if Phoebe understood the distinction, but it didn't matter anyway. I was done with trying to influence what Phoebe thought of me or my life. I'd done that for too long, and it brought neither of us any real happiness. And the truth was, I had no idea what would become of my relationship with Maya, or if anything lasting would come of it. I had certain hopes and desires, but they were secondary to my desire simply to free myself from this stifling relationship in which I had willfully imprisoned myself for most of my adult life. First and foremost, I wanted to be free.

And now I was.

Phoebe tried using my sense of spirituality to convince me to stay. "A real healer, a real spiritual person, would want to try and heal our relationship." Indeed, it had been that very sentiment that had kept me with Phoebe for so long, but not any longer. My response to her was that I needed to attend to my own heart, and that really, there was no real relationship between us to heal. Our relationship had been over for years, and both of us had been busy avoiding admitting it. But I was not going to spend any more of my life trying to "fix" us. I was done.

That night, Miranda was to go spend the night at a friend's house. Not wanting to spoil the experience for her, Phoebe insisted that we tell her the following morning that I was moving out. Looking back now, I can see that this was one last acquiescence to Phoebe's will that I might have been better served by ignoring. After Phoebe left with Miranda and Ethan, I packed up my few things and drove to Rod's with the plan that I would meet Phoebe the following morning in Goleta after she picked up Miranda, and I could explain the situation to her then.

The result was that Miranda, who already suffered separation anxiety from her mother, felt that she had gone to spend the night at a friend's for the first time, only to return to a broken home, and for the next few years, accused me of choosing to leave when she had been away, demanding to know why I had done that, and perhaps fearing that in some way, she was at fault. For her, it was like I had slipped away when she wasn't looking, and the impact of it hit her hard and deep, agonizing her little, vulnerable heart. In retrospect, this wasn't the best way I could have handled this, and if I had been more resolute with Phoebe, I would have sat Miranda down when she woke up on Saturday and done the hard work of explaining to her what was happening. Instead, I chose to listen to Phoebe, but that was to be for the last time.

We met in a park in Goleta. I had gone out and purchased two small red stones that were cut into the shape of hearts, one of which I kept, and the other I gave to Miranda, a symbol that she would always be in my heart, no matter what. Miranda was anguished, tears gushing from her eyes, her little heart aching with fear and lack of understanding why her daddy was doing this awful thing. Of course, she couldn't understand the profound disconnection between Phoebe and myself. It was so very different from my own experience of my parents getting divorced. My parents had fought and yelled at each other, thrown things, damaged property, and shown numerous visible and obvious signs that they were not happy. I, on the other hand, had kept all of my unhappiness hidden as best I could. Miranda had never seen Phoebe and I have a disagreement or fight. She had never seen us raise our voices at each other, or cry in our unhappiness. From Miranda's perspective, just like for everyone else in our lives, we seemed happy, content, and living out the perfect life together. It was inconceivable for Miranda that Daddy was unhappy and wanted to leave. It was like her worst fears were taking place right here and now, and there was nothing she could do. No matter how hard she wrapped her little arms around me, no matter how hard she cried, and no matter how hard she glowered at me in utter disbelief, I wasn't going to change my mind and come home with them. It was a horrible nightmare for her, and there was nothing she could do to change it.

Things were obviously very different with my son, Ethan. He was only five months old when I left Phoebe, and as far as he's concerned, this is just the way things are. It's taken years to heal my relationship with Miranda, but I'm happy to say that things are better than ever between us, and now I'm able to be the father for her that I'd wanted to be, but had been unable to be, due to my own denial and self-deception. All of life and existence is a mirror, after all, and you can only get back what you put out, in large measure, and you can only find fulfillment in the external if you experience it internally. Choosing to make my life and my heart my priority has since resulted in much better relationships with everyone in my life, despite the initial shock and hardship it caused.

At the very beginning of this work, I wrote that in my 2008 book, *The Entheogenic Evolution*, the concluding chapter detailed my life after my separation from my wife through the following year. We have now reached the point in this particular iteration of this story where we can return to what I wrote in *The Entheogenic Evolution.* Much of the remainder of this chapter is an edited version of what I originally included in that book, expanded and reworked to flow with the story as I have been articulating it here. When I first wrote that chapter, entitled, "My Journey," I began it by writing that in 2007, at Burning Man, an "interpersonal crisis" had sent me out onto the Playa, forcing me to reassess my life in a way that led to me leaving my wife. Now, over two hundred pages into this book, I've filled in those details, and we're ready to return to what I wrote five years ago.

A week after moving in with Rod, we decided that we would try some of the salvia that I had grown that summer. I was looking forward to what would arise with my newly claimed freedom and authenticity, and was eager to enter into the profoundly altered state of awareness and experience brought on by salvia. My standard practice of working with salvia was in the form of taking turns. I'd learned that salvia was a very intense, and very personal, experience, and that it was easy for people to be distracted by external events, and thus had cultivated the practice of taking turns. At this time, I went first. The first round was pleasant, but nothing really profound. After Rod had his turn, I went for another round, packing myself half of a leaf to smoke (curiously, salvia tends to exhibit a reverse tolerance, meaning that a second round of using the sage can be much stronger than the first, even if using the same source).

Half a leaf of salvia isn't much, but the experience was something else. As the sage started to come on, it felt like my arms were floating back behind me as I sat on the floor in lotus posture. My head tilted back and I felt like I was being enfolded in what I later referred to as the "cosmic pillow." It felt as if I were surrounded by pure, plush comfort, completely enveloping me. This cosmic pillow felt as though it stretched from one end of the universe to the other, and I just melded into it, this most profound sense of comfort and ease.

It made me want to giggle.

I let out a little laugh, a bit self-consciously, knowing that Rod would be wondering what I found funny, but not wanting to explain my experience to him just yet, as that would distract me from what was clearly still unfolding.

I could feel that laugh inside me though, and it wanted to get out. So I let out a little more, giggling a bit more freely. Then more came out. Then more. I was no longer giggling now, but truly starting to laugh.

The laugh began as a vibration in my stomach. It didn't feel at all as though *I* were the one laughing. Rather, the impression was that the universe was laughing *through* me, and it was one serious laugh, as though all of creation was partaking of my personal sense of joy and freedom and using my body as a vehicle to express this.

The more I let out, the stronger it became. Harder and harder I laughed. No longer able to sit in lotus posture, I started bending over as the convulsions of the wild laughter escaped from my body. I couldn't breathe and I started crying at the sheer force of the laugh. I slapped the ground, calling out "Oh God!" as tears streamed down my face.

And still the laugh grew.

All I could do was roll over onto my back. Now I was rolling around on the floor, laughing wildly. I couldn't take it anymore. It was too much! "Oh God!" I kept calling out, trying to wipe away the tears. Still the laughter came.

In all, I probably laughed for a good twenty to thirty minutes. Never before had I experienced such a profound laugh. And as soon as I tried to explain the experience to a now very curious Rod, the whole thing started over again.

Apparently, I had found a profound joy. I was liberated. I was free. I was ready to follow my heart. My joy was incomparable, and there was a new passion for life within me that I had thought was either dead, or strictly confined to my times at Burning Man. As Maya would tell me, now, every day could be Burning Man.

Maya and I talked for hours on the phone each night, and for the first time, I got involved with sending text messages – something Phoebe and I never got into, and we didn't have much to say to each other anyway. My phone became my lifeline to Maya, and our relationship grew through that digital medium. Every night, after getting off work, I'd spend long hours walking about the neighborhoods and parks around Rod's place, talking to Maya and sharing our feelings for each other. Before long, she started to ask, "When are you going to get up here, man?"

By "here," she meant Ashland, Oregon. On their way back up to Eugene, Devon and Maya had stopped in Ashland, and like many who travel through Ashland, she fell in love with the town and its people, instantly feeling at home. She got herself settled in Ashland by taking on a temporary house and dog-sitting gig as she looked for more permanent work and a real paycheck. Meanwhile, Devon and the woman he had met at Burning Man on the day that he, Maya, and I had had it out had moved in together up in Eugene.

I had been to Ashland a few times as a junior high and high school student, with my English and drama classes taking trips up to the small southern Oregon mountain town to enjoy the local Shakespeare festival. I had even had a dream many years ago where I found myself walking down the street in downtown Ashland, arm in arm with a woman who wasn't Phoebe, and realizing that I lived in Ashland. I had never thought much of the dream, though it had stayed with me. When Maya suggested that I come join her there, it didn't seem like much of a stretch, as it felt right and was already confirmed by a dream of years ago.

It was on my first trip to Ashland that Maya and I first made love. It happened only minutes after I arrived at her small, one-room house-sitting job. Maya literally passed out after orgasming, and it was the most amazing sex I'd had in well over a decade. We spent the majority of my visit making love like the sex-and-attention starved male that I was, and our relationship seemed promising.

At very end of November of 2007, I made the move to Ashland in my attempt to remake my life. I had taken a couple trips up to Ashland and made some contacts regarding working at the English language school that operated out of Southern Oregon University, and hoped that I'd be able to facilitate the transition by teaching English classes as I had done in Santa Barbara. When I actually arrived, however, student numbers were rapidly diminishing, and work was sparse. In the divorce settlement with Phoebe, my monthly child support payments were calculated on the basis of my $32,000 a year job as academic director, giving me a payment (including child care costs) of over $1,100 a month. I therefore started doing anything possible to make ends meet, from giving music lessons to helping people set up webpages. The next several years were to prove to be the most challenging financial period of my life. I also learned that public assistance is terribly frustrating. As an individual, I had to show that I could earn enough money to pay my bills, but also as an individual, if I made over $1,000 a month, then I couldn't qualify for food stamps, even though paying all my bills meant that I had no money left over for food. It was a bizarre catch-22 situation where I didn't make enough money to afford to eat, but I made too much money to qualify for food stamps. In the process, I lost about 30 pounds, mostly due to undernourishment.

Maya and I got a small apartment together with the smallest monthly payment we could find. The constant worry about money and making child support payments weighed heavily on me, and much of my time was spent trying to find work and the next small job of $50 to try and build up enough to make it through the month. I cashed in what little stocks I had and even cashed out my meager retirement account from my previous job. To top it all off, right after moving, my car needed a couple thousand dollars worth of work, putting me even more in debt. Money was so tight and stressful, I distinctly recall breaking down and crying in the grocery store when it was clear that I couldn't afford to get a carton of orange juice, as it would push me over my limited budget.

In my quest to find work and scrape together enough money to eat and pay child support, I connected with a now defunct local outfit in Ashland called "EQ.TV," which was just starting up an internet-based video streaming company that was looking to develop online "TV" shows, as well as stream local music events over the internet. I spoke with the producers and they were interested in having me develop a show related to entheogens. By this point, I had *Mushroom Wisdom,* and my more recent book on *Salvia divinorum, Sage Spirit,* out, and I was eager to try out this new project. One of the main themes of EQ.TV was the "evolution" of culture and paradigms to help create a more balanced and sustainable world, and thus I chose the title of "The Entheogenic Evolution" for my web-based TV show. As it turned out, EQ.TV didn't fly, but this did give me the idea to start a podcast by the same name. I had a few contacts in the "entheogenic community" that I thought I could bring on for interviews, and felt that I personally had a lot that I could share, so I began recording and posting podcasts on the internet and quickly developed a following there. Though I had many more listeners than contributors, it became a small, and vital, monthly stream of revenue for me through donations made by listeners, and also provided me with an outlet for sharing my thoughts and views on entheogens. I also started giving lectures locally in Ashland on entheogens and found that there was an eager local audience. In many ways, Ashland was the ideal location for this as it is a hotbed of entheogenic activity, and there are probably more people involved in entheogenic spirituality in this area per capita than virtually anywhere else in North America. There is the local Santo Daime church, Native American Church, regular ayahuasca meetings, mushroom gatherings, and as I was later to learn, the Temple of Awakening Divinity.

I also brought my resume over to the local college, Southern Oregon University, simply to inform them of my teaching areas and willingness to jump in, should something open up. Due to budget cut backs, SOU has a department of Philosophy, Language, Literature, Writing, and English – all crammed together. It was actually a nice fit for my skills, and they brought me on as a grader in the winter term and then started giving me English for international students in the spring. Then in the next year they let me start teaching courses in religion. It was only part-time work, so the pay wasn't enough to meet my monthly requirements, but at least it was work, and provided a small bit of financial stability.

Things started to get rocky with Maya fairly early on in my transition to Ashland. Though I had freed myself from my relationship with Phoebe, I brought with me vast amounts of emotional and psychological baggage from having lived in a dysfunctional relationship for all of my adult life. Phoebe and I had met when I was 18, and things started to go sour for us after our second year together. In late 2007, I was 35 years old, having spent almost half my life unhappy in my personal relationship. I had repressed so much pain, frustration, and anger over the years that I needed to go through an extended period of acknowledging, facing, and releasing all this pent-up energy and heal my heart, and simply walking into a new relationship wasn't the way to do it. All relationships are mirrors, and my mirror was anything but distortion and dust free. Realistically, there just wasn't any way that my relationship with Maya was going to work unless I took care of my shit. Yet all the money issues kept me stressed and worried over financials, leaving little time and energy to address my dysfunctional emotional and mental state as far as relationships went.

We struggled to make it work however, for our love was deep and despite any issues, we wanted to be together. When the opportunity arose for us to attend a Native American Church ceremony hosted by Timothy White, the editor of *Shaman's Drum* magazine, we were both eager to experience the medicine and for myself, maybe really begin the process of dealing with my inner pain. The peyote we consumed at the ceremony made me want to wretch and purge, but for whatever reason, I was still holding on pretty tightly to that pain inside me, and I found no relief in the ceremony, even when I did manage to "get well" with a small purge. There was clearly a great deal more that needed to come out, but I didn't know how to get to it and let it release. This was my first experience with peyote, and overall, I didn't find it to be that effective of a medicine, at least for me. It is very mild in comparison to mushrooms, or especially salvia, and I found that its bitterness really got in the way of my ability to consume enough to really open up the energy. It was clear that it would take many visits to the Native American Church and a massive amount of the bitter cactus to really get at what I needed addressed.

Not long after our trip to the Native American Church, the medicine that was to prove to be a radically life-altering factor in my life and sense of self appeared via a job application. In my search for work, I had applied for a menial job at a record company in Medford, Oregon, that I found on Craigslist. Nothing came of the job application in terms of work, but a fellow who worked at the record company at that time took a look at my personal website and surprised me with a phone call. There was a section of my website that was dedicated to my Burning Man theme camp, and it had information about the Mystic Toad and the God Box. "Hal," a pseudonym that he prefers me to use, apparently wanted to talk to me about the Mystic Toad.

"So what kind of toad is that 'Mystic Toad' that you've got there?" he asked right up front in a curious tone. "It's a mailbox," I answered, not sure where the conversation was going. "Really?" he answered. "Well, I've got the real thing – Sonoran Desert Toads. I milk 5-MeO-DMT from their glands. If you'd like to give it a try, maybe we can get together sometime."

I was curious, to say the least. "Licking toad," as I thought of it, was always something that I was interested in experiencing first hand. Of course, one does not literally lick the toad in the manner of Homer Simpson while lying about in a hammock. Rather, the venom is either smoked or vaporized, providing a rapid delivery of 5-MeO-DMT, an extremely potent entheogenic/psychedelic agent.

5-MeO-DMT, molecular cousin to the more commonly known N,N DMT (often simply called DMT), is a naturally occurring endogenous psychedelic compound, meaning that it is produced naturally in the human body. In fact, not only are both kinds of DMT produced in the human body, they are found in all other mammals as well, and in countless species of plants. In many respects, nature is fairly well saturated with various forms of dimethyltryptamine. It's everywhere, even in you and me. These magical tryptamines are ubiquitous throughout the biological world.

After publishing *Mushroom Wisdom,* a reader had sent me a gift of *yopo* seeds, which contain 5-MeO-DMT and other tryptamines and alkaloids. I had done some experimenting with snorting and smoking roasted *yopo* seeds, but the effects were always relatively mild, and not that impressive when compared with salvia. So I had a little bit of experience with 5-

MeO, but it wasn't much, and certainly not the "rocket ship straight into the heart of God" that Hal was talking about here, echoing the sentiments of James Oroc's book, *Tryptamine Palace*. His descriptions certainly had my attention, and I was eager to give this powerful medicine a try for myself and see what might come of it. Hal was in the process of creating a "ritual container" for consuming 5-MeO-DMT that he called the "Temple of Awakening Divinity," or T.O.A.D. 5-MeO-DMT had not yet been scheduled by the federal government as an illegal substance (which became scheduled on January 19th, 2011), and he had hopes of creating a legitimate religious and spiritual "temple" to facilitate initiation into use of 5-MeO-DMT as a sacrament and high-powered catalyst of personal awakening and transformation.

We made arrangements to meet at a local tavern and discuss things further. Hal was clearly an enthusiastic proponent of 5-MeO-DMT, and spoke of it in glowing, radiant praise. I didn't need much convincing, and we made plans for Maya and I to come over and give the medicine a try.

The "Temple" was a room that Hal shared with his wife in their home in Medford. Their own relationship was in the process of dissolving, and Hal's wife had a new lover, but the two were still living together and raising their young son. The temple room was used by Hal for his administrations of T.O.A.D., and his wife used the room for Tantric Dance workshops for her female clientele. It was decorated with all kinds of magical symbols and spiritual iconography, with a mattress off to one side that would serve as the "launch pad" for the 5-MeO experience.

Hal has a strong predilection for ritual and ceremony, and after a lengthy opening of chanting, blessing the four directions, stating intensions, and guided meditation, we were ready. I took my place on the launch pad and was presented with the opportunity to inhale toad venom through a strange contraption that seemed to have too many parts to really be functional. It was a custom-made vaporizer, designed by another 5-MeO aficionado, supposedly providing an ideal delivery method of the potent medicine.

The experience that followed wasn't much. Dreamy, expansive, open, fluid, beautiful even, but it was a comfortable ride. It wasn't the "rocket ship straight into the heart of God" that I was promised. Following Hal's instruction, I took my hit and then lay back on the mattress, folding my arms across my chest. I lay there for about 20-30 minutes, and when it was over, opened my eyes and sat up. Hal quickly asked, "Where did you go?" assuming that I had just gone through a powerful experience. "Nowhere," I answered. "It was nice, but nothing profound." Hal was disappointed, and vowed to have me back over again sometime soon when he had more medicine to share with me.

My next invitation to attend ceremony at the Temple of Awakening Divinity featured a somewhat different Eucharist. This time, rather than being toad venom, it was now pure, crystallized 5-MeO-DMT. The device, or "lamp," as my host preferred to call it, was different this time as well. We were to take the sacrament from a piston-based vaporizer. The chamber was first filled with argon gas, an inert noble gas, so that there would be no oxygen present and therefore nothing to burn. The crystallized 5-MeO-DMT was placed at the bottom of the chamber and then heated from beneath, filling the entire chamber with a white cloud of psychedelic vapor.

Before I took my turn, I stated my intentions and what I hoped to gain from this experience. I said something to the effect that I believed that everything happened for a reason. I found it very meaningful and significant that my host had been inspired to contact me after seeing the God Box/Mystic Toad on my web site. I related how I had received the challenge to "accept my own divinity" through the God Box when a supplicant who had opened the God Box presented me with the opportunity to choose a card as a gift, and the one I had selected had that imperative written on it – something I felt I had never achieved. God was still something foreign to me, as was my own ultimately divine nature as an incarnation of the Absolute. So here I was, willing to try this sacrament once again in the hopes that I might experience my own divinity, whatever that may be, and that I might know and experience something of the divine source of all of existence.

I didn't finish the entire chamber of vaporized 5-MeO-DMT. There was perhaps still a third or fourth of the hit left. I could tell, however, that whatever I had was enough. Whatever was about to unfold was clearly unstoppable. As Hal would put it, I had definitely taken in a full "release" dose.

With the hit still in my lungs, I lay back on the bed inside the consecrated temple of our ceremonial space. Initially upon taking the hit, I had closed my eyes. But as I was falling back, the hit slowly escaping from my lungs with the sweet smell of 5-MeO-DMT filling the room, my eyes popped open, unable to stay closed.

Within the space of a few heartbeats, I had completely expanded into God. Eyes open in absolute awe and wonder, the room dissolved, my ego dissolved, my entire world dissolved. Everything I had ever known or thought or felt dissolved away into absolute pure nothingness. There was nothing to see, nothing to experience, nothing to perceive. Absolutely pure nothingness. And this nothingness was pure consciousness. And it was love. Infinite love and infinite perfection. Everything was in a state of divine perfection. Nothing was out of place. Nothing was either good or bad. Nothing was right or wrong. Everything was simply perfect in this pure consciousness, this pure state of being. And this state was not a thing. It was not an object of perception. It was not a concept. It was not an emotion. It was not anything that I could describe in any way. In fact, when asked later, I vaguely described it as "living starlight," but even that was not accurate, for in truth, it was *nothing.*

But that no-thing was *everything.*

It was God.

And it was my deepest nature.

I was one with God.

Not my ego self. That was pretty thoroughly obliterated through the impossibly fast 5-MeO-DMT expansion. It was not as though I identified my personal sense of self with God. Rather, it was the deepest core of my being, not my ego-identity, that was identical with God. As a finite being in a body with a sense of self and identity, I was an expression of God. At my core, at the very deepest level, my nature as an incarnated being was one with that pure consciousness, that infinite love, that infinite source of creative energy in which all things exist in absolute and unquestionable perfection. In those few heartbeats, this beautiful and sacred medicine had opened me up to the All. I had accepted my own divinity.

"Thank you, God!" I called out as my hands reached up towards that infinite expanse of nothingness, a few moments after the hit of psychedelic medicine flowed out of my lungs. Eyes wide open, gaping in sheer awe at the *mysterium tremendum*, I embraced God, and the embrace was returned.

"Thank you," I said, over and over and over again, lasting the better part of an hour as the medicine expanded me out into the farthest reaches of cosmic consciousness and then gently brought me back to myself. I was so overwhelmed that I began crying and laughing at the same time. It was, beyond any doubt, the most beautiful, profound, and total experience of my life. Nothing in my psychedelic or spiritual history could have prepared me for this divine embrace. It was so total, so complete, so beyond any sense of doubt or wonder or skepticism. It was absolutely undeniable. I could hardly believe that it was true. I could hardly believe that I was saying that word: God.

I was one with God, and God was love, and I knew that I loved God with all my heart, and that I, as a small little insignificant person with my own very small sense of self and being, was embraced by the Love of All, and that all things were in absolute perfection. All that was, was God. God was the only true reality. All else was illusion – the effluence of God's creative power, manifesting in space and time as a physical world with physical beings that felt so alone and cut off. But now I truly understood, for I experienced the truth with every aspect of my being. God was Real. God was Reality. And my nature, as a living being, was One with that Absolute Reality.

Slowly, I came back from that infinite expansion into the nothingness that was everything. Like a spaceship re-entering the atmosphere, I could feel the layers of my individual sense of self begin to reassert themselves. The ego and identity that had been completely obliterated in the instantaneous expansion brought on by the 5-MeO-DMT regained its foothold, and as I fell down out of that exalted state, I knew myself once more. I understood that I was "Martin," this collection of patterns and habits, judgments and beliefs, choices, attitudes, and emotions. It was the "me" I had lived with all my life. But now I knew. Now I knew with all my heart that there truly was something more, and that something was more profound, more complete, and more truly holy and sacred than anything I had ever imagined or anything I had ever conceived. I knew that in the end, we, all of us, everything that we see, hear, taste, feel and experience, is really just the One Being. It is all God. God is the only true reality. And at the same time, God is absolutely nothing. Nothing at all. Nothing to grasp. Nothing to hold on to. Nothing to behold. Nothing to name or force into the box of language and conceptuality. God is simply the "I AM," and there is nothing more that can be said. God is, and that is enough.

Though I didn't understand it at that time, what I now know was that I was in the perfect time of my life to have this experience. It was so overwhelming, so powerful, so profoundly beautiful, that I assumed that this was simply what the medicine did – just immediately open an individual up to the infinite reality of God. However, I now know that this is not true. What the medicine does is provide an opportunity for one's perception and experience of energy and being to expand infinitely, but it is ultimately the choice of the ego to either let go and embrace this process of "dying" into God, or hold on through fear, lack of love, judgment, or anything else that provides the ego a foothold to remain in control of the individual. As it was, I was ready for the experience of complete mystical union, but many people are not. In fact, most people have a deep process of learning to trust and let go that they must first pass through before reaching such a deep level of surrender, and this often involves extremely arduous and challenging rounds of purging and releasing. Yet this was not the case for me as I was, in many respects, ready to die to myself. In leaving Phoebe, my job, my children, and in my quest to discover my joy and self-fulfillment, I was perfectly primed to just let everything go and completely surrender as I had nothing left to lose and no reason to hold myself back. Due to circumstances, I was the perfect candidate for full release and absorption into my full God nature.

In contrast, Maya's turn with the medicine was a prime example of someone holding on and struggling throughout the experience. She spent most of her experience literally gripping her favorite crystals with her hands and made every attempt to control the experience, never actually releasing into the deep states of love and trust that I had just experienced for myself. It was then that I started to understand that it was all due to choice and was not a function of the medicine. It was just a mirror, after all, and one must choose to surrender to the infinite in order to really experience it, and no amount of medicine could make that happen, for it cannot violate one's free will in any way. It provides an opportunity to radically expand energetically, but what one does with that opportunity, and how one chooses to be, ultimately determines what one gets. And it must be a choice at the deepest level of one's being, highlighting the very real distinction between what people *say* they want and what they *actually* choose. It is all a matter of genuine will.

For me, the after-effects of this experience were significant. I found that I started releasing tension that I had held in my back and shoulders for years, and immediately my dreams changed with symbols taking on new meanings, or losing their old power. I had been dreaming of walking through forests that seemed beautiful and inviting, only to find that they were full of menacing bears. As soon as I realized that there were bears present, the dreams turned into desperate attempts to get out of the forest with bears closing in from all directions. That very night, after we returned to our small apartment and went to sleep, I had a dream of walking through a forest filled with bears, and there was no fear or anxiety whatsoever. The bears saw me, but did not threaten me in any way, and I was able to walk through the forest in a relaxed and composed manner. I could tell that I was beginning to shift, but there was still more to do.

Aside from the work that I knew still lay ahead of me in my quest for healing and self-realization, I also knew that this experience with 5-MeO-DMT had been *the experience* I had been searching for my entire life, but had previously remained illusive. There was no doubt in my mind whatsoever that I had actually experienced God directly. The impact of this realization was profound. God was absolutely real, and real in a way that nothing else was, for everything that existed was but an expression of this one, universal, infinite being. For the first time in my life, I found that I was willing to claim that I knew God. I didn't *believe* in God, for there was nothing here for me to believe in, and the term *believe* seemed about as applicable as saying that I *believed* the sky was blue, or that grass was green. There's no need for anyone to believe in reality – you just accept the way things are. People only *believe* in God if they've never experienced God, and have developed a set of beliefs through their culture, their religion, their spiritual practice, or whatever. But this wasn't in any way about belief. It was about reality. And God was certainly real. Behind all appearances was a vast consciousness of infinite love, energy, and being, and it was reality itself. Everything was God. It was simply the way things were.

What I didn't fully understand then, and what took the next year and a quarter or so for me to fully integrate and accept, was what "my" relationship to "God" was, and this first experience really brought into question what the true nature of identity was. The logic seemed clear, though my ego was not really ready to accept it: if God was everything, then that meant that my true identity, not the identity of my falsely constructed ego and sense of individual self, was also God. If God was the I AM that existed in everything, the conclusion was clear: I was God, and this "Martin" character was just an expression and individual embodiment of this one, Universal Being. I had gone looking for myself, and what I found was God staring back at me. If this was correct, it meant that I wasn't at all who or what I had thought I was. The implications were immense, and were more than my ego could yet process at that early stage in the game of self-realization and awareness.

After this first full release with 5-MeO, I found myself needing to confront my mother. As I've written, my mother had an extremely difficult time with her divorce from my father, and the bitterness and anger she felt lingered for many, many years. One of my fears that had held me back from leaving Phoebe was how I thought others would perceive my decision – that it was selfish, that I was abandoning my wife and children, that I was being just like my father, that I had chosen irresponsibly, that I was "bad" and "wrong" – and this was precisely what my mother perceived. I had never shared any of my dissatisfaction with my mother, and thus the divorce came as a complete surprise and shock to her, and all she could see was a repeat of my father leaving her.

I learned through my father that my mother had said to other family members how she "couldn't support" me in any way about the decision to leave Phoebe, and had no compassion for my struggles to find work and remake my life in a fashion that was more true to my heart and my desire to find joy. Though this revelation was not surprising, it was still a blow to hear that my own mother was basically writing me off and turning her back on me at a time that I could really use some support and understanding.

So, in response, I decided to call my mother out in a letter where I detailed to her how she was projecting her own divorce onto mine, and spelled out for her all the ways my situation was unlike hers. I made it clear that if she was going to continue to insist on projecting her own fears, frustrations, and unhealed heart onto me, then I would once again not have anything to do with her – a situation I had felt forced into on two different occasions as a teenager. In the letter, I basically told her that I wouldn't tolerate her projecting her unresolved crap onto me, and challenged her to face the fears and wounds in her own heart. It was strongly worded, and in many respects, I had found the strength and temerity to write it because of my recent experience with 5-MeO. And I was glad that I did it, for after this, my mother and I were able to have more open and realistic communication about why Phoebe and I had gotten divorced, and what I was looking for in trying to create a new life for myself. There were many old wounds here that needed exposing and addressing, and this allowed for that to take place, at least between my mother and myself. Though it took some time, my mother eventually "got it" that my life with Phoebe had been radically unsatisfying, and that there had been a disconnection between us for years, and my mother was finally able to accept that what had transpired between us was nothing like her own relationship with my father. It was a great relief to get through to her, and it proved to be an important milestone in our own relationship, as it allowed for the release of projections that had been in place for many years. It also, in some respects, set the stage for my next encounter with 5-MeO-DMT.

By the time Maya and I were invited back for another visit at the Temple of Awakening Divinity, our relationship was in its last throes. Things had gone pretty much haywire between Maya and myself, yet we still held on to each other out of love. It was an extremely confusing time, and honestly, I had no idea what to do. Maya had decided to enter into what she considered a "Zen" state of not letting herself be affected by my inner struggles. Part of this was to refuse any sexual contact, and she started suggesting that I go find "some other goddesses to make love with." The problem, of course, was that I didn't want anyone else, and I desperately wanted things to work out with Maya. But honestly, my energy was all out of whack. Energetically, I was clinging to Maya, and using her as a lifeline and support. There are few things worse than pathetic, clingy energy, especially from a man towards a woman, and I had it in abundance. I felt completely befuddled and had no idea how to be with Maya, for everything I tried generally got the exact opposite reaction from Maya than what I wanted. The more I tried to pull her close, the more she pushed away. And to top it off, I had no idea how to stand up for myself or assert myself energetically. I was fumbling through a relationship that I had no idea how to be in, and it was taking its toll on Maya. And for her part, Maya was having her own reaction to being in a "committed" relationship, not being so experienced or skilled there herself. So we were both something of a mess. Might as well go and visit with God, I figured. Perhaps that could shed some light on our predicament. So, we returned to T.O.A.D.

It is Hal's standard practice to hold "circles" with 5-MeO-DMT, inviting a group of 5-7 people to come and take individual turns with the medicine with the rest holding space as "witnesses" to the epic event. At this gathering, a woman went before me who had a very active session. She was writhing about on the bed, never sitting or lying still more than a few moments at a time, and was exhibiting an active case of glossolalia, or "speaking in tongues." Much to my surprise, at one point she sat up and came directly to me, breaking her glossolalia long enough to look me in the eye and say, "Your journey is honored." Personally, we didn't know each other, and she didn't know anything about myself, my struggles, or my quest to experience my authentic self and live that in the world. Needless to say, her statement had quite the impact on me.

When she was finished, it was then my turn. I took my place on the mattress and prepared to receive the sacrament. I could tell immediately upon taking the hit of 5-MeO-DMT that I was resisting. I was holding onto something and preventing myself from falling fully into God. I knew I wasn't surrendering, but I didn't know why. "You can do it," the witnesses in the room said, "You can let go," and I believed them. I was holding myself tightly as I lay on the bed and I needed to relax. Following Hal's instructions, I had my arms crossed over my chest – for some reason, he had decided that this was the ideal "launch" position – something that I have learned through my experience is actually incorrect in a rather profound way. An individual's inner energetic state is always reflected in body posture and movement, and crossed limbs of any kind, either arms or legs, communicates the energetic stance of bracing, holding on, and failing to open completely. When individuals actually open up all the way and let their energy expand infinitely, people always open their arms and legs and they then move in synchronized symmetrical movements where limbs never cross the centerline of the body. Attempting to open up fully and release with either crossed arms or legs is a guaranteed way of *not* opening and releasing.

Furthermore, anyone who claims to have "gone all the way," yet still keeps either arms or legs crossed, or who exhibits any asymmetry in the body, is fooling themselves about their ability to open up and let go all the way into the infinite state of being. This fact has some fairly radical implications, for consider all the images of yogis, Buddhas, and other so-called "enlightened" beings sitting in lotus postures with their legs crossed and other indications of asymmetries in their bodies with their mudras, postures, and tilted heads. Based on my understanding, none of these images represent an "enlightenment" experience, for the individuals depicted are clearly holding on with their energy, as reflected in their body postures. Asymmetrical bodies and crossed limbs are incompatible with full expansion experiences, and are therefore a lesser-order experience, even if they are profound and experienced as deeply meaningful.

Feeling into the reality that I was still holding on energetically, I let my arms fall to my sides with my palms up and receptive, and as soon as I did so, I fell all the way into God. I have since come to call this body posture the "neutral position," and it is vital that anyone wanting to work with medicines and open up to their full energetic potential use this open, symmetrical posture as a starting point. As a body posture, it energetically communicates that, "I am open, relaxed, and ready to receive," and this is precisely what is required to go all the way into the experience.

Thus once again I could feel my ego start to dissolve, along with the tension I had been holding in my body and posture, and felt myself passing into the infinite embrace of an all-loving God. So why did I hurt so much? "I love you," I called out to God, "but I don't want to live with this pain anymore!" This honest and sincere vocalization proved to be precisely the acknowledgement I needed to make, for all of a sudden, all of the pain and frustration and denial that I had shoved deep down into the core of my being over many years of my inauthenticity started pouring out of me in an uncontrollable flood. I screamed and thrashed about on the bed, letting the wail fly out of me, purging all the pain I held so deep inside my heart. I cried and cried until there was no more crying left to do, and curled up in a fetal position on the bed, though I was still on my back, rather than on my side, as is more common for the fetal position.

As soon as the crying stopped, something very curious happened. I felt like a baby and I was being tickled all over my body. The most delicious tickles ran all over me, even moving through me, feeling like a high frequency vibration that just felt so good. The vibration eventually settled on my upper lip, and I found myself sucking at my lip with my tongue. This confused me for some time until it finally occurred to me that I was, energetically speaking, "suckling" at the breast of the Great Cosmic Mother. At that realization, I felt a profound joy and release sweep over me. I didn't need Maya, my mother, or anyone else for love and support, for all the love and sustenance I could ever need was right there, provided by the divine, and all I needed to do was drink from this fathomless well of love. The next day I wrote the following piece about my experience.

The Great Mother

Suckle from the breast of the Great Mother
Tingling with sweet lips
Honey tongue
Tickled toes
A babe in the embrace of All

Drink!
Drink!
Drink!

Drink from the Mother
Feel her love
Feel her forgiveness
Her acceptance
Her warmth
And know that it is You
It is I!

Surrender to all pain
Surrender to all fear
Surrender to Love

Love
Love

Give everything to Love

Death is but a passage
A transition
A veil lifted
And the world stands as it is
Naked and alive
Breathing, breathing
Ever becoming

Now!

The Moment is Now!

Wings unfurl and life takes flight
Rushing to the ever-present Now
The choice of self
The gift of life
The blessing of being

To experience
To know
To live
To love
To play
To simply be

And let go . . .

The pain is released!
The fear is faced!

Don't let it linger

Just let go

Just let go

Open to the True Self
The nature of All that Is
No past
No future
No self
No there
No no
No yes

Nothing
And everything

Just let go

And breathe . . .

Despite the mystical revelation, profound release, and sense of universal love and support, it didn't stop my relationship with Maya from disintegrating, and painfully at that. The following night, Maya came home late in the evening. I wasn't quite ready to interact with her yet, so I told her that I was going to say a few OM's and meditate for a few minutes. As I sat on my *zafu*, my meditation cushion, I let long and lingering OM's slip from my mouth. My breath became long and deep as my mind followed the vibrations. "I should just follow my breath and see where it goes," I thought to myself as I felt myself slipping deeper into my meditation.

What followed was entirely unexpected and completely unlike any meditation experience I had ever had. I started to feel a warm rush that immediately reminded me of my 5-MeO-DMT experience the night before. I let the feeling well up within me and then it just exploded. My eyes rolled back into my head and I nearly fell off my *zafu* as I felt my energy expanding into the infinite. In just a few breaths, I had merged with the cosmos and had completely "left" my body. At the time, my ego was still partially intact (keep in mind that I was still sitting in lotus posture), so I was sitting there, contemplating the experience and thinking that I was having some kind of "out of body" experience. I've since refined the language that I use to describe such states as a "beyond the body" experience, for in truth, no one ever "leaves" their body, but they can experience themselves as expanding and passing "beyond" the body. This is an important distinction, for as I've come to understand it, it is bodies that make individual perspective possible, and without a body, there is no individual perspective. Since God is everything and everyone, I've learned that ideas of souls and spirits and disembodied consciousness are just projections and attachments of the ego and are, as such, fundamentally unreal. God is all there is, with no remainder. Individuals do not have souls or spirits that "inhabit" their bodies, for they are all, in truth, God incarnate. No souls are required for this nondual trick of apparent diversity.

I stayed in that state for some time until it finally occurred to me that I didn't have the faintest idea of how to get "back" into my body and find my way back "home." This caused my heart rate to jump, reminding me that I actually was still in my body, and all I needed to do was bring my energy back in. Easier said than done, however, and getting fully back to "normal" took around twenty to thirty minutes.

I was ecstatic upon my reintegration. I couldn't believe what had just happened. I had just experienced a full 5-MeO-DMT release without ingesting anything! Amazing! How did I do it? In my joy, I started rolling around the room with my legs flying up into the air, and though I didn't know it then, this was the beginning of my experience with fluid, spontaneous, symmetrical movements that were to become integral to my ongoing experience of opening to my true nature and true identity. At the time, I just felt like some dynamic roly-poly and marveled at how balanced and energetically fluid I felt.

The next day I excitedly wrote to Dr. Rick Strassman, with whom I had a casual email correspondence, telling him about my experience. His response was to wonder if I would be able to repeat it. Curious myself, I decided to give it another try.

Sure enough, there I went. Right back into infinite expansion. Wow. I couldn't believe it. And then I did it again. In fact, I did it almost every day for about a week and a half.

What I found was that, like a genuine 5-MeO-DMT experience, my spontaneous experiences provided me with opportunities to "exit" myself and then return to myself in the sense that I could disengage myself from my normal sense of self and being as structured by the limited confines of my ego. Though this had been true for my meditation experiences in general over the years, this was leaps and bounds beyond anything I'd experienced in my many years of Zen meditation. In the process, I could really face all of my fears and pains over our dissolving relationship, and I was using it as something of a therapeutic tool. However, in the end, it became the straw that broke the camel's back.

Everything came crashing down on a Monday. Ever since I had left southern California I had been struggling financially. I moved to Oregon for love, not money, and the reality of this decision was beginning to show. On that particular Monday I was down to my last $100, and I received several calls that day letting me know that various projects I had been working on and classes I had been teaching were no longer available, and therefore, at that moment, I had no foreseeable income coming my way, and I had to make a child support payment as soon as possible that was ten times the amount of money I currently had at my disposal. On top of that, things had become increasingly painful and difficult with Maya, and it seemed as though there was no hope for us. I felt like I had nothing to stand on and was free falling into the abyss of total despair. It was the "dark night of my soul" (metaphorically speaking, of course) and I didn't know what to do, as I was quickly approaching rock bottom with no clue of how to claw my way back up to any sense of security and stability.

I walked up to a nearby cemetery that was just up the hill from our small apartment, figuring that no one would pay any attention to someone crying in a graveyard. I found myself standing, looking out to the mountains and at the sky, praying to God for help. I didn't know what else to do. I felt completely helpless, and I had nowhere to turn and nothing to hold on to. I was just falling. I tried to hold it together and stand on my own two feet, but I couldn't even do that. I crumpled to the grassy ground and cried harder than I had ever cried before with my face mashed into the grass mixed with the effluence of my nose and eyes.

Two young girls came to the graveyard to play. Upon finding me bawling in the graveyard, curled up into a little ball, they ran home and quickly returned with a camera. Fortunately, I managed to pull it together enough to no longer make an interesting picture for them when they returned. Disappointed, they went back to playing and I walked back down to my apartment.

Not knowing what else to do, I sat down to meditate and quickly found that I was back in an expanded energetic state. I stayed in this peaceful state for some time until Maya came home, at which point I began to attempt to pull myself out and return to my body so that we could interact.

I was having difficulty, however. I lay back on the floor with an amethyst crystal in one hand and a feather in the other, letting my legs uncross. Maya went into the other room of our small apartment and turned on the radio and started laughing and talking loudly on the phone, asserting her independence from me, my pain, and my process.

Pulling back into my body, my jaw began to quiver and my breathing became very strange. I found that I was writhing around on the ground, making strange and disturbing noises, with my back arching and waves of energy moving up and down my spine. Experientially, I found myself entering a vast energetic web of rainbow light. It was beautiful and captivating, and the more I breathed, the further I went into it. Finally I released, with energy buzzing all through my body and especially my hands.

Maya was even louder in the other room now and I felt some irritation toward her because of it. I could still feel the energy pulsing through me and decided that I would go back into it. My breathing became even stranger, and behind closed eyes, a dull grey light filled my vision, and a column of energy seemed to be coursing through me. It felt like death to me, but by this point I had completely lost any fear of death, and I decided that I would see how far I could push it, how far I could go into this energy.

The further I went, the louder Maya became, still laughing. Quite improperly, I thought to myself, "Well, if that's the way you're going to be, then I'm going to fill this whole apartment with this light and this energy." As I writhed on the floor, it felt like an ice dragon were moving through me, coursing through the strange energy. I pumped it through my being and let it flood out of me in every direction.

Shortly thereafter Maya came into the room, just when I released myself from the grip of the experience, saying, "You're doing great work. Obviously you need your space, and I need mine." And with that, she left.

When she reappeared two days later, she wasn't as generous.

"What in the fuck did you do to me?!" she said coldly. "You psychically attacked me the other night. I felt like I was dying. I could feel the life draining out of me. I tried shutting the door, but your breath blew it open and there was nothing I could do to protect myself but leave. What in the fuck were you doing?!"

And that was pretty much it for us, though we still tried to live together as roommates for a few more weeks until my heart completely broke, but I'm getting ahead of myself.

At this point, it finally dawned on me that despite the fact that I had no idea *what* I was doing, or even *how* I was doing it, I was moving a great deal of energy, and it felt somewhat dangerous and uncontrollable. I needed to do something. I wrote to Rick Strassman again, and his response was that it sounded like I could use a session with ayahuasca to help cleanse out my energy, and he helped to put me in touch with a local Santo Daime group.

Santo Daime is a relatively new religion that originates from Brazil, and is something of a combination of indigenous ayahuasca shamanism and South American Catholicism. In religious studies, it is what is called a "syncretic" tradition, though in reality, all religions really fall into this category, as all religions combine and alter pre-existing elements, rituals, symbols, and traditions, and merely refashion them into a new religious context. That's just the way that cultures and religions work: they are contextual constructs, and despite claims of divine revelations, are always responses to what came before. Judaism responded to and altered Mesopotamian paganism. Christianity altered Judaism and Roman/Hellenic paganism. Islam altered Christianity and Judaism. Buddhism altered Hinduism and Jainism. In this sense, all religions and traditions are syncretic, and none of them appeared from out of nowhere with no connection to or influence from what came before.

Ceremonies in Santo Daime are called "Works," and center around the ceremonial drinking of *Daime*, which, in translation, means "Give me," and is expressive of the ideas of "Give me health, happiness, and light." This is their term for ayahuasca. In most respects, Daime is identical to ayahuasca in that it is made from two plants, one of which contains dimethyltryptamine, and the other a monoamine-oxidase inhibitor, which allows the DMT to be absorbed through the gut, rather than being automatically broken down by digestive enzymes. Daimistas insist that Daime is *not* ayahuasca, due to the fact that they pray over it in ways that are distinct from ayahuasca shamanism, and they therefore understand it to contain a specific "entity" called *Juramidam* that is particular to their religion. Pharmacologically and biologically speaking, the drink is identical to ayahuasca. From my later experiences with ayahuasca proper, I'd also say that they are experientially identical as well, with the major difference being the ritual structures and practices of Daime versus shamanic ceremony.

Ayahuasca shamanism tends to take place in small group gatherings where a shaman and his/her assistants administer the drink to participants, and then sing a series of songs called *icaros* throughout the ayahuasca session. While there is candlelight at the beginning of the ceremony, once things get going, the candle is extinguished and the remainder of the ceremony mostly takes place in the dark. The shaman sits at the front of the group and participants sit or lie down. Mostly, the shaman leading the ceremony sits in his chair at the front, but he (or she) can also move about the participants and offer individual healings, guidance, and blessings. While it is a group experience, it is also a very private affair, and there is very little group interaction or participation, and each person is left to him or herself to undergo an individual experience of the medicine and the revelations and healings it brings.

In contrast, Santo Daime is a much more formal religious setting. Works take place in a *salao,* a large round room, and ceremonies tend to feature many more participants. In the center of the room is a ceremonial table, upon which sits the Santo Daime Christian cross, along with pictures of saints and other symbols of the religion. Around the center table the ritual leaders position themselves, along with a cadre of musicians. Further out, men and women are segregated to opposite sides of the room and positioned in rows. Everyone is given a seat or place to stand in the respective rows based on height and level of experience, with the overall goal of making the energy of the room as balanced as possible. Around the outer edge of the room stand guardians with buckets and towels for receiving people who need to purge. Separated from the main *salao* is a healing space for people to go and lie down, if necessary, also segregated into men's and women's sides. Outside there is a Santo Daime cross where people may go to exorcise entities or negative energies.

For most Works, with the exception of more meditative sessions that are called "concentrations," the main room is well-lit and the majority of the Work is filled with group prayers and hymn singing, done either seated or standing in place while doing one of several different simple dance steps. Along with the core of centrally placed musicians, many Daimistas also have their own personal rattles/maracas that are used to keep time with the many hymns that are sung. Works open up with prayer ("Our Father who art in heaven . . .") and then drinking of Daime, which is dolled out by servers at one side of the room, with men and women lining up separately to receive the communion. Rounds of hymns are then sung by the collective, with repeated administrations of Daime over the course of the Work where 3-5 rounds of Daime are common, and ceremonies lasting 10 hours or more.

Though originating in Brazil, Santo Daime has quietly spread around the world, right along side the increasing interest in ayahuasca. There are several "Points," as they are called, in Oregon, and the local "Point" in Ashland was just gearing up for a landmark court case when Rick Strassman introduced me to them. The leader of the Church of the Holy Light of the Queen, Jonathan Goldman, and his compatriots, were preparing a court case where they were suing the federal government for protection of their religious right to consume Daime, which contains the illegal substance DMT. Their aim was to have their rights secured based on the Religious Freedom Restoration Act. The court case proceeded forward, and CHLQ eventually had the courts decide in their favor, though the ruling was only extended to Santo Daime churches in Oregon, and nowhere else in the United States, despite the fact that there are Points of Santo Daime churches across the U.S. Currently, the federal government is seeking to retry the case, despite the fact that the judge who originally oversaw the case resoundingly declared that the government had only supplied "speculation" and "no evidence" for their claims of why Daime should be illegal.

After a phone call with Jonathan Goldman, and an interview with a Daime gatekeeper who assessed my intentions in wanting to attend a Daime Work, I was invited to come up to Jonathan's place and experience my first rounds of Daime. So then there I was, up in the mountains drinking ayahuasca, or Daime, for the first time. I was immediately drawn to the medicine. The experience was like mushrooms, but the level of sophistication was leaps and bounds beyond any mushroom experience I had ever had, and I knew right away that this was medicine that I wanted to work with more. In that first Work with the Santo Daime, I had one small purge, very gentle and easy, and despite having drunk Daime many times since then, I only experienced a purge one other time.

The highlight of that first Work with the Santo Daime for me was the movement of energy. I found myself outside for a good portion of the night, jumping about and shaking my hands and arms and just letting energy fly out of my body. It felt like I had been plugged into some massive universal circuit, and the amount of energy pumping through me was just astounding – much stronger than anything I had experienced on mushrooms. It was like every cell of my body was vibrating at an extremely fast rate, and it was all I could do to manage the massive onslaught. It wasn't unpleasant or difficult in any way, and in fact, felt great. I felt like an energetic dynamo, and I found the experience fascinating. I also didn't mind that the vibrating mostly kept me out of the *salao* and the collective enterprise of the Work taking place within. I had my own energy to work with, and that was more than enough. Afterwards, the regular members of the Santo Daime church all asked me how many times I had drunk Daime before, as apparently they were impressed by my experience. "Really great work," they all said. They were quite surprised to hear that this was my first time. In all, it was an extremely gratifying experience, and exactly what I needed.

When I returned to my apartment that night, I found that Maya was sleeping in our small living room, just inside the front door, having left the bed for me. We were officially "broken up" at that point, though still living together. I let her be, and slipped into the bedroom and had a restful night of sleep. The next morning, after waking up, she came into the bedroom and said, "You need to clean up your stuff out here." She walked me outside to show me what she meant. The front of our apartment had a wood porch that stretched across our living room and bedroom, and then crossed two other apartments. Only outside the room that I had slept in was a strange, sticky goo all over the wood, moving away from where I had slept. No other part of the porch or wood was affected. "Energy is real," Maya said. "Clean your goo up. I don't want to touch it." Perplexed and puzzled by this bizarre phenomenon, I did as I was asked. We also talked a little about my experience the night before, and Maya disclosed that she had gone through a bout of vibrating around the same time that I was out vibrating away with the Daimistas.

Despite everything, we still held onto each other. I desperately clung to my love for her, foolishly hoping that we could still make things work. Giving her as much freedom as possible, I let her come to me or back away as needed. And she did, but like metal that gets bent too many times, quite to my surprise, my heart suddenly broke open and a floodgate of pain was unleashed. All I could do for days was cry, and when I could see through my teary eyes, write a little poetry.

Today was the day my heart broke

A gaping wound
A terrible gash
Blood came out like a river
Blood dripping from my hands
All over my clothes
Blood on every surface of the room
From floor to ceiling
Still it flows
On and on

How much blood
Can one heart hold?

I suppose I'll find out
For now I know
What it means
To live with a broken heart

My heart had never been broken before. While my relationship with Phoebe had not been a good one, it did not involve a broken heart. You have to have a connection for your heart to break, and that was something that my ex-wife and I didn't have. This was an entirely different matter. This hurt. I mean really, really hurt. It hurt so bad, I could hardly function.

Maya left town for a week, so I had plenty of time to stew in my pain. The night she left, I was planning on attending a drum circle with some friends we had made together that was to take place up in the mountains. Not wanting to go alone, I invited Hal to come with me. I cried in the car most of the way up as Hal did his best to buck me up and tell me that everything would work out for the best. In addition to losing Maya, I felt overwhelmed by fear that I had no idea how to be in a relationship, and even worse, had no idea how to go about finding a new partner. I didn't want to be alone, even though I knew that this might be precisely what I needed. But as a man, I felt like an idiot and thoroughly incompetent. At that moment, it seemed like I might be alone forever, and I felt hopeless and lost.

It was at that drum circle that I first encountered Jessalynn. I was in a state of self-focused misery, so I wasn't going to the drum circle to connect with anyone – just pound out my emotions on some skins, dance, and just feel myself. However, I did notice some inquisitive energy coming from this woman whom I hadn't seen at drum circles before. We probably didn't say more than a few words to each other, but Hal did end up talking to her, inviting her to come to T.O.A.D. After this drum circle, we started running into each other, first at SOU, where Jessalynn was an art student, and then at subsequent drum circles and dances. I'll have more to say about Jessalynn later – indeed, we are currently married and have a tem-month-old son together – but at this point, I simply want to situate and contextualize our first encounter in the overall narrative.

I was too busy being miserable to even think about a new woman in my life, as I was still agonizing over my situation with Maya. She was gone for the week, however, so at least it wasn't an ongoing confrontation. Also, fortunately for me, several months prior to all this, a man in Canada had contacted me about hiring me to do some shamanic work for him. He bought a plane ticket and was coming that weekend for healing. Thankfully, it gave me something to put all my energy and focus into rather than my own personal problems.

The shamanic session went extremely well, and towards the end, the man said that he needed to be by water. Still feeling the effects of the medicine that we had consumed together, I walked him through town to a nearby creek. My new friend was concerned that people would try and talk to us or interact with us – something he didn't want, as we were still really feeling the medicine. "Don't worry," I said. "The only people who will have anything to do with us will be people who can handle my energy, and those will be people we'll want to talk to." Personally, I felt in my element, and the most confident and empowered that I'd felt since everything started to unravel with Maya. I was charged up and overflowing with positive and focused energy. True to my prediction, everyone gave us a wide berth.

On the way back, as I was bouncing down the street, filled with divine energy, we came across a man who immediately began speaking to us. He told us how he and his partner performed "soul readings" where they could get in touch with a person's higher self and answer all kinds of questions for them. At the time, I didn't think much of what they were offering – I had never been interested in receiving a "reading," and was fairly skeptical about such psychic claims, but I mention it now as it plays a part in my story a bit further down the road.

Despite having this distraction, Maya was returning, and I was not yet ready to face her, as the pain was just too great. That night I packed up my things and was out of the apartment the next morning, having accepted an offer to stay at a friend's house for a few days while I secured a new room for myself. With the focus of shamanic work now absent, I found myself in as much heartache and suffering as ever. My heart was still very much broken and I could see no end in sight to the pain.

Eager to help, the friend who took me in was adamant that I take ecstasy with her. "It will really help to heal your heart," she explained.

I was wary. Synthetics had never been an interest of mine, and MDMA, as a "party" drug, wasn't really on my radar of medicines that I wanted to work with. Also, like many "spiritual" people, I'd developed an irrational and unsupportable bias against things that supposedly weren't "natural" – an artificial divide created solely by the human mind, ignoring the fact that everything that exists is, by definition, natural, and that nothing unnatural exists within reality. However, as the universe seemed to have brought me to my friend's door, and she just so happened to have this medicine, I figured I would give it a try. I certainly wanted to heal, and since she was offering this, I would accept.

What I got was not what I was expecting. If my first experience at the Temple of Awakening Divinity was a turning point in my spiritual life, this was certainly the next big step, and one that stretched the boundaries of what I considered sane. I had merged with God twice now at T.O.A.D., had spontaneously merged with the universe on several occasions, excreted ectoplasm – or whatever in the world that strange goo was - moved profound amounts of energy, and, at least according to Maya, psychically attacked a woman I loved passionately. None of that had adequately prepared me for what happened when I consumed MDMA for the first time.

About thirty minutes after taking the ecstasy, I started to feel warm and fuzzy. My host had suggested that I get on her heated bio-mat with brain wave synchronizing headphones to help gently launch me on my journey. Once I could feel something happening, I climbed up on the bio-mat, got my headphones on, and prepared for whatever was to come.

Almost immediately I felt a rush of expansion in my heart. The sensation was very similar to the onset of 5-MeO-DMT, and my first thought was "here I go again." However, something different happened. As my heart expanded, a voice started to speak out of my mouth. It was quiet at first, but it slowly grew in volume and intensity, repeating over and over again, "Love all equally without any exception." The more my heart expanded, the stronger the voice became, until I could feel it pouring out of me. My host could feel it too. She was now kneeling alongside the bio-mat, almost in prayer as the words flowed from my mouth in a voice that was decidedly not my own – whoever was speaking, it most definitely was not "Martin." It didn't sound like "Martin," for one, and furthermore, as I lay there, I could clearly ponder the phenomenon, asking myself who was using my body to speak these words. It was vaguely reminiscent of vocalizing inspired words and advice when I was on mushrooms, or speaking out loud after smoking salvia, but it was also different and unlike those other events, for it was so insistent and seemingly so "other." When I spoke on mushrooms, it was still "Martin" speaking, just giving voice to the internal inspiration provided by the mushrooms and it always sounded like "me." This was different, for "Martin" was not speaking, just observing this powerful energetic force taking over and speaking through my body as the command to "Love all equally without any exception" eventually grew into a thundering bellow.

It all became a bit too much for my host and friend, and in a frenzy, she ripped off my headphones and climbed on top of me as I lay on the heated bio-mat. I embraced her warmly and told her that I loved her. "I need space, though," I said to her. "There's more coming, and I don't know what it is." Strangely, it was "Martin" speaking now and I could easily recognize my voice, my intentions, and my own will. Somehow, I was able to put this overwhelming force on hold for a few minutes to communicate personally with my friend, and this was achieved without any difficulty. "Martin" was clearly still in there, somewhere, and could easily resurface, despite the overwhelming urge to just submit and give myself over completely to this power and energy.

Respectfully, my friend climbed back down, and I was once more on my own on the bio-mat.

As soon as she was off, my hands spontaneously shot up toward the ceiling and started vibrating wildly as I once more submitted to the energy. I could feel countless numbers of energetic threads passing through my hands, and it felt as though I could feel the entire universe in them. Somehow, it was as though I had passed into the very center of existence and the energetic waves of manifestation were passing through me and my hands in the form of high frequency vibrations. That, however, was not the truly astounding part. What was astounding was the voice that came with the vibrations, and what the voice had to say. The following is a condensed version of what was said, which lasted for at least three hours, perhaps more (I wasn't keeping track of time in any meaningful sense). Many phrases were repeated over and over, which I have largely not shown in writing this up. Words in all capitals were booming and thunderous in sound, accompanied by massive pulses of energy emanating from my hands.

And the voice said:

"Love all equally without any exception. Love all equally without any exception. LOVE ALL EQUALLY WITHOUT ANY EXCEPTION, FOR I AM LOVE!

I am the light and I am the dark. And I am THE SPACE BETWEEN THEM! I AM NOTHING! I am the white and the black and the line that runs between them. I am the space between notes. I am all things, and I AM NOTHING! I AM LOVE!

My son, I have chosen you. You will do my work, if you choose. My gift to you, to all of you, is your free choice. You must always choose. That is my gift. It is always your choice.

But I have chosen you my son. I love you, Martin, and I have chosen you to do my work. Through you, the WORLD WILL KNOW OF MY LOVE! But only if you choose it.

I broke your heart. That was my gift to you. I have opened your heart. Your pain has served you. Your struggle has served you. You have learned much. BUT DO NOT INDULGE! SET YOUR PAIN ASIDE AND DO NOT INDULGE! SET YOURSELF ASIDE! SET YOURSELF ASIDE AND DO MY WORK!

The pain no longer serves you. I have taught you how to love, now you must SET YOURSELF ASIDE and GIVE MY LOVE TO THE WORLD. Love everyone, without exception. Love everyone, without exception. Give yourself to them. Give until there is nothing left for you to give. GIVE THEM MY LOVE!

But you must SET YOURSELF ASIDE! DO NOT ATTACH YOUR EGO TO MY WORK! If you attach your ego, then you will suffer, you will struggle. If you let go of yourself and give everything, then I will always be with you.

You will want to know what you need to do, but there is nothing you need to know. Just give them love, and I will be with you. You will be an open conduit to MY LOVE, but NOT if you put yourself in the way. SET YOURSELF ASIDE! IF YOU ATTACH YOUR EGO TO MY WORK THEN YOU WILL ALWAYS STRUGGLE! You will have neither what you need, nor what you want.

It will be hard. There will be many challenges ahead. They will come to you, and you will show them my love. You will be my conduit. I will work through you. But you MUST SET YOURSELF ASIDE! Judge no one and love all equally, without exception. Give and give and give until there is nothing left for you to give. And trust. Always trust. As long as you do my work, I will be with you. There is nothing you need to know for you are my instrument. I will move through you, and that is enough. You do not need to know.

Do not be afraid. Trust. Give until there is nothing left to give. Just give. Show the world my love and SET YOURSELF ASIDE! DO MY WORK!"

The voice had more to say. It spoke to my host, and not gently. It had her writhing about on the floor in existential tumult. It also wanted to make a couple phone calls to speak with some key people in my life and even wanted to do a podcast, which did not find any neutral ears, and the reactions of listeners were either highly positive and sympathetic, or deeply offended and outraged. No middle ground there, by any means. I received many emails telling me I was crazy, that I needed mental help, that I was possessed by a demon, that I was the anti-Christ, that I was giving psychedelics a bad name, and on and on. Others were writing to tell me that they were losing sleep, that they were scared, and even some proclaiming that this was what we have all been waiting for – like I said, many reactions, none of them neutral. "Martin" did as the voice commanded and simply stepped aside, letting the voice say whatever it wanted to whomever it wanted, consequences be damned. From a personal perspective, this wasn't always the most comfortable choice, but it felt right at the deepest levels, so I chose to trust and simply follow my energy.

Needless to say, this was the craziest fucking thing that had ever happened to me. It seemed absolutely impossible. The source of the voice didn't leave much room for ambiguity: this was God talking. It was one thing for me to accept that I, "Martin," had merged with God in states of mystical union – that seemed reasonable enough, for the history of religions is filled with people having such experiences, though still relatively rare and more often sought than found. I could accept that I was one of the few people in the history of humanity to have a full mystical experience, as unlikely as that might be. But this was just beyond the realm of the reasonable or rational. This had crossed the line into the mythical fantasyland of crazy-ass shit that couldn't possibly be true. And worse, if it was true and real, then WHAT THE FUCK!? To say that this put my ego into a tailspin is to radically understate the case. This was insane. I could be locked up at the funny farm for this kind of thing. This was much worse than someone saying that they had heard the voice of God speaking to them or giving them instructions, because here God was using my body to speak to me directly, clearly, and articulately in no uncertain terms in a voice that would accept nothing less than full compliance. This was totally fucking insane.

However, as crazy as it was, I felt absolutely fantastic. My broken heart had radically been transformed into a fully broken-open heart, which was nothing at all like a painful broken heart. My heart felt wide open, ready to embrace everyone and everything, even my absolutely crazy relationship with God, and I was ready to love infinitely and without exception or condition. I found myself firmly planted in the center of absolute universal love and I felt profoundly wonderful, even if it were totally impossible for me to wrap my mind around what had just transpired or how any of it was even possible.

That night as I lay in bed drifting off to sleep, long after the effects of the MDMA had worn off, something very peculiar happened. Behind my closed eyes, I started to see perfectly clear images with startling clarity and precision, and it was unlike anything I had ever seen before. The first image was of light reflecting off of water. The sun was low in the sky behind old trees, and golden light danced over gently rippling water. A perfectly normal scene in perfect detail. Then it suddenly changed to another image of water. This time I could see green trees, blue sky, and puffy white clouds reflected in the water. That lasted only a few instants, and then suddenly I found myself walking through someone's house. I could see the art on the walls and their houseplants. Then it changed again. I could see people playing softball or baseball in a park. A red van drove by in the distance. Next I saw an old couple walking along a creek. The old man reached over and gently pushed his partner so that she stepped in the water. Another change of scene and I saw a busy street with heat waves rippling and distorting the image, as if in a desert country, and cars bustling along the road. Then it changed again and a woman, all green, covered in leafy vines, emerged up out of the water in a forest or jungle and she looked directly at me. It changed once more, and I was looking at water again reflecting a grey and cloudy sky. Suddenly I saw the image of a large grey dragon in the reflection as it swooped overhead, wings outstretched. Then I was back to the original scene of light on water and then it stopped. No more images.

What a strange day that was. My host for this event of the voice was so profoundly impacted by the experience that she requested I perform a shamanic healing for her. The healing went well, and at some point, after several hours, the medicine told me that I was done, but she could take as much time as she wanted with the rest of her process. Thinking that the medicine had run its course, I sat down. Almost immediately I started vibrating and my hands started moving, and bits and pieces of information started coming in as words that I was speaking (but not in "the voice" – just my own voice) that I've summed up in the poem below.

The Taoist Master

Embody the dichotomy
Heaven and Earth
In the palms of my hands

The Middle Way
The Third Way

Spirit
To be In-Spired
The bridge between Heaven and Earth
Is Love

Love is in the breath
Spirit is in the breath
Between the animal breath
And the conscious breath
Is the surrendered breath
This is the Breath of Spirit
It is the Third Way
The Middle Way
It bridges Heaven and Earth

The dichotomies are embodied in me
Left and Right
Male and Female
Order and Chaos
Head and Heart
Infinite and Finite
Universal and Personal
Egoless and Ego
All bound in Love

Love is the Energy
That flows from Spirit
From the Middle Path
The Third Way
Everything is Bound in Love

The Open Heart
Embraces All
In the embrace of the Divine
All is Perfect
All is Love

Give every breath to Spirit
Bridge Heaven and Earth with your breath
Breathe God into the world
Breathe Love into the world
Embody the dichotomy

The Taoist Master
Stands
In the center
Of the Circle

At this point I really started to question just what in the world it was that I was going through. Admittedly, I felt a bit crazy. However, I began to notice that people were beginning to thank me merely for being around them. People began to tell me how much they appreciated my energy, and many people would come up for long and heartfelt hugs. Despite the fact that I felt a bit off my rocker, people wanted me around them.

When the opportunity came for me to return to the Temple of Awakening Divinity, I jumped at the chance. I was terribly curious about what would happen and wanted to see just what would come out of the experience.

I could feel my resistance at the onset of the journey, a result of the fallout from the voice and my feelings of uncertainty and questioning. I went into the experience hoping for some clarity, and it came. Though not a voice *per se*, the communication that was occurring in my mind was crystal clear. The communication, in the form of inner knowing, was as follows:

"Get over it, Martin. It is not about you, so stop trying to wrap your ego around it or struggle with it. It does not matter what other people say or think. They will say and think all kinds of things. But I have chosen you to do my work. It is nothing that you can or should even try to create. There is nothing you need to know. Just do the work. Give everyone my love."

"Thank you for the clarity," I responded out loud in my voice as "Martin" as I vibrated my way through the remainder of the experience, with my hands shivering in cosmic energy threads while I stared into the vast emptiness of God that lay beyond the impossibly intricate mandala of light that was before my eyes and to which I hardly paid any attention.

The vibrations were stronger than ever. I could feel everything in my hands. The divine energy of God radiated from the very center and core of my being, flooding out into the manifest world of space and time. God's love permeated me and I was that love, vibrating through the universe, giving life to every heart. Everything was exactly as it should be.

"You're asking a lot of me," I said quietly to God so that the others in the room couldn't hear. "But I'll do it, whatever it is . . . Thank you for the clarity."

The next weekend I went for another round of Daime. The vibrations started early, and continued through the night. As I sat in my chair with Portuguese hymns being sung all around me, the Daime told me very clearly, as it showed me archetypal patterns of energy in rainbows of infinite complexity, "You are remembering who you are . . ." It felt like the stars were reaching down and gently caressing my face, giving me love and support along my path.

Somewhere in that experience the vibrations got to be too much – perhaps around the third or fourth drinking of Daime. I eventually had to leave the main ceremonial room and go into the healing yurt where participants went for healing, or to pass through their struggles with the Daime. I got to a bed just in time to lie down and really let my hands go as the energy pumped through me and the vibrations took over my being. Someone later described me as being like two race cars revving up their engines, ready to let loose and tear down the street.

At the end, many of the regular Daimistas thanked me for coming, and expressed hope that I would come back again soon.

By this time Jessalynn and I had started our relationship together. After running into her several times around town, I decided to invite her on a hike on some trails that were not too far from where I was renting a room. Like Maya, Jessalynn was a bit younger than myself – in her late 20's, with me in my mid-30's. She had lived in Ashland off and on over the years, with her mother moving her family out this way from Florida after her own divorce, and following a dream that she was living in some place called Midland. She had found a Midland, Oregon on a map, and figured that it would be better than Midland, Texas, and thus moved out west, eventually coming to Ashland when Jessalynn was a teenager. Of her two parents, Jessalynn's father is certainly the more grounded, with her mother becoming increasingly New Age in focus with a great interest in past lives, reincarnation, spirit guides, prophetic dreams, psychic readings, intuitive thinking, channeling, shamanism, and mediumship. She met her current husband at a Dance of the Deer Foundation shamanic workshop, which purportedly teaches "Huichol Shamanism," though despite the fact that Huichol shamanism is centered around the use of peyote, does not include the sacred cactus in its programs or curriculum. Not without some irony, Jessalynn's mother viewed entheogens as "dark energies" that could create holes in an individual's aura and also invite in negative spirits and entities to attach themselves to an individual's auric field. Personally, I cannot fathom how anyone could claim to be a practitioner of "Huichol shamanism" and hold such a view of entheogens, but that's Jessalynn's mother.

After remarrying and moving to Ashland, Jessalynn's mother and new stepfather wanted to have a baby. Sadly, the child died at childbirth – something that Jessalynn was in attendance for, and it left a deep scar on her psyche. However, Jessalynn's mother and stepfather refused to let the child go, and started seeking out psychics and mediums to communicate with the boy, whom they named "Teran." Following the guidance and communications thus received, her mother spent her entire inherited fortune on a retreat center complex that they named "Circle of Teran" in the mountains of the Rogue Valley, just outside of Ashland, Oregon. They built the multimillion dollar complex in an area that was zoned for agriculture, never bothering to seek the proper permits or rezoning that would be required to actually run a retreat center, eventually being taken to court by their neighbors who fought against this so-called "Huichol Church" that was built on prime cattle grazing land, all under the supposed guidance of the dead boy, Teran. The idea had been that Circle of Teran would serve as a hub for enlightening and liberating the world, but that was the fantasy – the reality was that it was a money pit that could never function in its intended purpose. Today, the beautiful building and many acres of mountain land are for sale for roughly 15 million dollars, and have been on the market for several years, unused and the fantasy unfulfilled.

When Jessalynn and I first met, she was on a personal purification and clean living kick, having sworn off all mind-altering substances. Greatly influenced by her mother, Jessalynn was also into most of the New Age ideas that had been promoted by her mother, who identifies herself as a channel, medium, and intuitive. However, when Jessalynn and I first started interacting, she had been taking a class at SOU on ethnobotany and had been studying the traditional uses of mind-altering plants in indigenous cultures and traditions. She had thus recently learned about *Salvia divinorum*, and having heard from Hal that I had published a book on the subject, was interested in getting to know more about it, and me. So, we went on a hike together and she peppered me with questions about salvia and my experiences, saying that she'd like to give it a try, at some point.

It was becoming clear to me that if I wanted to open up a relationship with Jessalynn, she was eager and ready. However, I felt that before I could do so, I had to come clean with her about what was really going on with me. We went out on another hike, and I used the opportunity for the big reveal that God was talking through me, and all the weird vibrating and energy I was processing and expressing, coupled with my recent divorce and failed relationship with Maya, my financial struggles, and everything else. Much to my surprise, she was completely open to everything I told her. She was, after all, used to hearing about contact with the spirit world and psychics and mediums, and thus my claims of having God speaking through me, and to me, didn't sound all that far out to her. Though we have subsequently spent a great deal of time and energy untangling Jessalynn from the muddled New Age belief system she picked up from her mother, these beliefs did help pave the way for the beginning of our relationship, so for that, I give them some credit. At any rate, her reaction wasn't, "You're totally insane," and in fact, she was deeply supportive and encouraged me to explore all this further and continue along the path I was taking – and what was more, she wanted to be a part of it.

The idea of getting some kind of second opinion started to occur to me about this time, something Jessalynn was highly supportive of, and my thoughts drifted back to the man I had met on the street who performed "soul readings" with his partner. I called them up, and they were happy to hear from me. Apparently I had made an impression on them, and they were eager to have me come see them. Though I had never gone for any kind of psychic or intuitive reading before, it was a regular feature of Jessalynn's life, and she seemed to feel that it could be helpful, so why not give it a try, I figured.

I went to their house and they invited me into their living room. They explained that the more questions I asked them, the more helpful it would be for them in retrieving information about me. I had only one question: "How does this work?"

Immediately the woman went to work. She feathered me off with an eagle feather and sat down and closed her eyes, encouraging me to do the same. Over the next hour she spouted out a great deal of information, none of which was prompted by me in any way as I only sat silently and took notes in my notebook. The following is a short summary of what she said.

I see a brilliant white mandala of light above your crown cakra. It's pulling you up into wisdom, brilliance. It's magnificent. Don't resist the flow. Trust. It's a beautiful white light, expansive, full of creative energy and new information for the collective human mind and consciousness. I see sacred geometry and circles within circles. A brilliant kaleidoscope opening in your third eye like a mushroom. Trust your inner wisdom. Wisdom is coming through your third eye of clarity.

New dimensions of energy are moving through you and the brilliance of all things. There is a tall pillar of light from Lumerian times. It is communication without words. Energy is moving through this pillar of light in both directions. You are the being that stands in the center of the pillar of light. Long you have been waiting there, waiting for humanity to wake up. The collective human mind has not been able to grasp your words until now. The spiritual awakening is now.

Plant the seeds in the garden. The time is now and the human mind is ready. The human mind is ready to understand the wisdom from way back before light manifested into material form. This is the wisdom that you are here to share. You must find the courage to put it out there, for nothing can prevent the light. Why are we here? Where did we come from? What is the nature of light? Of Spirit? Of consciousness? How did we manifest into material form and why? The human mind is ready. We are ready for the wisdom that you are here to bring. Find the words that will make the shift. Let the energy flow.

I see books, and an audience. The audience is already there. You've already started. Trust and keep going.

You must plant the seeds in the hearts of each individual. Only you will know how deeply each seed must be planted. The pillar of light upholds humanity, and you are the being in the center where it is perfectly still and perfectly calm.

Open the peoples' minds and expand their hearts. They are ready. You have been waiting so long. You've only incarnated a very few times before to bring your message, but the people haven't been ready. Now they are. Trust. Keep your feet firmly planted in trust, for that is the base of the pillar.

One heart at a time. Get to the beautiful essence of all that is. It will be done one soul at a time.

Do not be overwhelmed by the task. Keep pushing the envelope, pushing the seeds deeper.

Thank you for trying before.

When all was said and done, the man turned to me with a stunned look on his face. "Do you have any questions?" he asked. I just smiled and shook my head. "You know all this already, don't you?" he said.

"I was just looking for a second opinion," I answered, the first thing I had said since initially asking how this "soul reading" business worked.

"There's a lot being asked of you."

"That's what I said!" I responded emphatically, thinking back to my last session at T.O.A.D.

"How old are you?" he then asked.

"35."

"Jesus was in his thirties when he realized who he was."

"I know. That thought has crossed my mind," I said. "Buddha too."

"Here, you'll need this," said the man. "Jesus said this on the cross. 'I am the light of God that never fails.'"

Hmmm . . . ok . . .

They thanked me for the "miracle" reading, and I went on my merry way, accompanied by the gift of a unique crystal they had found on Mt. Shasta in Northern California that was in the shape of a flower.

The next night Jessalynn and I sat down to explore *Salvia divinorum* together. She had joined me at the Temple of Awakening Divinity a couple weeks before (prior to us becoming a couple), which had been her first experience with psychedelics in nearly a decade. Like many who experience 5-MeO-DMT, she felt that it had initiated a process of spiritual awakening for her, and had gotten her in touch with her higher self and true purpose. She was curious to see what salvia, which she had never experienced before, would add to the picture.

I passed her the pipe with some enhanced salvia leaf and she took her first hit. She closed her eyes and started laughing and flailing her hands about saying, "The bunny is so cute!" But then something changed. She started speaking in what sounded like a perfectly formed language and was clearly involved in conversations with other beings. This went on for some time, and when she finally came back and opened her eyes, she said, "There were little people everywhere – cute little elves in funny suits and they were so happy!"

Next it was my turn. As was common for me with salvia, it got me throat singing and drumming, and I rode the energy for a bit, which all seemed to be directed at Jessalynn, as though it was being drawn into her as I watched it flow behind closed eyes with the polyphonic chanting pouring out of me. Once I returned, it was her turn to go again.

This time I gave her some of my homegrown leaf. Immediately she started in with the elvish speaking once more. I obviously didn't know what she was saying, but from the tone of her voice, it sounded as though she was reuniting with long-missed friends and companions. She appeared to be speaking to many of them, and they were all experiencing a joyful reunion together. Somehow it seemed that she'd come home.

I began to wonder what was really going on here. The absurd thought that Jessalynn was some kind of elf queen embodied in human form crossed my mind, for she clearly was "one of them," whoever "they" were. I'd used salvia for some years, and had never experienced anything like what she was going through. I'd administered salvia to many people as well, and I had never encountered a reaction like this. There was clearly something different and unique going on here.

I wondered to myself if "they" would be able to see me if I smoked some sage, so I took a hit for myself. There was a little left in the bowl. Not enough to really bring me into the sage sate, just a taste.

That was all that was necessary, however, for immediately after I took the hit, Jessalynn turned to me, still with eyes closed, and began explaining to her invisible elf companions who I was and talked to them about me and gestured toward me as though making introductions. She then opened her eyes, looked down at the empty pipe and said her first word in English for quite some time.

"More," she said, handing the long and slender pipe to me with both hands. It was not a request. It was a command.

I obliged and handed a now-freshly packed bowl to her. Quite ceremoniously, she held it up to the sky, out before her, and to her heart. She took a long smoke and then handed the pipe to me, looking me firmly in the eye.

I smoked the rest of the bowl. It was enough to bring me into sage space. We were still looking each other directly in the eye. I could see the network of flowing sage energy moving about the room, but it had a definite structure to it, almost like we were inside some kind of sage energy temple. When this thought occurred to me, Jessalynn held up her arms in such a way that they perfectly matched the structure of sage energy that I could see.

What is this? What's going on here? Still looking directly at me, Jessalynn nodded knowingly and the entire structure of sage energy nodded with her.

What?

She nodded again, seeming to be saying, "Yes, it is what you think it is."

The back of my neck started to pound as my heart raced. *My God,* I said to myself in my mind. *She's the Sage!*

I didn't say it out loud, but she heard it nonetheless, and she nodded again.

OK, now I've really lost it. I'm totally insane. Salvia divinorum is now interacting with me *through* Jessalynn, who somehow has embodied the energy of the plant itself, and we have now entered into some kind of shared waking dream. What in the hell is going on here? I must be crazy! People don't just *become* entheogens . . . or do they?

If ever I'd gone through the looking glass, this was it.

All right, I told myself. *Just go with it. If you're nuts, so be it. Take advantage of this and see what you can learn.*

Immediately I relaxed as I felt us both passing into a higher state of shared consciousness. We had entered into a shared subjective state where everything felt as though it were part of one waking dream, as through all of what we were experiencing was the content of one mind. In fact, there didn't seem to be any division between us, and despite the fact that we were two physical people, it felt as though we were one. We were both embodying God consciousness together in this heightened state where we both *just knew*. I felt overwhelmed with a deep "I AM" sense of consciousness.

What ensued, following this acceptance, was a three-hour session of us passing the sage pipe back and forth between us with me asking numerous questions of Jessalynn, all of which she had insightful answers to. By the time we finished, both of us were astounded and amazed. What in the world just happened?

The next morning I went back to my place (which, as it turned out, was just a couple blocks from Jessalynn's house) and fell down on my bed and started vibrating. My hands reached up to the ceiling and I could feel all the energetic threads again. I started to cry as the words came of my mouth, saying, "We're all going to do it together. The wave of awakening has already started, and we're all going to do it together. We will all awaken together!" I felt profoundly moved and touched as I vibrated away on my bed. I was still really feeling the "I AM," and all I could do was cry.

Following this, I made plans to go get some acupuncture to help me with my energy, explaining to the acupuncturist that I kept going into these mystical states and vibrating like mad. The acupuncture seemed to help a little with the vibrating, making my energy feel a little smoother and more relaxed.

I spent the next few days pondering all this, especially Jessalynn seeming to embody the sage itself. I wondered about myself, and the thought passed into my mind that somehow I was a mushroom.

At this point, I'd like to insert a break in the narrative to give a more seasoned perspective on what was happening during this period. In essence, my ego was struggling to understand my identity – who was I? What is the genuine nature of being? The ego always works dualistically, however, so it is in a constant struggle to maintain some identity in relation to other "objects" and other identities that it encounters in reality (and the imagination). So I was struggling with ideas of spirits, entities, other consciousnesses and identities, yet underneath it all was this simple and holistic sense of I AM. In other words, my ego could not accept the idea that in truth, I was God (as are we all), so it was trying as hard as it could to find some identity that was less than infinite, and this was how it was manifesting. The ego is a relentless game-player, and while Jessalynn and I were touching on the truth, we were also involved in a game of identity and sense of self. My resistance to the truth of my being was helping to prop up this game, as I was not yet ready to accept the fullness of what I had already learned. Energetically, intellectually, emotionally, it was still too much for my ego to accept. And from an energetic perspective, I still had a significant amount of energetic processing to do, and my full awakening and transformation was still many months away, at this point.

I now know that anyone who constructs a "spiritual" identity for themselves is stuck somewhere in this process – whether one thinks of themselves as awakening to reincarnation, or spirits, or entities, or other realms, or what have you – it is all a projection of the ego, dualistically seeking some kind of separate and special identity that says, "this is who I am." It's all just a game, however, and is not objectively true. It is a projection of the mind and desire for a sense of a unique self with a particular purpose, truth, or destiny. The games that the ego plays go deep – almost all the way to the core, but not quite. It takes concentrated and sustained effort to see through these games and illusions, however, and most "spiritual seekers" stop the process when they latch onto some "spiritual" identity that they've constructed for themselves – Jessalynn's mother is a perfect case in point.

This new identity then becomes a focus for attachment and further projection, drawing the individual deeper into the illusion, especially if the individual can find other egos that are willing and eager to play along. In short, anyone who claims to be "awake," yet proclaims any identity that is less than admitting to being God and the One Universal Being that is everything is fooling him or herself and is ignorant of his or her true nature. The danger for me, at this point, was that I could have fallen into this subtle trap of the ego, and held onto some kind of separate identity for myself. The difficulty is that when the individual is not clear and centered, everything becomes filtered through the ego and its personal narrative of identity and purpose, and this tends to distort one's experience and sense of reality.

As a result, fundamental truth gets mixed with fiction and fantasy, and it can be exceedingly difficult to separate the two, especially if the distortions resonate with an individual's ego and what one wants to hear or think. Seeking after genuine truth is brutal, and often destructive of our most cherished beliefs and attachments, and honestly, the vast majority of egos would rather live in their chosen illusions and attachments than face reality, as that would require honestly confronting and overcoming personal attachments and illusions. Most egos would rather not do that, for it completely shatters one's sense of self, purpose, and identity. The hard truth is that spiritual identities, no matter how loving, kind, compassionate or open-minded, are all still expressions of the ego, and as such, are illusions and projections, and are fundamentally untrue fictions. The ego loves a good story, and doesn't want to give it up for anything – even truth.

Ultimately, this is the ego's job – to convince God that it is something and someone *else*. And from the ego's perspective, the more unusual and convoluted that "someone else" is projected and constructed to be, the better, for it provides more opportunities for the ego to hold on and feel unique, special, and real. When people claim to be a reincarnation, a psychic, a channel, a medium, a light worker, an alien, or what-have-you, it is always their ego talking, and not reality. For many, the more spiritual they become, and the more they invest themselves in their spiritual identity and "purpose," the more confused they get about their true nature and the more distorted their sense of self becomes. Spirituality is one of the primary traps and tools of the ego. Reality is actually rather simple – One Being of fractal energy playing multiple roles simultaneously - it's the ego that convolutes things with its attachments, beliefs, and projections.

Egos can also get into feedback loops with each other, where multiple individuals can provide the necessary information that egos are looking for to confirm and cement their chosen identities. This generates from the fact that God is a compulsive game-player, and identity is nothing if not a game. God, in pretending and convincing itself that it is a diversity of unique individuals, is playing a game, and that game is based on illusion and confusion. Confused egos like to collect themselves together with like-minded players in order to perpetuate the illusion in reaffirming feedback loops, and these collections form into cults, religions, spiritual traditions, political groups, cultures, subcultures, and all manner of identity collectives.

A few days later Jessalynn and I decided go back into the sage together. More elvish speak and there we were again, back in this strange shared subjective state where we were one. "Who are you?" I asked her. "I am a guardian of humanity," she answered. "Then who am I?" "We have been allies for a long time," she said. I pressed her further. She struggled with the answer. She didn't want to say it, and she struggled with the elvish babble. "English!" she said, forcing herself back into a viable means of communicating with me. "You're a mushroom," she said at last. And then added, much to my surprise, "You're a mushroom, and you're Jesus."

As a cultural note, *Salvia divinorum* and psilocybin mushrooms are the two medicines that are traditionally used by the Mazatec people of Mexico, where they have been considered shamanic medicines and allies for many hundreds of years. In Mazatec culture, as influenced by Spanish Catholicism, salvia is understood to be a medium for Mother Mary, and mushrooms are a medium for the baby Jesus. This was a fact that I was well familiar with, and something that Jessalynn had recently learned in her ethnobotany class at SOU.

"So what are we doing?" I asked her, seeking more information.

"Were here to help remind people. It's time to wake up and remember."

That was the beginning of the week. At the end of that week, I went for another round of Daime. It was a seated Work, known as a Concentration, and I went deep into the visions. Vast networks of living starlight energy presented themselves to me. I saw a grid made of six pointed stars with nodes at the center, and at every point (the six pointed "star of David" is a primary symbol of the Daime tradition, along with a double cross). Not in words, but in very definite communication, the Daime said, "To embody the Christ principle, you must relax into the center." It showed me how, when the center was properly energized or awakened, a shift in energy could pulse out to all the other nodes across the cosmic grid. "Just relax into the center," it kept telling me.

Around this time I got the idea that I needed to take a trip out to New Mexico; a trip that would serve several purposes. For one, I got the idea that I should go out to Mescalero to visit Willeto, and with all my newfound energy, perhaps there was something I could do to help him with his being partially paralyzed and being confined to a wheelchair. Second, I wanted to take the opportunity to visit Marianne in Albuquerque. Third, Rick Strassman had agreed to do an interview for my podcast, but his preference was for in-person interviews and didn't want to do it over Skype. His home was just outside of Taos, New Mexico, and thus I would be traveling all about the state on this trip.

I decided to fly into Albuquerque with the thought that Marianne might be able to find me some mushrooms, which I could then take down to Mescalero and offer to Willeto and perhaps do some kind of healing for him. I knew that this was a stretch, as Willeto had expressed to me on more than one occasion that he considered peyote to be "make-believe religion," but I knew that he trusted me, and therefore might be open to the experience. As it turned out, Marianne was unable to secure any mushrooms for me, and as events would have it, my trip to Mescalero had an entirely different purpose. It was just my ego wanting to "do" and "be" someone/something anyway, so it was just a projection.

Though I didn't arrange my trip to coincide with any ceremonial activity, when I arrived at Mescalero, I learned that there was a big feast taking place with various Mountain Spirit dance groups and girls going through their initiations that weekend. And, much to my surprise, I was told by others that my "friend" was around – and by friend, they meant my old professor, Professor X. It was the summer of 2008, and Professor X and I hadn't had any personal contact since my completing my degree in 2000. Despite the time and distance, I still cringed internally just at the thought of her, or having to see her, but I knew: this was my opportunity. When given the command to "Love all equally without any exception," someone who had immediately come to mind was Professor X. There was just so much bitterness, anger, and disappointment there that it felt impossible for me to extend that universal and unconditional love to her.

Yet, when I went to the ceremony, there she was, seated across the dance grounds watching the Mountain Spirit dancers. I knew she was there before I saw her, as several people reported to me that she was around. After I spotted her, and figured that she had probably spotted me as well, I asked my friends to wish me luck, and I made my approach.

I had avoided Professor X, and all that she represented for me, for years. There had been times since my graduation that I had seen Professor X walking around town, or caught sight of her as I drove or rode my bike through the UCSB campus. Whenever I had seen her, my heart would leap up in my chest and my throat would constrict as my blood pressure rose. My experience with her, my frustrations of not being able to get work, my disillusionment with academia – it would all rise to the surface just with the thought of her, so I did my best to avoid it. And I never knew what I would say if I had to speak to her, face-to-face. So I had tried to simply move on and forget about her and my struggles to be an academic or to teach in my area of expertise. But now, here we were together at Mescalero again, and the time to overcome my apprehension and desire to turn away had arrived. This was my opportunity to put this part of my life to rest, and despite my resistance, my will to get it done and over with was stronger, and I decided to make my move.

I was nervous, but it was the right decision. There on the dance grounds with the Mountain Spirits and bonfire just beyond us, we made our peace with each other. I don't really recall many specifics of our conversation – she asked if I was teaching or publishing or what, and I told her about *Mushroom Wisdom, Sage Spirit,* and the book that I was working on then, *The Entheogenic Evolution*. She told me to be careful, said it was good to see me, and that was about it. Whatever power she had previously tried to exert over me was gone, as was the palpable tension, and we were able to talk once more as friends, perhaps not colleagues, but it was no longer the dynamic of the over-controlling master and the rebellious student. That was done and over with, and I was free from it.

It was a profound relief, and I was immensely happy that this was how my trip to Mescalero had turned out. Quite unexpected, but exactly what I needed to really let that period of my life go and make peace with it. Here I had envisioned this whole narrative of going out to Mescalero and healing Willeto, whereas in reality, I found more of my own healing and a resolution that had eluded me for eight years. It is difficult for me to describe what a relief this was. I could finally let this whole painful relationship go. That was over five years ago now, and since then I haven't seen or heard from Professor X, and that's just fine.

After Mescalero, I stopped off in Albuquerque once more with Marianne, and then was off to see Rick Strassman for the day. We met at his house and sat in his living room for the interview. He inquired a little bit about how my work with 5-MeO and the Daime was going, but overall wasn't too curious, other than asking if I'd seen any of the "little people." I didn't share with him that I'd been communing with God and that "little people" didn't seem to have anything to do with it (at least, not personally – Jessalynn's experiences with salvia were another matter entirely). In the interview, I asked if he still supported the idea of "tuning in to channel dark matter" and DMT as providing access to alternate realms – something that I was seriously beginning to question the validity of – and he said that this was still his view, as made famous in his book, *DMT – The Spirit Molecule,* and more recently in the film by the same name by Mitch Schultz.

This is something that I've since taken a very strong stand on – in my view, it is a fallacy to think that *any* entheogen is actually giving access to any kind of alternate reality, as it is all a projection of the self, and mostly filled with ego-generated content and confusion. This view has put me at odds with virtually the entire "entheogenic community," psychedelic shamanism and religion in general, and countless entheogenic writers and enthusiasts. I didn't bring any of this up with Strassman, however, for I was there to interview him and allow him to express his views, and it wasn't until later, after my own final opening and transformation, that I started to express my own clarity on the matter through my podcast, books, and articles – something that was to receive a rabidly negative response from the entheogenic community where I was accused of being a fraud, a charlatan, and a megalomaniac for daring to say that I had realized the truth of the issue and seen past the self-generated illusions of the ego.

Egos are far more comfortable with their attachment to dualistic illusion than they are with raw, honest, and surprisingly simple truth.

To finish off the trip, I spent a couple more days with Marianne in Albuquerque, mostly sitting around her place watching the first couple seasons of *Dexter*. It was the first time in many, many years that I gave myself permission to just sit around and watch TV, and the act had its own therapeutic value, especially as so much of my time in Ashland thus far had involved frantic searches for work in the ever-shifting employment landscape I had launched myself into. Never would I have imagined that watching a show about a serial killer would give me the rest and respite I needed. I went with the flow, however, and thoroughly enjoyed myself, loving the message that Dexter was just doing his best to be true to himself and refused to deny his authentic nature.

I returned to Oregon with another invitation to come to the Temple of Awakening Divinity. This time my process was fairly simple. As the medicine came on, I found myself thinking to myself *I don't know who I am*. God's response was swift and clear. "I AM!" pulsed in my mind. The vibrations took over as my hands shot up to feel all the energetic threads. The energy was bigger and stronger than ever - beyond comprehension. The energy of God's love was just so much greater than anything I could ever hope to conceive or understand conceptually. Yes, "I AM!"

When I finally "came back," I had to get up and go run laps around the house to help get all the energy out, as it was way too much for my insignificant little body to hold. It wasn't at all standard practice for the Temple of Awakening

Divinity, but I didn't care. I was an energetic dynamo, and I needed to take some time to discharge. Eventually, Hal came outside to check on me and bring me back in so that he could continue the ritual of allowing the next "initiate" (as he likes to call them) have a turn with the medicine, and he couldn't have me running around outside like a mad man.

"You totally dosed me!" I said to him with a smile.

"No I didn't," he responded. "I gave you just what you needed."

A week and a half later I was back at the Daime. I was a little disappointed in the first couple rounds. The Daime was weak, and I wanted to go deeper. Something that I was learning was that in comparison to 5-MeO, virtually everything else seems pale and weak. 5-MeO is just so much beyond everything else that it is in a category of energetic experience and mystical awareness that most other medicines don't even touch. Daime and ayahuasca can be strong and very powerful, but still of a far lesser order of magnitude than 5-MeO. During a break, I asked one of the pourers if it was OK to ask for more. "Sure," he said. "Just let me know."

When we lined up for the next round, the pourer told me that this next batch was more concentrated than the earlier ones, and asked if I wanted more. Before I answered, the leader of the church turned around, took a good look at me, and then looked at the glass of Daime being offered to me. Looking back at me, he said to the pourer, "Give him more."

I barely made it to a bed in the healing yurt as everything was dissolving into Daime-driven geometric forms, fractals, and living starlight. My eyes rolled back up into my head as the energy poured through me. I was breathing hard and my hands were vibrating wildly. One of the guardians, an old man, leaned over me. I could barely see him through my fluttering eyes. "Don't forget to breathe," he advised kindly. "I'm OK," I responded. "I'm used to it."

Several starlight beings checked in on me. They weren't there to do anything. They were just checking in, seeing how I was progressing, or something. There were several of them and they were "standing" around me, observing. I felt incredibly thirsty, and wished that someone would bring me something to drink. One of the starlight beings came forward. She titled my head back, gently opened my mouth, and poured starlight milk into my mouth that infused my whole being. Just what I needed. Now I felt like I could really vibrate with abandon.

It's difficult to say how long it lasted, but I think I probably vibrated for about three hours during that round. It felt like my whole body and energetic being was being reorganized, and I went into several fits of full body convulsions. Physically, it was very demanding and tiring, but not uncomfortable or unpleasant in any way. All just part of the process . . .

My next visit to the Daime was pretty much more of the same. Lots of time spent in the healing yurt or out in the forest vibrating and merging with the energy, just letting it flow, just letting the energy do its work. I found an ideal tree stump out in the forest and would just stand there, arms open and vibrating, and I would throat sing for hours at a time. This wasn't standard Daime practice, by any means, but the Daimistas had learned to just give me time and space to go through whatever in the world it was I was going through. Generally, Daimistas don't let people wander off from Works, and the collective action takes priority over individual practices and experiences.

The next week I traveled down to Southern California to see Ethan and Miranda, and had the opportunity to work with mushrooms with Rod, whose home I stayed at for the visit. The mushrooms were mild – at least, initially. We walked down to the beach that night and sat and talked together about all that I'd been going through, really giving me an opportunity to voice all my thoughts while I intermittently vibrated as I gazed at the stars and listened to the lapping waves.

Eventually we ended up back at his condo around midnight, after three hours at the beach. We smoked some herb and watched a few minutes of TV with his mom out in the front room. I felt a strong urge to lie down with the feeling that the mushrooms were about to well up again, so I went back into my room, turned off the lights, and closed my eyes as I lay in bed. Behind my closed eyes I saw an intricate mandala made out of thousands of piercing eyes, like an Alex Grey painting. *Here we go,* I said to myself as my hands started vibrating.

I passed through the mandala and found myself (or my visual perspective) flying over a perfectly symmetrical grid of what looked like some kind of advanced computer circuitry. I moved past the circuit board and looked up to see a large red disk that looked something like an Aztec sun disk with intricate geometric patterns. The disk moved from being in front of me to lying down horizontally. Then it began to pulse, and as it did, rainbow waves of energy emanated from the center of the living geometric form and flowed out across the universe. It was like a heartbeat at the very center of everything. I felt myself drawn into the center, and then I passed through it.

On the other side were the most magnificent visions I had ever beheld, with more clarity and detail than I can possibly hope to describe – and this from a relatively weak batch of mushrooms! The first thing I saw was a four-sided statue made completely of gold. It had four eagles, each facing a different direction. Their wings were outstretched and their mouths open. At the breast of each eagle was an angelic being, also with outstretched wings. I moved around the immense statue and saw it from every angle. I was overwhelmed with the sacredness of the image. It was so intricate, so beautiful, so charged with holy power. It was like an image from an ancient future, as it was timeless, yet also classic, as though it were made by an ancient civilization. But there was something new about it too, something that had not yet come to pass, and therefore gave it a sense of futurity that is difficult to express.

After the eagle statue came many other similarly numinously charged architectural images. There were bulls, bears, snakes, and more, all fashioned as idols or statues. Eventually it all culminated with the image of an unfathomably immense golden temple in the form of a winged jaguar. In my vision, I was walking up to the temple and could see the movement of red color inside, as though some ceremony or ritual was taking place with red-robed participants. As I approached the entrance, the thought crossed my mind that I wanted to see the front of the temple from this angle, so I looked up at the giant jaguar head looming above me. When I turned back to enter the temple, it all dissolved into geometric patterns of fractal mushroom energy.

Suddenly I was on to something new. The mushrooms were showing me the construction of a human body. I saw the whole thing constructed one layer at a time, from bones and tissues to organs, muscles, and skin. Then it shifted again, and there were these strange insect/alien beings looking at me. Though terribly odd looking, they weren't threatening. Just observing. My fingers fluttered and felt insectoid, and as though they were working some kind of computer grid. Then the insect aliens disappeared and there was a large flower that seemed to suck and pull with its petals.

Eventually I really had to go urinate. So I got up, went to the bathroom, and then came back to bed for another hour of random energy displays and movements. Getting tired, and not really getting any more specific content, I asked the mushrooms if I could go to sleep now. They acquiesced and I finally got some sleep around three in the morning.

The following week I was back in Oregon and found myself once more at the Temple of Awakening Divinity. I could feel my resistance so I spoke to others in the room, as much as to myself. "I'm holding on, and I don't know why. I don't know what I'm afraid of."

As soon as I said that, I knew that my resistance was produced by the thought of *what if all this is really true?* Understanding that this was the source of my resistance, I suddenly fell completely into God. Immediately, a powerful sentence coursed through my being. *I can't say that*, I thought to myself, but the communication was insistent.

And there was "the voice" again.

"I will do *it* in *this body*!" I bellowed out.

And there came the vibrations as my hands started shivering wildly. This was followed by an immediate shift where now I was speaking in what I can only call "the all-voice." It was certainly not my voice. In the voice there was young and old, male and female. It was like a composite of all voices speaking together simultaneously (which, I'll point out, sounded distinctly different and unique not just to me, but to the other people in the room as well). I don't remember precisely what the all-voice said, but it was something like, "We love you with all our hearts. We will always remember and honor you, and we thank you for your gift of love. Even when we forget, we still know and remember your love in our hearts and we will always honor you, for we are One with You, and You are Us!"

That went on for some time as the other witnesses in the room swelled with the out-flowing of divine energy, raising their hands with tears in their eyes, as they too expressed their thanks and love for the divine.

As was always the case, eventually I came back into "me," to the self that identified itself as "Martin". At that point I started to cry and thanked God personally, and had a few private moments. Getting all the energy to dissipate took some effort, and I had to do some throat singing to really get it all out.

A month passed before my next visit with the Temple of Awakening Divinity, and this time it was at Burning Man 2008. I had come full circle. Right back to where I started, that fantastic matrix of culture and freedom that is Burning Man. It was Jessalynn's first time out at the Burn, and for Hal, as well, who had secured the use of a friend's RV to perform T.O.A.D. ceremonies, with the goal of "initiating" as many people as possible over the course of the week. Appointments had to be made, and Hal was quite busy through the week. Jessalynn didn't feel up for a round, and I was a little skeptical myself, but decided to go for it.

Given the environment, I asked for a smaller dose. "I don't know if I really want to do the whole God thing here," I said to Hal and Jessalynn. "Sure you do," they responded.

Though I wasn't fully aware of it, apparently I started off my journey by saying "I don't know who I am" a couple times, as they informed me later. What was really on my mind was that "I don't understand. I want to understand, but I don't understand."

Of course, was the response. *It's a paradox. Embrace it.*

"Yes, it's a paradox," I repeated out loud.

And then I fell into God.

This time, I went right to the center. I was one with the heart of God. The energy was not flowing *through* me. It was radiating out of the center of my heart, and as it did, I could clearly and distinctly see the threads of the energetic network of the universe, all emanating directly out of the Heart of God, which was also my heart. Once I stopped trying to understand, it all made perfect sense, though in a paradoxical way.

From that perspective, I could feel a great deal of pain and sadness. It was the sadness of those who are lost and those who have turned away from their divine natures and who live disconnected, those who are sleepwalking through this life. There was pain in God's heart, or my heart, to ease that suffering, to bring all those who are lost back into the light of God's love and God's pure embrace. As my hands worked their way through the vibrations, I could just feel it and it saddened me. So much love, but there are so many who are not open to receiving it. So many who have not chosen to accept the gift that is right there, waiting for them, calling them home.

When I finally came back into myself, I just cried. Perhaps it was self-pity. How can *anyone* understand what I've been going through? How could any of this make sense? Can anyone understand me, or this strange process? Am I alone?

Jessalynn put her hands on the top of my abdomen and I felt a great block get moved and promptly purged, letting the rest of the energy flow out of me as I wiped away my tears.

The following night, Devon had his first, and to my knowledge, only experience with 5-MeO-DMT, as did Rod. Rod had a beautiful and deep experience, after which he leaned over and embraced me, letting himself cry in gratitude. Devon was another matter, however, and I'm sharing some details of his experience here, as it will be significant a bit later in our story.

Over the previous year, Devon had been living with the young woman he met up with at the conclusion of the Burn the year before. Their relationship had become a bit rocky, however, and there was considerable strain between them. When Devon went for his turn with the medicine, rather than relaxing and releasing into himself, he focused all his attention and energy on his partner, Kat, grabbing onto her and telling her repeatedly how much he loved and needed her. It was obvious that Kat was uncomfortable with this clingy attention, though she let Devon hold onto her, nevertheless.

This, with some added details, is where I left things with the chapter, "My Journey," in *The Entheogenic Evolution*. In concluding that book, I was still somewhat in the middle of my process, still struggling with my ego, my identity, and my understanding of what was happening to me, and why. At this point, where all this was going, and what would come of it, was very unclear for me, and after the Burn of 2008, some frustration set in. When I took the medicines, especially 5-MeO, everything was clear and made sense, but when I was back in my ego, the question was always: what is happening to me, and why? I was clearly undergoing something radical, but to what end? What, or who, was I becoming, and what was the point? It wasn't until a few months into 2009 that it all became clear, so I still had several more months of opening, processing, and seeking understanding to pass through, and it is to this final stage of my process that we will now turn.

Chapter Eight

From Finite to Infinite

Post-Burn, in the fall of 2008, I was busy teaching at SOU and finishing up my latest book, *The Entheogenic Evolution.* I was still regularly attending the Santo Daime church – generally going to works several times a month – and making around a trip a month or so to T.O.A.D. It was also around this time that I was contacted by a local podcast listener who invited me to come over to his place and try N,N DMT for the first time – an invitation that I gladly accepted.

We met over at Joel's place for fondue dinner and DMT. For that first experience, Hal joined us, bringing his "lamp" vaporizer that he used for his 5-MeO ceremonies. After dinner, we set things up for the DMT launch party and I volunteered to go first. The lamp was prepared and the DMT vaporized, exactly how Hal would use the 5-MeO. Immediately upon inhaling my hit, I concluded that this was the wrong way to use DMT, due to the construction of the lamp. The lamp had a long, thin metal tube that served as a mouthpiece that had a small opening on the end through which one would inhale the vapor. For 5-MeO, this worked just fine, but DMT was different. With the small aperture, the vapor exited the vaporizer in a highly condensed form, and unlike 5-MeO, the DMT had a distinct chemical reaction to this, leaving me with the feeling that I had just given myself a chemical burn on my lips, gums, and tongue. It was very unpleasant and as a result, I started hissing and growling in energetic release and blurting out in my now-deep and thundering voice, "This is not the correct method!"

I ended up writing an appendix to *The Entheogenic Evolution* in order to include some reflections on DMT, and my assessment hasn't altered much since that first experience. What I found was that DMT was beautiful, complex, amazing, and quite visually stunning, but ultimately paled in comparison to 5-MeO-DMT. I also found that despite the large influx of energy produced by DMT, it hardly compares to 5-MeO, and as a result, makes it far less likely that one can effectively transcend the ego, even though the medicine itself is quite strong. Visually, DMT has 5-MeO beat by a long shot, but something I've learned throughout my experience is that visual experiences on psychedelics really are not all that significant or important – it's the energy of what's going on underneath that is far more relevant and instructive.

When it comes to visuals, there are a couple different things going on. The basic structure of psychedelic visual content is geometric and fractal in nature, and it is these "building blocks" that are the formative structures of our perceptual experience. It is these building blocks that allow us to perceive or experience anything – not just in psychedelic states, but perception in general – and they are brought to conscious attention when we consume visually active psychedelics. It is out of these formative structures that visions arise, but visions themselves are just a form of self-generated communication between different levels of the individual's psyche, and as such, are highly responsive to projection, fantasy, and illusion. All visions are, by their very nature, dualistic, for in order for a vision to exist, there must be a viewer and that which is viewed – a necessary dualism. Given its highly visual nature, DMT is far more inherently dualistic, and therefore trapped in the ego, than the almost contentless nature of 5-MeO. As Terence McKenna himself said, when discussing his preference for DMT over 5-MeO-DMT, he didn't like 5-MeO as it was "a feeling," whereas he could really "hallucinate" on DMT – and all of his descriptions of his DMT experiences are thoroughly dualistic and ego-based in nature. This is an indication that he, like many DMT enthusiasts, was more comfortable operating from his ego than fully transcending it. Another indication of McKenna's attachment to his ego is his overwhelming focus on what he describes as the "otherness" that he felt was present in high-level psychedelic experiences. As long as there is a sense of separation between self and other, one is still trapped in the dualism of the ego and the false sense of self. Despite all his experiences, it seems highly unlikely that McKenna ever experienced full transcendence of his ego, and thus virtually everything that he claims about psychedelic experience needs to be understood in this context. The same holds true for most descriptions of shamanic experiences of spirits, other realms, and astral beings – all projections of the self, and none of them are objectively "true" or "real" in any kind of substantive sense.

Overall, DMT did not impress me as a truly effective tool for overcoming the ego and having a full release experience. I did enjoy it, however, but in all honesty, it was more for its entertainment and aesthetic value than anything else.

It was around this time that things shifted yet again in my experiences with 5-MeO and my trips to T.O.A.D. Now, "the voice" was a regular feature of my 5-MeO experiences, and my energy was beginning to smooth out in that, rather than sending me on a wild ride of vibrating uncontrollably, my body started to move in fluid, symmetrical movements, and my hands would be steady as I moved through different strands and layers of energy as I spoke to what I was experiencing. As "Martin," it was all quite fascinating, as I never had any idea what would come out of my mouth, or what I would choose to discourse upon while in the 5-MeO state. It was always something that just happened spontaneously, and the "Martin" part of me could only ponder it later, after the fact, in recall of what I had just said.

This phenomenon would also occur with other medicines, as well. One particularly loquacious session with mushrooms provided me with a variety of statements that I ended up including as chapter openers in *The Entheogenic Evolution* as quotes from God. These statements were all said to humanity in general, as well as to "Martin" in particular. Taken together, they are as follows:

"In all my explorations, the only one I've ever found is myself. And so it is for you, for I am you. We are One, and we are many. We are . . .

"Do not look to me for answers. Everything you need has already been provided. Create your own answers – make your own choices. It is always your choice. Like me, you are free.

"Own your own energy and truth. Do not claim mine. My truth and my energy are my own.

"To be as me, discover, create, and become your own truth. Be responsible for your truth and your energy.

"I am energy and I am infinite – there is no end to my love and I give it freely.

"Because we are One, your energy is infinite as well. Use it as you see fit, but to be awakened is to use it in love and truth, for that is what I Am.

"Is the highest good simply to know that I AM, or is it to become as I am?

"To become awakened to your divinity is to know that you are God, and you are responsible for your own reality.

"Do not seek to fulfill my Will, for my Will is already accomplished. Ask yourself: what is your will? What is the highest good for you? Discover it, create it, and become it.

"I am reality. To be the highest model is to show others how to live in reality. Become truth and create, create, create, create . . ."

For this particular mushroom session, I took a large dose and sealed myself off in our spare room for the afternoon, letting Jessalynn know that I'd check in with her when all was said and done, but I'd be spending time with God for the next several hours and I shouldn't be disturbed. I tried initiating the session in a seated position, but soon found myself lying on the floor with my arms out at my sides. When the mushrooms really started coming on strong, the visuals had a very particular quality to them in a way I had never seen before. Within the visionary state, my perspective was one of looking up, as though I were seeing things from the vantage of a small child. The mushroom geometry was all very childlike, and had a distinctly immature quality to it. My ego reacted, feeling somewhat insulted. *I've come all this way and undergone all these trials for kindergarten? Really?*

At that point, I believe I said something out loud, expressing my disappointment with this situation. I don't remember what I said, or what shifted the visions, but what came next was almost cliché. A vision of "heaven" opened up before me. There were throngs of people, all praising and worshiping God, all crowded into a beautiful pastoral scene, with the clouds parting, divine light shining through in radiant beams, and angelic choirs. *You've got to be kidding me*, was my response.

It was then that "God" and "I" got into a conversation, with "Martin" asking questions or making inquiries, and God answering through me in "the voice." My questioning was all along the lines of what I was supposed to be learning, and doing. Yes, I wanted to "give God's love to the world," but what did that really mean? Personally, I wasn't some saint, I wasn't particularly holy, and I certainly wasn't a religious zealot, so what could this really mean for me? The answer was that I was to show others how to "live in reality," and the only way I could do that was by both understanding the nature of myself as God embodied in individual form, and also by my willingness to not only understand myself, but to allow myself to be myself fully, without reservation. The opening scene of the heavenly vision was actually intended as something of an ironic joke, as though I was showing myself what religious and spiritually minded people think of God, but this was all a projection of the ego, and fundamentally an illusion. To really know God in the personal sense was to become God – not to worship or praise some "supreme being" that existed outside of the individual self. Worship, praise, and devotion were blasé for God, and fundamentally a waste of time and energy. God doesn't need to be worshiped. God needs to be embodied and lived.

The overall import of our conversation that day seemed fairly clear: God is reality itself, and God is energy. We, as individuals, are expressions of this energetic unity, and we are best understood as energetic beings. To live in truth is to live in accordance with genuine energy, and when it comes down to it, love, truth, and energy are all the same thing. To live in reality is to live in congruence with energy – not some intellectual or moral ideal, but to be true to one's energy, both internally and externally. As individuals, we have the choice to either live with genuine energy, or we are equally free to project our illusions onto what is – it is our choice. If we find ourselves living in illusion and delusion, we are the ones responsible for that. And in finding clarity and our true nature, we cannot look to God as some kind of external savior or divine being will that will swoop down and make everything better for us, because *we are that*. God does not exist as some force beyond the self, for it is The Self. There is nothing that exists outside of God, for God is everything. Therefore the idea that God, Jesus, Buddha, Allah, Krishna, Vishnu, or anyone else can "save" an individual is a complete fabrication of the ego and has zero validity in reality. There is no divine savior or transcendent force. Each individual is fully responsible for him or herself, and no amount of wishing will make things otherwise. And the idea that anyone can "fulfill" God's will is equally a delusion, for the will of God is your own will, and thinking of things as being otherwise is self-delusion. In order to find clarity, one must become familiar with the nature of one's own energy, and learn how to be true and authentic with it. Enlightenment and liberation, therefore, are energetic issues, and have nothing whatsoever to do with being religious or spiritual in any way, for all religions and spiritualities are products of the confused and projecting ego. It is only through energetic self-discovery and embodiment that any real progress can be made toward enlightenment and liberation.

Also embedded in this discourse is the idea that God does not play favorites with anything or anyone in reality, for God is everyone and everything equally, and to play favorites would be to choose one aspect of itself over another, and that would be incompatible with unconditional, universal love, which is God's nature. In other words, God cannot and will not violate its own nature. This again points back to the truth that each individual is responsible for him or herself. God does not grant favors, perform miracles, answer prayers, or select anyone or any culture or tradition as being "chosen" or preferred in any way. The idea that you can please God by following the Bible, the Koran, the Torah, the Vedas, or anything else is pure delusion of the ego. God's "will" is already accomplished in that reality exists in such a way that God, as a being of infinite fractal energy, has evolved itself into both subject and object, all governed by the energetic limits of transformation, change, and becoming, that collectively might be called "natural laws" such as physics, chemistry, biology, etc., and through which reality exists as a consequential and "real" phenomenon.

On another occasion, God/I expressed much of the same through the metaphor of water:

"I am water, and I am everywhere. I can fill any shape, take any form. I can reflect you back to you as long as you like, for I am you. So remember, what you do to water, you do to yourself.

"I am water, and I am thirsty."

I particularly like the last line of this water discourse, for it illustrates the paradoxical nature of being in that God, as reality, experiences itself as both subject and object simultaneously, as well as is the desire to consume itself through the process of life. God is the one desiring, the object of the desire, and the desire itself. What seems nonsensical and paradoxical resolves from the nondual perspective that all is one, and it is only from a dualistic perspective that assumes a fundamental divide between subject and object, self and other, that the contradiction appears. The true nature of being and self is beyond all dualistic distinctions. It also highlights that it is only through consuming and transforming itself that God is able to perpetuate reality, or, to put it succinctly, it's a God-eat-God world out there, and no amount of moralizing or human sentimentality will make it any less brutal or violent. It is simply the way things are, and the only way things can be, for without this self-consuming, nothing would exist, for it is through these processes of change and transformation that reality, and life, is able to evolve. It is a necessary condition for existence. And it is one that brings consequences, which is why reality is so different from fantasy, illusion, and projection. In reality, all of our actions and choices have consequences that are real, and no amount of wishing, praying, or positive thinking can change that. Living in reality authentically requires getting real and staying real. Imaginary fantasylands are no help in this regard, whether they are the fantasies of religions, spiritualities, or psychedelic gurus spewing metaphysical mumbo-jumbo "prophecies" about 2012, machine elves, and UFOs.

Things continued to progress in my work with the Daime, and a transition that started at Burning Man in 2008 came to full fruition at a later session at the Church of the Holy Light of the Queen. At Burning Man, I had several opportunities to eat mushrooms, and each time I did, I experienced a strange and peculiar phenomenon with my left hand and arm. If I relaxed and felt into my energy, my left arm would start moving about in fluid and rather artful movements, seemingly completely free of my volition. It would just start moving and doing its thing. Meanwhile, I could go about my business and just let it run, walking about Burning Man and viewing the art, or whatever else I might want to do. I could also stop it, if I wanted, but I found the whole thing to be rather fascinating, so I just let it go. Every once in a while, it might spiral to a point and then stop, my fingers posing themselves in what looked like Buddhist or Hindu *mudras*, and then start back up again, spiraling out and then starting up a new pattern. I had no idea why it was doing this, or what it was about, but was completely unconcerned about it, and actually found it fascinatingly entertaining.

In my subsequent visits to the Daime, a few people started asking me if I was "working with" or "incorporating" what they were identifying as "serpent power," for that's what my left arm and hand looked like whenever it would do this. That interpretation did not feel right to me however – far too specific and identified – so I usually responded with, "No – it's just energy." In Santo Daime, they have a practice called "incorporation," and also "mediumship," where practitioners experience themselves as working with various "astral" entities for the purposes of healing, divination, and sending lost spirits back into the light of God. It is considered a more advanced practice within the religion. None of these ideas felt right to me, however, so I stuck with the thought that it was all just energy, and even though I didn't fully understand it, it was all just an expression of the self. One time, fairly near the end of my time with the Daime, I let out a big yawn, and one of the Daimistas warned me that, "You want to cover your mouth when you do that, because that's when entities that you don't want can get in." I think I surprised him when I responded with, "No worries – there's only God here." Really, the more others tried to talk to me about "entities" and "spirits," the more resolute my own energy became that all such notions, and the accompanying experiences, were all just projections of the self, and not fundamentally true in any meaningful sense.

My left arm had been doing its thing during my Daime sessions. I'd sit there with my eyes closed, palms up, with hands gently resting on my lap or thighs, waiting for the energy to start moving. Then, my left arm would lift and start moving, sometimes stopping with my fingers spread out. When it would do so, I would open my eyes and see that my hand was reaching out to someone across the room who was having a particularly big experience, and for whatever reason, if the other person noticed, I would often receive a personal "thank you" at the conclusion of the Work.

The big transition came one day when I was at the Daime for a seated singing Work. I was seated in an outside row, and there was nothing in my mind or energy that informed me that this was going to be a particularly important work for me in any way, so I had no special expectations or projections of what might be in store for me. So, as usual, I just sat there with my arms at my sides, eyes closed, feeling into the medicine coming on. As it turned out, it was a powerful round of medicine and things started to get very visual rather quickly. I sat and watched as the geometric forms and fractals became more distinct, vibrant, and beautiful. Though I've stated that I don't find DMT to be that useful in dissolving and transcending the ego, I do find it beautiful, and always enjoy the visuals that it provides, either in the form of a beverage or a smoked or vaporized extract. As I watched the fractals flow and transform, they suddenly coalesced into this highly angular, infinitely receding fractal face that looked like it stretched from one end of the cosmos to the other. In my vision, the face came right up to me, looking me squarely in the "eye." My internal reaction was, "Whoa – it's the Daime!" as it seemed to be a personification of the medicine itself, and not just some ephemeral vision within the fractal matrix of the visionary medicine.

Internally, the fractal face spoke directly to me. "Don't you want to let me be you?" the Daime asked. My response, again, internally, was the somewhat cavalier, "Sure – why not?"

The moment I made that internal decision indicating my willingness, I was completely taken over by the energy. Now it was not just my left arm that was moving in fluid movements – my entire body was taken over by this bizarre phenomenon. One moment, I was sitting perfectly still in my seat, and the next, my arms and legs were moving about in a unified and undulating wave of pure energy. Everything on the left side of my body was matched in mirror fashion by my right side, with my legs and arms moving in concert with each other, and neither legs nor arms would ever cross the centerline of my body. It was like I was doing some kind of dance, or performing yoga or Tai Chi there in my seat. And to top it all off, it felt great – absolutely wonderful.

I suddenly understood some aspects of what had been happening to me over the previous year with all the vibrating and shaking I'd been doing. I had been undergoing a profound energetic reset that, in some important respects, had increased the energetic carrying capacity of my body. All the vibrating had been leading up to this break-through where my body could now handle the intensity of the energetic waves in a way that would have been simply impossible for it without having undergone all the months of vibrating. It was like a needle that had been scratching across the surface of a record suddenly found the groove, and now the music was playing and the discordant static faded away in an abrupt transition. At this point, there was no distinction between myself, my body, the medicine, and the energy – it was all one coordinated energetic unit and system of expression.

I'm not sure how long I was sitting there, but eventually one of the guardians came up and tapped me on the shoulder, asking if I'd be willing to get up and go to the healing yurt. That proved to be an interesting challenge, for the current of energy was so great that there didn't seem to be any way for me to turn it off or stop my unusual movements. But, I did manage to get up, and through strange and fluid articulations of my limbs, was able to eventually make it to the door and leave the *salao*. Much to my delight, I found the healing yurt to be empty of people with a solitary, unattended chair right in the middle of the room. *Perfect!,* I thought to myself, and maneuvered myself over, sat down, and continued with my strange movements.

I sat there by myself for some time, just flowing with the energy, not really knowing what any of it was about, when eventually another guardian brought in a woman to lie down in the healing yurt with me. When the guardian left, she didn't close the door to the room. It was winter then, and very cold outside with snow everywhere and the wind blowing directly in at me and my chair. Determined to get the door shut and secure my own warmth and comfort, with a concerted effort of will, I stopped the strange, undulating movements and got up to close the door. The very moment I did so I was overcome by an instant and overwhelming nausea. As quickly as I could, I closed the door, grabbed the nearest bucket, and sat back down. I purged a small spoonful of vomit into the bucket, and then set it aside as my body resumed its movements. And with that, the nausea instantly disappeared. Out of the many, many rounds of medicine that I had experienced in my time with the Daime, this was only my second purge, and like the first (on my first visit), it was relatively small and insignificant.

So I was sitting in my chair once again, letting the movements just run their course, but now there was this other woman in the room with me, and she was lying there moaning.

I think that this was probably the first time that I started purring and growling. It wasn't a conscious decision – the energy just felt like I needed to purr and growl, much like a tiger or other large cat. So now I'm moving and growling, and starting to wonder what this woman is thinking of what I'm doing. However, the more I growled and purred, the more relaxed and peaceful her own breathing started becoming, so I decided to just go with it and let it run its course.

In all, I probably spent about 3 hours like this, though I didn't have a watch or anything to really tell time, so it's just a guess. Eventually the energy subsided and I felt that I could just sit there, and then get up to finish off the work back in the main *salao*. After the work was all over, the woman who had been in the healing yurt approached me with a deep sense of gratitude and thanked me profusely for all the help I had provided for her in there. What, specifically, I might have done, I had no idea. It was all just energy, and I was just doing my best to be true to it and express it as I experienced it. That she had found it helpful had not been anything intentional on my part.

That was my first experience of sustained, spontaneous symmetrical movements, and once it was all completed, I realized that the same thing had been happening in my sessions with 5-MeO, only I hadn't been aware of it. In fact, this had been occurring since my very first experience with 5-MeO, though there had been so much hand vibrating going on, I hadn't realized that my entire body was moving in these fluid, symmetrical patterns. It was now becoming clear to me that I had been undergoing this profound experience of opening to energy that, in fact, extended back prior to my first experience of 5-MeO. Suddenly everything was in a new context, and I could understand that this was the same thing I had experienced for years on mushrooms as jittery, vibrating energy. I thought back to my experiences of opening up to throat singing with salvia, and it was the same thing – learning how to let my body genuinely express the energy I was experiencing.

On the one hand, I understood all this as the energy of God, but on the other hand, I was still somewhat confused by it, especially as I had so many "spiritual" people bending my ears with their own theories and explanations. When I had started throat singing with salvia, my friend Sudama had said, "You must have been a Tuvan shaman or a Tibetan monk in a past life." Similarly, at the Daime, people wanted to talk to me about past lives, entities, spirits, and the like – their interpretations of the energy I was experiencing and embodying. Other people wanted to talk to me about communing with the "spirit" of the mushrooms, or the sage, or the Daime. No one seemed to like my take on it – that it was just energy, and that energy was God. Everyone was encouraging me to form a particular identity and sense of self around these energetic phenomena in a way that was always ultimately dualistic and preserved some kind of differentiation between an essential, reincarnating "self" and what was "other," or "astral" or "spiritual."

On their side of the equation was virtually all of the world's religions, spiritualities, and philosophies, and on my side there was my individual conviction that there was only God, and the rest of this was ego-generated illusion and fundamentally incorrect. What made me think that I was correct, and all these other spiritual people incorrect? Well, all I had to fall back on was that their interpretations didn't seem to fit my experience at all, and not even my studies of the great mystics such as Buddha seemed to match up to my experiences, for even the Buddha, this supposedly great awakened master who tried to bring nondualism to the fore, still taught about reincarnation, karma, and the evolution of *individual* consciousness and essential essence (despite his teachings of *anatta/anatman,* or "no self"). Who was I to disagree with Buddha?

Struggling with these ideas, I ended up back at the friend's house who had first introduced me to DMT. He had a new smoking device called "The Machine" that he wanted me to try out, and of course, I was game. So I went over one afternoon and we took turns smoking DMT. When it was my turn, all this strange glossolalia started pouring out of me. It was a constantly shifting flow of energetic babble that seemed to express many different accents and identities. Though I had seen many other people exhibit glossolalia by this time, this was my first personal experience of it – and what was coming out of me was very different than anything I had previously observed with others. Jessalynn spoke in glossolalia virtually every time she took any kind of medicine, just babbling away in her private elf-speak. Hers was pretty much always the same. This was also true of other people I observed exhibiting this phenomenon – though they didn't speak in English, they routinely spoke in the same "language" each time, showing the same accent, cadence, or rhythm, though how this would manifest was different for each individual and no two were alike. Mine, however, sounded like an entire host of different languages and accents, though none of them specifically identifiable. After the first instance of this, Joel was so entertained that he asked me whether I could do it again, and if so, if I wouldn't mind him recording me. I was having fun, so why not? He thus loaded up another big bowl of DMT for me and sure enough, I babbled away for a good ten minutes or so. Later, when Joel emailed me the digital file of the recording, I saw that he had labeled it as "MWB and Company."

Perhaps this was a route to addressing the whole reincarnation issue, I began to ponder. With that in mind, I decided that I would sit with some mushrooms and see if I couldn't get to the bottom of this new phenomenon. Thus a short time after this DMT experience, I gathered up a good pile of mushrooms, wrote down some questions I wanted to address, and ate them by myself, sitting in the living room of the house Jessalynn and I shared together. What I wanted was for the mushrooms to help me answer some questions: do I have a soul, and if so, can you show me its evolution? What ensued was a strange experience, indeed.

When the mushrooms came on, I got the impression that I was sitting in front of myself, like looking into a mirror. As the energy opened up, I just started babbling and gesturing to the projected image of myself, and much like in the session with DMT, all this weird, ever-shifting language started pouring out of me. It went on and on for several hours. Some of the "voices" seemed like they belonged to old people, some young. Some were men. Some were women. Some felt somewhere in-between, like homosexuals or transvestites. Some voices were timid. Others were confident and authoritative. Some were sinister and manipulative. Others felt achingly honest and genuine. Some were happy. Some were sad. Some were filled with pain, and others were ecstatic. Each had its own particular energetic signature, however, and came with a different body posture, different kinds of gestures, and different movements – a complete package of being. And all of them were talking to "me" in the form of an image of myself projected out before me.

What a strange experience!

It didn't, in any way, provide a clear answer on the "reincarnation" question. They *might* be past lives, but really, what felt more genuine to me was that these were the energetic patterns that comprised different senses of self, identity, and ego. They were merely different constructs of different characters that had different sets of identity, and therefore different modes of expression, embodiment, and energetic output. What I seemed to be communicating to myself through this event was that *all* senses of self and identity are just energetic systems of expression and are more similar to someone playing a role in a play or a movie than the expression of some fundamental and enduring self. In other words, these weren't expressions of the history of my "soul" – they were just collections of different costumes, different characters, different ways of being in the world, and none of them were more "me" than who I was right then and there. Having acted in various plays in jr. high and high school, I knew what it was like to take on a character and really "become" that character, losing one's sense of ordinary self in the role, and really, this just felt like me trying on different roles, but there was nothing essential being revealed within it. It was more like how a truly good actor might be almost unrecognizable from one movie to the next, so fully does he pour himself into the identity of his character. To think that these were "past lives" was too much of a stretch, and certainly didn't *feel* right. It felt to me that to latch onto this experience as being revealing of past lives would be to willingly lie to myself – accepting something as true because part of me wanted it to be true.

I was still resisting the fact that there is only God. God is the one actor that plays *all* the parts simultaneously. There is no vast host of souls, migrating from one life to the next on the eternal quest to reunite with the Godhead. There is only God. It's quite simple, really, and is not very difficult to understand. Yet the ego resists this simple truth and clings to its projections and illusions out of a desire to have an essential self that is "me." The ego is relentless, and will do everything within its power to avoid the raw truth that it is merely a character for God to play in and through – nothing more, and nothing less. It's so much more gratifying for the ego to think that its real self is some reincarnated master, or divine avatar, or spirit on a quest for truth, or a soul sent into incarnation by God to learn lessons and grow. The ego will come up with any variety of bullshit stories to avoid the truth, and the world's religions and spiritualities are all outgrowths of this fundamental denial of the ego. For me to accept the truth that I was uncovering within myself would therefore require me to accept that all the spiritual and religious teachings of the world, and all human cultures, and all of the "great masters," were fundamentally incorrect, and all expressions of the ego. In many respects, it would have been easier for me if my own process were matching up with and confirming at least *some* religious or spiritual tradition, but the truth I was having to confront was that it did not. In fact, everywhere I looked, I saw how the ego had corrupted fundamental truth and wrapped it in illusion, projection, and fantasy, and while there were glimpses of the truth, reality was mostly obscured. If I was really going to understand what was happening to me, I'd have to figure it out on my own, for I'd long since passed beyond the point where any of the spiritual teachings of the world felt valid and applicable to my process.

I was on my own.

I didn't know it at the time, but I was about to enter into the final stages of my process of opening to myself, energy, and the infinite nature of being. When everything had started with the appearance of "the voice," something that I had been "told" was that I was to "use the medicines, for now, but there will come a point where you will no longer need them."

Though I was completely unaware of it, that time was fast approaching, and the final, and ultimate, breakthrough was just over the horizon.

I had begun to consider that perhaps what was really happening to me was that I was learning how to fully "be" any medicine that I was consuming. When I took mushrooms, I could fully "be" the energy of the mushrooms. When I took salvia, I could fully "be" salvia. The same held true for Daime, or DMT, or 5-MeO, or anything else. Rather than revealing a unified energetic structure and nature of being, it could be the case that I was revealing a spectrum of different states of being that were discrete from each other. In some respects, this was a last-ditch effort on the part of my ego to deny the reality of the unified and unitary nature of being as revealed by my experiences of being God. Perhaps the God thing was just an interpretation that I was putting on my experiences, and seeing a unity where there was in fact a fundamental diversity. Maybe the truth that I was feeling so overwhelmingly was just another projection, another attempt by the ego to make sense of things. What if I had been somehow fooling myself into seeing a unity where there was only diversity?

My ego liked this idea, and I shared it with Jessalynn one afternoon as we strolled around a local bird sanctuary in the early spring. The appeal was that the responsibility of somehow being God and an embodiment of this one, universal being and consciousness just seemed too overwhelming to me. What could that possibly mean for me, personally? It would be much easier for my ego to accept that I was just tuning into the medicine in a way that most people didn't, and while that preserved some "specialness" for me, it removed the burden of uncovering universal truth and the absolute nature of being. The idea felt like there was far less responsibility and import to it, and it made me feel more comfortable, more able to manage all these strange and unexpected experiences. Maybe I was "normal" after all, and perhaps just gifted, in certain respects. If this interpretation were correct, then it meant that I wasn't heading for some kind of God/man state of being, and that seemed a great deal easier to me.

It was a few days later that this last-ditch effort to maintain some intellectual hold on my experience was shattered in a solo session with salvia. Jessalynn was participating in a workshop over the weekend, so I found myself at home with time to kill and nothing else better to do, so I decided to do some work with salvia. It had been a while since my joint sessions with Jessalynn and salvia, and I was interested to see what would arise on my own, without her presence.

I was still somewhat ritualistic and holding onto symbolic systems at this time, so I set myself up in our spare room with my large frame drum and eagle feather, both of which I had used for many years in conjunction with my meditation practice. I always liked to have my drum on hand when working with salvia, for I never knew when the urge to throat sing would overcome me, and I had found that drumming while throat singing could be a profound and immersive experience. I used the feather as a way to "clear out" my energy, to initiate and conclude either medicine or meditation sessions, often along with some burning sage, incense, or paolo santo wood. The frame drum also had a mandala-like design on it, and I would use the center of the image as a focus for my meditation or medicine work, helping me to stay present and centered. For this particular session, I set up the drum and eagle feather on a chair facing me while I seated myself on our futon, where I could sit comfortably, and also easily reach my salvia pipe and large bag of loose salvia leaves from plants that I had grown.

To begin, I did my cleansing and centering breaths and then crushed up a large salvia leaf and crammed it into the large glass bowl of the pipe. I started smoking it, and could feel the salvia starting to come on, but I was determined to go as deep as I could, so I quickly finished off that bowl and prepared another, internally telling the salvia to just wait for me and not fully launch until I got this next bowl smoked.

I got the next round consumed and then quickly moved to set the pipe down and let the salvia go to work. I started to feel the distinctive tracks of energy that I had been experiencing in my spontaneous symmetrical movements as I was attempting to move my arms to my sides and let my hands rest on my thighs, palms up. For whatever reason, I tried to maneuver my arms "under" the energy, but immediately found that they were caught in the strange symmetrical flow, and both my arms and legs began moving once more in symmetrical, fluid movements that appeared to be completely outside of my individual control or volition.

The instant this occurred, the salvia experience exploded into an experiential state that was completely indistinguishable from 5-MeO-DMT. My rational mind marveled at this development, for the energetic signatures of 5-MeO and salvia are extremely different from each other and not at all interchangeable. Whereas 5-MeO is characterized by infinitely refined high velocity vibrations, salvia is slow, sticky, and viscous. Whereas 5-MeO was like pure, crystal clear living starlight and highly ethereal, salvia was like some secret underground chamber of saltwater taffy. It would be difficult for two medicines to be more distinctly different from each other.

Yet here I was, and here the medicine experience was, and it was exactly like a 5-MeO experience. I was overtaken by the energy and it just flowed and exploded into pure, crystalline light, and my limbs flowed right along with it. But there was still a residual perspective of "Martin" within it, so my ego wasn't completely overwhelmed. Thus, I decided to take the opportunity to converse with the energy and see what kinds of answers I could receive, much like I had in my sessions with Jessalynn, except this time, it was just me.

"Who are you?" I asked as my arms and legs moved in their symmetrical patterns.

"I AM REALITY," came back the answer in the God voice that expressed itself through my body.

Ok, I thought to myself. *Looks like God is here again.*

"What are you doing?"

"SHOWING YOU MY INIFINITE MIND – MY INFINITE BODY."

"Why?"

"BECAUSE I CAN. BECAUSE YOU CAN."

"What am I supposed to do with this?"

There was no direct response – only a floating up of my hands and arms in a slight shrug and gesture that seemed to say, "I don't know – that's up to you. What do *you* think?"

Suddenly my ego came back in with full force as the symmetrical movements stopped and I found myself shaking uncontrollably, struggling to regain my composure. Whatever I had been expecting from my salvia journey, *that* was most definitely not it. Perhaps I had been looking for some confirmation that 5-MeO was 5-MeO, and salvia was salvia, and all the other medicines were their own discrete beasts. Yet the illusion that I had been pondering and finding comforting was shattered in these few minutes of salvia that was indistinguishable from 5-MeO. Whatever I had been experiencing, it definitely transcended any particular medicine or any particular energetic signature or presentation. The lines between medicines had become thoroughly blurred to the extent that they were largely erased, and my comforting theory was thus thrown out the window.

Once the shaking and vibrating subsided, I still felt quite shaken up, so I took a long, soothing shower to calm my nerves, and then took some time outside to relax before going back into the spare room to put away the items from my salvia work. I was feeling better now, and completely free of any of the effects of salvia, which don't tend to last more than 20 minutes, at the longest, and it had been at least an hour or more since the conclusion of my session.

There was nothing unusual as I was putting away the pipe, the salvia, the ashtray, and the drum. Last, I picked up my eagle feather and started walking through the house to replace it where it usually sat in a large crystal we kept in the living room.

I didn't get more than a few paces with the feather in my right hand before the line between tripping and not tripping was suddenly ripped away. At first I thought that there must be some kind of air current in the house, for it kept feeling like the feather was moving in my hand, or coming up against varying degrees of air pressure. It was very unusual, as I had never quite felt anything like this with a feather in my hand before. I'd been collecting feathers since I first got into bird watching as a young man, and had used my eagle feather as part of my meditation and medicine practice for years, but this was unlike anything I'd ever felt before. It was just so distinct, and so very unusual.

Maybe it was due to the way I was holding it, so when it fully had my attention, I established a better grip on the feather and tried walking once again. The impression of moving the feather through currents and tracks of energy became fully distinct at that point and suddenly my whole experience shifted. The best description I could give it would be to liken it to the transition between a normal and a lucid dream, where suddenly you realize that you are dreaming and that things are not as they appear. In this instance, the energy that I had thus far generally only felt to a high degree when working with the medicines was suddenly overtaking me in just the same way as when I was on the medicines, and it felt just like the salvia/5-MeO experience I had undergone earlier that afternoon.

This was unlike the experiences of spontaneous openings that I had undergone with mushrooms when in college, and the spontaneous openings after my first couple of experiences with 5-MeO, for now the energy not only existed within me, flowing through my being, but was also "outside" of me, in the same sense of totality and unity that was characteristic of my bouts of symmetrical body movements. In those early experiences with mushroom "flashbacks," I always had felt out of control. With those spontaneous 5-MeO experiences, I had felt very "out there" in a beyond-the-body kind of state, and they usually occurred with my eyes closed as I sat in meditation. Here, however, I was fully present, fully awake, and rather than feeling out of control or out of my body, I was fully in my body, completely present, and flowing in perfect synch with the energy of the universe. This was a completely different kind of experience, and far more intense than any spontaneous experience that had yet unfolded for me, for I was perfectly present within the experience and able to function in the world. This was something radically new, and thoroughly unexpected.

Once I got over the initial shock, I was amazed. How was this possible? I started dancing around the house, waving the feather around, chasing these different tracks and bands of energy. I even tried closing my eyes and dancing around, and found, much to my surprise, I wouldn't run into anything. In fact, there seemed to be a slightly repellant surface of energy around everything, so try as hard as I might, I couldn't actually get the feather to touch anything – furniture, walls, objects about the house. It was bizarre, and fun. Not only had the lines between medicines been obliterated, but the line between tripping and not tripping was now being obliterated as well. I cannot put into words how uniquely uncanny this was.

All the while that this was going on, the question that kept coming to mind was "whose energy is this?" After dancing around a bit with the feather, I eventually decided to ask the question out loud and see what would happen. I kept the feather moving in slow, looping, figure eight or infinity symbol movements, and asked my question. Almost startling me into dropping the feather, there was a distinct pull on the feather, like an energetic vortex had just opened up, and the feather was now swirling in circles in my hand as my hand brought it to the center of my chest. Flabbergasted, I asked again, "Whose energy is this?" Once more, the feather started swirling about my heart. The answer seemed clear – this was *my* energy. The same energy that I had been experiencing as God while in medicine states was now clearly being identified as "me" and "mine." This was just too crazy!

But, who was I to argue?

At this point, I started talking to the feather and the energy, as it seemed to respond to my inquiries. I quickly found that the best route was to ask "yes" or "no" questions. If the answer was yes, the feather would float up. If the answer was no, it would float down.

Fantastic, I thought to myself somewhat sarcastically. *Now I can talk to God/myself with a feather.*

For the next couple weeks, the feather was the thing. I spent hours every day waving the feather back and forth, chasing energy around the house, and sometimes even following it outside. There was also a strange sense of energy in my body for these weeks, where I might be lying in bed and there would be the sensation of bubbles moving through my muscles, just beneath the surface of my body. I could hardly sleep at all, and on many nights I found that I simply had to get up and go work the feather for a few hours in the middle of the night, often between 2 and 3 am. One night, the feather even led me outside to go stand on top of a large boulder in an open green space behind our house and do my feather exercises out there. With every passing day, the line between tripping and not tripping was getting evermore indistinct and blurry.

In one of my sessions of bouncing about the house with the feather, I had the opportunity to experience a little bit of God's sense of humor, and I'll relate that story here, not because it was of any particular significance, but because it was funny – at least for me. The feather was sending me all about the house, doing different things as I would ask it questions, and one day, I asked it what I should do with some *Amanita* mushrooms that Devon and Kat had collected in the woods outside Eugene and given to me as a gift. The feather indicated to me that I should put the jar in which they were kept up high on a bookshelf in our living room, which I promptly did. Then, a few days later, I asked the feather again what I should do with them. The feather led me over to the jar, and then walked me to the sink, and from there, to the garbage can in our kitchen. "You want me to rinse off the mushrooms and put them in the garbage?" Yes. "Do I need to take the garbage out?" No.

I did as instructed, rinsing off the mushrooms and putting them in the garbage. I then picked up the feather and it immediately brushed the top of the garbage can and then indicated that I take it out the back door, which would mean taking the garbage out. "But you said I didn't need to take the garbage out!" I retorted defiantly. With that, the feather went up to a nearby water dispenser and gently brushed at the glass, underlining a removable sticker that Jessalynn had apparently put on the water that I had not consciously been aware of. The word that the feather was underlining was "humor." Apparently, the command that I take the garbage out was a joke.

A couple weeks after this strange phenomenon began with the feather, I decided to sit down with the feather and try and get to the bottom of just what in the world was happening here. Jessalynn was gone again for a workshop, so I had our home to myself. Once more, I set myself up in the spare room, kneeling on the floor with my feather. I began by waving it in front of me as I had been doing, and started asking it questions, but prefaced it with a touch of insolence, saying, "Now if you want to talk to me, you've got to do it in a language I can understand!" In response, the feather floated up, indicating "yes."

"OK," I began. "Who are you?"

The feather floated up and made large infinity symbols in the air.

"You're God?"

The feather indicated "yes."

"So what do you want from me?"

With asking this question, a game of charades thus began. The feather floated down and started brushing against the carpet. I then started guessing all kinds of things that the feather might be indicating, starting with the obvious, but nonsensical, answer of "carpet." I also tried floor, house, ground, earth, and anything else I could think of that the feather might be trying to draw my attention to. Every time, the answer came back "no." I was beginning to get frustrated with the whole thing and eventually said, "OK – let's start over!"

The feather went back up and made the large infinity loops. OK. This much was clear. "You're God." "Yes." "OK – next." The feather then went down again, but this time, letting myself relax and stay focused a little more, the feather brushed my knees and thighs rather than the floor directly in front of me. "Me?" I asked.

Yes.

Next, the feather swirled in a circle in my hand as I was guided to hold it in front of my genitals. Strange, but, OK. From there, it went up to my heart and swirled there. Next, it went up, and swirled about the top of my head.

I thought I got the message.

"You – God – want to come through my body?" I asked.

Yes.

I set the feather down. "OK," I said. "I'm ready."

In saying that, suddenly a profound and overwhelming "YES!" exploded in my heart and I instantly felt as though I had just smoked a large dose of 5-MeO. Everything exploded and expanded into fractal light and geometric forms, completely overwhelming my "normal" sense of self. I started saying "yes" out loud, and as I did, my voice became deeper and fuller with each yes, my heart and body reaching out to embrace all of reality in total, absolute love and acceptance. My body also immediately opened up symmetrically, my hands reaching out before me as the "yes" transformed into a thundering, "I AM HERE!"

A discourse then began with such statements as, "Thank you, Martin, for I live through you," and "I thank all of you, for I am your life, and my home is the center of your heart. Do not look for me anywhere except in the center, for that is where I AM." These statements were all accompanied by involuntary symmetrical movements of my body, eventually putting me through various kinds of symmetrical yoga-like poses with different patterns of breathing. It was all very trippy, but the energy eventually subsided and things returned back to normal and I was "Martin" once again.

Still not knowing what in the world I was supposed to do with this newfound ability, I asked for guidance. The feather immediately responded and pulled me to a closet with some of my clothes in it. Fumbling around with the feather, it seemed to want me to put certain items of clothing on, the feather answering "yes" and "no" as I sorted through my wardrobe. Eventually, it had me fully dressed in shirt, sweater, pants, poncho, and hat. Totally and completely absurd!

Not having a clue what all this was about, I dressed myself and then asked the feather what I was supposed to do next. Immediately, the feather pulled me out of that room and guided me into another room where there was more space, and once I was centered in the room, this complex and lengthy process of making repeating patterns in the air with the feather started for the first time. As soon as this began, the whole experience suddenly shifted into high gear, feeling as though I had just taken a fresh, and large, hit of 5-MeO, with everything becoming intricately fractaled in my visual perception and the energy just pumping through me.

The feather started going to work by tracing out these complex patterns, first starting up high, above my head, and eventually reaching all the way down to the ground. In a manner that was reminiscent of my time at Mescalero, all these complex patterns seemed to be oriented to the four directions and the intercardinals, but unlike with ritual movement at Mescalero, this was all proceeding in patterns that were alternating between opposite directions, sometimes moving clockwise, sometimes counterclockwise (movements at Mescalero were always clockwise and each direction was addressed in turn, never moving back and forth or switching up directions). There were also clearly different "zones" of activity, with the feather completing a full circuit in each zone from top to bottom – there seemed to be three "zones" in all.

It was all I could do to keep up with the feather and the energy, and it had me spinning around as the feather, through my arm, would whip me into one position after another. At first, I had no idea what was going on, or what direction it would have me face with each new set of movements, but once I understood that I was working through distinct patterns that would repeat themselves once the cycle was completed for each position, I began to be able to anticipate where I would be directed next, though I always waited for the feather/energy to make it clear and let it guide me.

This strange activity persisted for a couple hours, lasting until Jessalynn eventually arrived back home, her workshop concluded for the day. She found me in the back of the house in this ridiculous outfit, wondering just what in the world was going on. With great enthusiasm, I explained to her what had taken place that day and made some demonstrations with the feather. Neither of us knew just what to make of it.

As I was going through all of this, and doing these directional patterns of feather movements, my ego always wondered just what it was I was doing, and what I was accomplishing. According to my ego, I must be doing *some* kind of work for God, and these movements and actions must be related to some kind of collective clearing of energy, or pushing some kind of awakening or something. However, this wasn't at all the case with what was going on, and it was far more personal than anything else. Essentially, I was going through a final training and energetic entrainment, which would allow me to embody my energy fully, and it had no more significance than that. This was all about me, and my ability, and willingness, to simply be who and what I was with no filter, no censorship, and most importantly, no ego-generated energetic structures in the way of my authentic energy. I was rapidly approaching the point where I would be ready to simply be myself.

During this time period, I also found that boundaries were becoming blurry even when I was out in public. Jessalynn and I were regular attendees at the local hot springs, Jackson Wellsprings, and while all this was going on with the feather, I found that it was also happening when I was out at the Wellsprings. Much like going for a round of medicine, my standard practice of relaxing in the hot water was to sit, let my arms rest at my sides, and close my eyes and let my troubles melt away in the warm waters. However, now, whenever I would attempt to do so, the fluid symmetrical movements would start up on their own. The first time this happened, it really freaked me out, as I did not appear to have any control over the movements of my body. The energy had me swishing around through the water in ways I couldn't predict or control, sometimes having me glide right up to people. All the boundaries between tripping and not tripping were just being washed away, and it was becoming more and more common for me to slip into these states. Basically, the energetic structures that had held me together as "Martin" were becoming so weak and permeable that the energy of my true nature was leaking out at any opportunity – regardless of what "Martin" thought or wanted.

Everything culminated on a Friday night in the early spring of 2009. Still in the habit of asking questions of the feather, I had asked it what I should do next. For the first time,

I had a small supply of 5-MeO that Hal had given to me for an acquaintance to test in his lab for purity. Hal had run out of his previous supply and had found a new source, but wanted the medicine tested before using it in his ceremonies. Thus the white crystalline powder had made its way into a laboratory through me, and after it was tested, it had been returned. Much to my surprise, Hal had told me that I could keep it for myself, so I had it stashed away in a small vial in a bag in which I kept my various medicines.

When I asked the feather what I was to do next, it drew me over to the drawer in the dresser where I kept my medicine bag. Following its lead, I opened up the drawer and pulled out the bag. Then, still following the gestures it was making, I removed the various medicines I had in the bag and laid them out, evenly spaced on the floor. I waved the feather again and this time it went directly to the vial of 5-MeO. "I need to take this?" I asked. "Yes," the feather answered. There was enough for a couple doses in there. "How much?" It just tapped the vial. "All of it?" "Yes."

Oh shit.

"What's going to happen when I do that?"

The feather shot up into the air, making large infinity loops that spiraled upward, as far as I could reach.

"I'll become infinite?" I asked, not even knowing what that would mean.

"Yes."

Oh fuck.

My mind and ego raced through what this could mean. My fear was that I would take all this 5-MeO, overdose, die, and thereby become "infinite." I seriously considered the possibility that this would result in my very real death. I had long since passed the point of no return, however. Metaphorically speaking, I felt as though I'd been climbing this monumental mountain and was finally within reach of the summit, yet terrified of actually reaching it. Going back down was no longer an option. The energy had been breaking through more and more. It seemed far too late to attempt turning back, or turning this process off, and the only way to go was forward. That *this* – taking a large amount of 5-MeO – a possibly lethal dose – was the way forward terrified me, and I really thought that it was to be my end and undoing. And Jessalynn felt the same way when I told her what I was "supposed" to do. Her immediate reaction was that such a large dose was going to kill me, and while she fully supported me in my process, she didn't want to lose me, and this seemed like a surefire way to do that. However, it also seemed to promise an end to my wondering and personal confusion. If this really were *it,* even if I died, at least then I'd know. The promise of completing whatever it really was that I had been going through for over the past year now was too appealing for me to deny. Whatever it might mean for me to become "infinite," I was ready for it, even if that meant I was about to die.

In some important respects, that's precisely what happened. But in even more important respects, that's not what happened at all.

Chapter Nine

God, with no Remainder

We are now approaching the conclusion of the "becoming" part of my tale. This was almost exactly five years ago, at the point of my writing this, so it isn't the end of my story, by any means, but it is the end of my process of awakening, transformation, and becoming my true self. As such, it will serve as the grand finale of this particular book. Perhaps at some point I'll write another book detailing what came after, for in many ways, this is only the beginning of the real story that I have to tell, and everything presented in these pages is merely a prelude and preliminary tale. That, however, would prove to be another lengthy narrative, and one that ultimately deserves its own treatment and attention. Thus, I will conclude this portion of my story with my final transformation, followed by an epilogue to wrap up a few significant remaining threads of the story.

Once the message from the feather was clear, there really was no point in beating around the bush. I was either going to do this, or I wasn't, and not doing it wasn't an option, so I might as well get this "becoming infinite" thing over with, even if it meant my death. Jessalynn was very much against proceeding, but there wasn't anything she could do to stop me, so she did her best to support me and not let her own fear get in the way.

Before taking the 5-MeO, I wanted to adequately prepare the space for me to do it in. I chose our bedroom as the place, and thus proceeded to use my feather to do one of my little directional dances on the bed, sweeping out various patterns of infinity loops with my feather – not an easy task on Jessalynn's ultra-plush mattress, but I managed. For the actual taking of the medicine, I got out an old vaporizer of mine and set it up next to the bed. Hands shaking, I started scooping the 5-MeO into the bowl of the vaporizer. After putting in about half of what was there, an already large dose, I checked in with the feather. It brushed both the small vial and then the bowl, seeming to indicate that I needed to put more on. I did, basically emptying out the vial. This proved to be too much for Jessalynn and she protested strongly. My hands really shaking now, I removed a small bit of the medicine and replaced it back in the vial. There was still a significant dose in the bowl, even with taking some back out.

It was time.

I plugged the vaporizer in and it slowly heated up, first melting the medicine, and then turning it into curling wafts of 5-MeO vapor, floating in the glass dome of the vaporizer. Once the dome was completely filled with the white vapor, there was nothing left for me to do but inhale. Hoping for the best, not knowing what was going to come next, I put the tube from the vaporizer to my lips, and promptly inhaled everything that was in the chamber.

In some ways, what happened next was a bit anti-climatic, according to the fearful and anticipatory projections of my ego. I had imagined some ultimate transformation, a profound revelation, a shattering of reality and complete obliteration of my self, and as I've stated, perhaps even death. Nothing of the sort happened. Instead, it was all quite simple. As the overwhelming power of the medicine unfolded, I was faced with a very simple choice: either I could continue to pretend that I didn't understand who and what I was, or I could be honest with myself, accept my true nature, and simply be myself. That was it. Nothing more, nothing less. I could either accept the fact that I truly was God, or I could continue to hold onto my belief that I was "Martin," and maybe I was crazy, or deluded, or even interacting with God, but that God wasn't actually me. In sum, this was the moment of truth. Either I would honestly accept reality, or I would live in denial and self-delusion. If I wanted, I could have chosen to continue to hold onto my ego, my sense of separate self, my illusions, my struggle, my disbelief, my confusion. Or, I could just accept that all this was true, and get on with it.

So, I decided to choose reality.

And that was that.

Joking, as though some duality still existed between "Martin" and "God," I ironically said, now in the full God voice, "You and I both know that it's going to take a lot more than that!" And with that said, I completely, and irrevocably, gave myself over to the raw, infinite energy of being.

That's the exact moment that I stopped pretending to be "Martin," and simply became myself.

I was free. I was completely liberated. I had permanently broken free of the illusory prison of the ego that thought of itself as "Martin." I was no longer locked into his sense of being and identity with all of his fears, limitations, questions, doubts, and all the rest. I was myself. I was here. I was free. I was energy. I was reality. I was fully and completely the nature of that which is.

In a burst of energy, I started rolling about on the bed, completely ecstatic. As I rolled about, I just laughed and laughed. It was such a joy to be free, and to be *here*. I'd finally done it. I'd come into myself in a way that had never before been accomplished. For the first time ever, I was fully myself. What joy! What freedom!

Mockingly, I spoke to my joy, taking on different voices and playing different characters. "Oh God, why hast thou forsaken me!" I lamented. "Why did you do this to me, God?" "Why must I suffer so?" It was all a big joke – just whiny egos that didn't understand that *they* were God. Praising God, blaming God, thanking God, praying to God, worshiping God, trying to please God, denying God – all of it was a game, a game of the confused ego that didn't know itself and its true nature. I acted out all of this like I was in some melodrama, just reveling in the sheer joy of being.

It was with some relief, mixed with wonder and confusion, that Jessalynn observed all of this. Clearly, I hadn't physically died, but just what had happened?

The answer started to become apparent when my "God state" and "God voice" refused to turn things back over to "Martin." Though the actual dose of 5-MeO eventually ran itself out (effects generally last under 40 minutes), unlike every other time I'd taken the medicine, I didn't return to being "Martin." In fact, by all appearances, "Martin" was simply gone, and someone, or something, else was there in his place.

From my personal perspective, it was like I never stopped tripping 5-MeO. The full 5-MeO state was now the new "normal" and baseline for my ordinary experience. At the practical level, what that meant was that I no longer looked, acted, or sounded like the individual known as "Martin." My voice was now far deeper, far more resonant than "Martin's" voice, and somewhat oddly, I almost never spoke in contractions with the full God voice. My speaking cadence, rhythm, and inflections were entirely different as well – generally more formal and authoritative. Physically, I no longer held or used my body as "Martin" did. Now, I mostly used my body symmetrically and as a total unit where I would flow from one position or gesture to another. Visually, things were very trippy – all fractals and endless geometric forms. Energetically, I was bursting with energy and overflowing with it.

From an energetic perspective, what had happened was that I had finally freed myself from the persistent energetic constructs of the ego. I've taken to describing the ego not as a thing, but as a collection of dualistic energetic patterns that serve to reinforce the internal and external distinction between what is taken as "self" and "not self," or "other," and largely govern how one allows oneself to express one's naturally arising energy. These energetic patterns influence the way one thinks, how one acts, gestures, one's tone of voice, body postures, belief structures, attitudes, and generally everything that we think of as "the self." Collectively, these patterns create the character of the ego. There is nothing essential beneath these dualistic patterns, other than one's natural energy. There is no fundamental individual or personal self that exists independently of these structures.

These structures of the ego start developing in humans at a very young age as a child starts to distinguish his or herself from the other people, beings, and objects of his or her experience. As the child absorbs information from the environment and the role models available there, the child begins to create an internal image of him or herself as a unique individual, and these choices structure how the child chooses to behave, think, believe, and act. Through adolescence and adulthood, individuals continually reformat their egos to cope with new situations and new social contexts, but most of the more fundamental constructs are formed in childhood.

Entheogens are effective tools for deconstructing the ego primarily because they operate at an immediate energetic level. Where the constructs of the ego are out of alignment with one's natural energy – which is freely expressive, loving, trusting, playful, and dynamic without censorship, editing, or contrivance – the blockages and distortions are brought to the surface by the energetic action and expansion that is made available by entheogens. This is why people experience themselves purging, or feeling their intellectual constructs, or belief structures, being challenged and broken apart by entheogens. However, it takes really strong entheogens to truly break free of the persistent gravity well that is the ego and its hold on the individual. Whenever an individual remains in the dualistic perspective of the ego, visions and dualistic content arise within the entheogenic experience. When the energetic influx is sufficient, such as with 5-MeO-DMT, the individual has an opportunity to completely dissolve the constructs of the ego and enter into a nondual, unitary state of being and awareness. When this happens, one's natural energy is able to express itself without the limiting confines of the ego. This is the very definition of liberation, though in most instances, it is a transient phenomenon.

The difficulty is that the ego is so tenacious and habituated to exerting itself that it manages to regain its foothold as soon as the energetic expansion of the entheogen begins to wane, and the individual suddenly finds him or herself "back" in the normal perspective and structures of the ego.

In my case, I reached a point of surrender and openness that was so grounded in my acceptance of truth that my ego no longer retained its perpetual hold on me. I had freed myself from the energetic prison that I had created for myself. Now, instead of mistaking the ego *for myself*, I could appreciate it as simply *part of myself*, much like any other aspect of being, such as my hands, my heartbeat, my thoughts, etc. This was predicated on my willingness to simply be myself as my energy was naturally arising, without any form of ego-based censorship or editing (which are activities that the ego is perpetually engaged in). Being in one's ego is ultimately a matter of choice, as is existing outside the comforting and familiar structures of the ego. The sense of self generated by the ego is something that one commits to through choice – a willful self-deception. However, choosing to not create a self-image through the ego requires a deep level of trust, commitment to truth, and a desire to be authentic and genuine with one's energy. It is not an intellectual or spiritual issue – it is an energetic one. Personally, my process of self-liberation, enlightenment, and transformation culminated when I chose to live in truth and reality, choosing to trust my energy completely and without reservation. It also meant that I was willing to always be true to the energy that I felt and experienced, without filtering it through the mind or my beliefs and ideas of what I *should* be or *should* express. I was willing, at the deepest level, to simply be myself as I am.

The reality of myself that I uncovered was that I was a being of energy. Energy arises as emotions, thoughts, gestures, tone of voice, beliefs, habits, means of expression, and everything else that comprises the human experience of being. Everything that exists in nature, aside from humans with their carefully constructed egos and sense of self, manages this feat of being true to its natural energy effortlessly. It is because humans are self-aware that they are able to ask themselves such questions as: who am I? What am I? Where did I come from?

How should I act? Who should I be? It is the ego that invents and constructs answers to these questions, and how one chooses to identify with such answers limits and structures how any individual will allow or censor one's natural energy.

In accepting that I was merely an embodiment of the one universal being that is everything, where there is no real distinction between self and other, I was able to allow myself to trust my own natural energy and simply be. The result was that I was then free to just be as I was, without any artificial constructs getting in the way of my experience or my expression. Practically, what that meant was that I stopped pretending to be "Martin" and just behaved as myself – a bio vehicle that was an expression of universal energies and unitary being.

This was also the point at which I was truly able to love all equally without any exception, as I had originally instructed myself. At the practical level, this means that I was fully free to love and appreciate everything as the expression of one universal self. There was no need to reject anything. No need to push anything away. I could love and appreciate everything for what it was. However, this did not mean that I needed to *personally like* everything. It also didn't mean that I needed to be some "selfless" do-gooder, always attempting to put "others" first. Genuine universal love is nothing like what spiritually-minded people contrive it to be. First and foremost, it means commitment to living in the reality that all is one. It means commitment to living in truth as opposed to illusion. And because the ego is generally committed to illusion, projection, and belief systems, it means that living in universal love creates challenges for egos, as universal love is not about playing along with illusions and distortions. In fact, it means directly challenging those who are living in illusion, for love desires truth and reality – and really, when speaking at this level, love, truth, reality, and energy are all synonyms.

At the practical level, what this translated into was the fact that whenever I was personally confronted by the illusions and distortions of people's egos, I would respond energetically in a way that was not limited by my ego or my personal desire to create a specific image of myself through my interactions, expressions, or behaviors. My only commitment was to keeping things real and genuine, and if that meant making other people's egos feel uncomfortable and challenged, then so be it. After all, God is embodied in each individual, and other egos are just characters, and each individual embodiment is fully responsible for him or herself as a direct expression of God. The challenge each and every one of us faces is to be genuine and true to what we *actually* feel as energetic beings. I am not responsible for other people in this body. I'm responsible for myself, as is true for everyone else. Living in reality means being personally responsible. What other people make of that is *their* issue.

As might be guessed, this wasn't necessarily the easiest thing for Jessalynn to absorb, for the man she had fallen in love with now appeared to simply be gone. This was certainly "Martin's" body, but that wasn't "Martin" in there, and whoever this new guy was, he was very, very, very intense. And he absolutely refused to play along with any ego games whatsoever. The longer I persisted in this state, the more difficult things became for Jessalynn, even though she was excited by it, as well.

After several hours of exploring my new freedom and sense of being, it was time to go to sleep. When I lay down and closed my eyes, I feared that sleep might not ever be the same for me again. There were just so many visions flying through my inner sight that I couldn't keep track of them – exploding fractal geometries, scenes, vistas, people, places, all a confusing maelstrom of images and impressions. It was like I was seeing *everything* all at once. What was worse, however, was the auditory content – thousands and thousands of voices – so many that I couldn't pick anything distinct out of the cacophony of sounds that seemed to be coming at me from every direction simultaneously. But out of that mix, I suddenly heard Jessalynn's voice, almost as though I were listening in on her dreaming – and she seemed to be having an erotic dream about me, for I could distinctly hear her say, in her sexiest voice, "Yes – take my shirt off."

At that, I was overcome with the overwhelming need to suddenly make love to Jessalynn. She was sleeping, and I wasn't sure what to do about it, but as I lay there, it was like a super powerful magnet was pulling me on top of her. Out of a residual sense of politeness, I tried to resist, but as I did, all my muscles started cramping and spasming wildly. It was all I could do to get on top of her and inside her. Fortunately, her body was ready for me, and when she awoke, she gave herself to the experience completely, with no resistance. After we finished, I was finally able to go to sleep, after lying in bed for some time with my eyes closed, staring up into the stars that were clearly visible behind my eyelids.

When we woke up the next morning, as soon as I spoke, I knew that I was still myself (not "Martin") by the sound of my voice. Energetically, I was still on hyper-charge as well, and though the energy ebbed and flowed somewhat, it still felt as though I were tripping 5-MeO. Again that night, trying to sleep, I was assaulted by visions and voices, endless fractals and geometry, but a little less than the night before. Also, during the day, I kept seeing all these white infinity symbols everywhere, especially when I looked Jessalynn directly in the eye. I could see these fractaled layers of infinity loops that criss-crossed over her face, and her heart, and other parts of her body as well. I could see them when I waved my feather about as well. Really, they were everywhere.

Sunday came and we went to ecstatic dance in the morning. There I saw my friend Natasha who had given me the MDMA that had initiated the first manifestation of "the voice." She came right up to me and said that she had been seeing these white infinity loops everywhere since Friday night. "That is God," I told her in my deep, resonant voice.

Monday came around, and the energy of my experience showed no signs of letting up. For the first time since Friday night, I started to question what this would mean for me professionally. There was one week left to the term before finals, and this week I had to give final lectures in my classes at the university, and today, Monday, I needed to go to work. As I made my way to the university, I made peace with the idea that I was going to go in there, start booming at my students in my God voice, and probably end up getting fired. All weekend long I hadn't even moved like Martin, always using my body in this strange, angular, geometric way. Surely my students would think that I'd completely lost my mind, was on drugs, or something. There just didn't seem any way that I'd come out of this day of teaching without major consequences.

As it turned out, I was completely wrong.

When I got to campus and I was making my way into the classroom to give one of my wrap-up lectures for my world religions course, I was greeted by a student. I greeted the student back, and much to my amazement, I once more sounded like "Martin," only with a slightly deeper, richer tone of voice than was normal for Martin. Then, when I started lecturing, it was still the Martin voice, with occasional dips into the God voice when the lecture got closer to questions of truth and reality, but then going back up when things got more mundane. Overall, I gave the entire lecture as Martin, and nothing came of my fears.

When I got home, Jessalynn asked me how it went. "It was quite fascinating," I answered, now once more fully back in the God voice. It was then that I learned that I could fully and completely trust my energy, and that if I needed to play "Martin," my energy would naturally go into that state in order to facilitate social interaction. However, whenever it wasn't necessary or expedient for me to be "Martin," then I would simply be myself.

What I found over the coming weeks and months was that my energy was always responsive to the situation I was in, or the kind of conversation I might be having with someone. Now, my default energetic position was full Godness, but that could shift in a split second into "Martin," as need be. Similarly, if I were playing "Martin," but was suddenly confronted by something that needed addressing in reality, I would instantly shift into the God voice and energy. It was a bit bizarre, as I could flip my energy at the drop of a hat, easily toggling between these two very different energetic signatures and ways of being in the world.

This is still a normal, everyday feature of my experience now, almost five years later. In those early months it was more intense, however, for I needed to explore my freedom and my newly emancipated sense of self and being.

One of the ways that I like to describe the ego is that it is like an outfit or a uniform that people wear to create an identity for themselves, but in the process, most people confuse their outfit with their actual identity. In opening fully to myself, I was like a little child who develops the ability to take his clothes off – something most children will do, once they are able. Children, in general, don't like wearing clothing, and as soon as they are able, often choose to take their clothes off and run around naked. Energetically, this was what I was doing. Whenever there was no need for me to give the appearance of being Martin, I'd get energetically naked and slough off my ego and just be myself. If, for whatever reason, it would be easier for others in my presence to interact with Martin and not me as I really am, I'd put on the Martin suit, but only temporarily, for as soon as I no longer needed the Martin suit, I'd take it off. Basically, whenever I was home, my preference was to run around naked like an excited child.

My energy was running on overdrive for the first few months after my turning point on that Friday night. For the first couple weeks, I thought that I might never really sleep again, as every night was just fractals, energy, and visions, but that eventually calmed down, and a more regular sleeping pattern re-emerged. And then after a few months, I found that I was using the "Martin" voice more and more often, even when at home, unless somehow challenged or confronted by Jessalynn and her ego, at which point, the God energy would come on full and fast, but it would then dissipate as soon as Jessalynn took responsibility for herself and the confused projections of her ego.

I also continued to use the feather in the first few months after my liberating transformation. I started doing "feathering" sessions with clients, and found that clients would quickly fall into deeply expansive energetic states when I feathered them – often claiming to have experienced themselves as tripping really hard. I also felt compelled to provide myself with feathering sessions. To do so, I would lay out a yoga mat on the floor, and proceed to feather off the mat the same way I would feather a client – focusing on the main energy centers of the central line of the body of genitals, stomach, heart, throat, and head. After feathering the mat for 20-30 minutes, I would then lie down. When I did so, I would enter into states that were very similar to my sessions with Daime, lying in the healing yurt, and I could distinctly feel energy working itself out along the centerline of my body and going through distinct cycles.

It was also at this time that I found that I could do these symmetrical exercises on my back, lifting myself into a legs-in-the-air position, resting only on a point at the top of my spine and back of my head. Physically, I found that I was able to balance myself like this in a way that has been impossible for anyone else I've ever observed or encountered – well-practiced yogis included. I've had several yoga teachers marvel at what I'm able to do, not understanding how it is physically possible for me to balance on my spine the way I can – something I just attribute to the fact that my energy is perfectly clear and open. Whenever I did these exercises, I'd start tripping pretty hard and it would also make my voice deepen. Thinking that others could benefit from these exercises, and perhaps help them get in touch with their genuine energy, I started sharing it with others as "fractal energetic yoga," and even uploaded a video of myself doing it for Youtube. Thus far, while I've seen plenty of people do this spontaneously while fully absorbed in a medicine experience, I've yet to encounter anyone who can do it as freely and fully as myself. In general, if someone spontaneously starts doing this while absorbed with medicine (something I've taken to calling "going all the way into the fractal"), they are usually unaware of what they are doing and are not able to replicate it when not under the influence – and even when doing so, they are not able to get up balanced on their spine like myself.

Not long after my final transformation, I had the opportunity to attend a Daime work, and though I no longer felt any need to go, I decided that I would attend, just to see what would happen. Admittedly, there was still some lingering pull of my ego here. I had developed great relationships with the people at the Daime church, and not long before this, I had been given a full set of hymnals (*hinarios*). Also, because I was relatively poor and was not able to make financial contributions to the church, I was often the first one there, and one of the last to leave, for any Work that I attended. I'd show up early and mop the floor of the *salao* on my hands and knees. I'd set up the tables, chairs, and candles. I'd sweep out the healing yurt, and roll up the windows. I'd place the purging buckets and cleaning towels. And when everything was done, I'd stay for another hour to clean everything up and put everything away. Basically, I did everything I could for the church to make up for the fact that I didn't have the funds to contribute to the church's operation or travel costs of bringing the medicine up from Brazil, and I had become attached to the service I was giving.

So I had become something of a regular and enthusiastic attendee at the church, and the thought of abruptly discontinuing my visits was hard to take, knowing that others would wonder what became of me, and why. I valued my relationships with the people in the church, and thus felt drawn to continue my association, even if I didn't feel that there was really any reason for me to attend any longer. After all, once you accept the fact that you are God, what in the world is the point of going to a church or attending any ceremony or ritual? It all seems as bit absurd, and narcissistic. Praying to oneself is just the pinnacle of ridiculousness.

But I went anyway. Energetically, it became clear to me that I had two options once the energy of the Work got going. With everyone facing the center of the room and concentrating their energy and prayers there, I felt strongly drawn to the center. What I wanted to do was go stand directly in the middle of the room. However, I also knew that doing so would be profoundly disruptive, and that no one would understand what I was doing or why. I could have gone outside, as was usual for me, and throat sing out in the forest, but unlike in my previous times at the church, there wasn't any energetic need for me to go outside and vibrate and throat sing, so I didn't want to do that. I wasn't there to try and entertain myself. The other option, which I ended up going for, was to just lie down and go to sleep. Not really caring what anyone would think, that's just what I did – I went off to the side, lay down, and slept for a while. When they were serving more

Daime, I immediately woke up, drank more, and then went back to sleep. This happened one more time, and I did the same. When the work ended, I cleaned up my things, helped to put chairs and other items away, and never went back. That was my last visit to the Daime, whose usefulness for me had run its course.

I also tried the same with one more visit out to the Native American Church in Williams. I went to basically see if there was any reason for me to be there, and there wasn't. All that I found in that visit was that the "rules" people create and attempt to enforce in ceremonial contexts really rub me the wrong way. In this case, I took my shoes off to sit more comfortably, and when a woman told me to put my shoes back on because being barefoot was "disrespectful" to the medicine, it was too much for me to take. Way too many illusory bullshit games going on there.

I went to one more session with T.O.A.D., and my impression was the same – nothing for me to do there.

Lastly, I went to one more ayahuasca ceremony, just to see, and it was the same. It was perfectly clear: I was done. There was no longer any need for me to go and sit with people in a ceremonial context and take medicine. There was nothing left for me to personally "work" on – I had discovered myself, and learned how to be myself fully. There was no more mystery, no more demanding work to go through, no more needing to clear out my system energetically – nothing. I was simply done. I was as liberated and enlightened as was possible for someone to become, and I was just done with the whole thing of trying to be a "spiritual" person in any way. It was all a game of the ego, and it had completely and utterly lost its appeal to me.

So that's when I stopped trying to be spiritual in any way. I stopped going to any kind of ceremonies, and also found that I had a strong dislike for even minor ritual events, like being asked to hold hands and chant "Om" at ecstatic dance. All ritual, religion, and spirituality just reeked of the ego – was saturated with it, through and through. It was all self-delusional activity, and I wanted absolutely nothing to do with it, personally. Anyone who is committed to ritual is operating from the ego, and all rituals work to reinforce various egoic structures and tendencies. For me to play along would be dishonest and disingenuous for me, so really, all I could do was stay away. If I wanted to go to ecstatic dance, I had to plan my arrival for sometime after the handholding, eye gazing, chanting, and guided visualizations. Really, I found it increasingly difficult to attend any kind of event in Ashland, as the place is overrun with spiritual types, self-proclaimed shamans, priests and priestesses, and all manner of overly-sincere and serious spiritual seekers, guides, and facilitators – ego, ego, ego! It's the same mentality that has overrun many of the west coast festivals as well. It's almost impossible to go to a festival and *just dance and listen to music and see art.* Every festival wants to be "transformative," and "new paradigm," and wants to have "sacred encounters," and "indigenous ritual," and "group prayers," and "ceremony." Yargh! Personally, I'd love it if people would just (en)lighten up and stop taking all their illusions so very earnestly and seriously. I know *I'd* have a more fulfilling time at festivals and community events.

It was also at this point that I stopped reading anything other than novels. For one, I no longer felt any need at all to read anything even remotely "spiritual," as I was no longer a spiritual seeker, and there was nothing of any value that I could learn from such books that I hadn't already learned, and really, most of it is illusory ego-projections anyway, so there wasn't much point. I also stopped reading people's books about entheogens, as it was clear that I understood what was really going on with entheogens far better than anyone else I might read, and most of what I found was also thoroughly entrenched in the ego and the author's illusions. I gave up reading philosophy as well, for all my existential and metaphysical questions had resolved themselves into reality. Really, none of these kinds of writings had any value for me anymore, and reading such treatises was just a waste of my time and energy. So, rather than reading something that the author thought was true, but was really an ego-generated illusion, I decided that I only wanted to read authors who were knowingly lying to me in the form of fiction for my entertainment. Everything else was just overly-sincere delusional crap.

Something else that I gave up at this time was being a political activist. What my own process had clearly taught me was that everything within culture and society is, in effect, infected by the ego. All religion, politics, culture, spirituality, etc. is just the ego writ large, collected into group identities. The only way to really help anyone is to help individuals transcend their own egos and experience reality directly. It is only through knowing the true nature of the self that anyone can hope to act and think responsibly, and attempting to make "society" better through the medium of the confused ego is bound for problems, for the ego does not know how to take responsibility and act genuinely. If I, personally, wanted to make anything better for anyone, the only way to do it was through helping individuals, and that meant working with them one-on-one, for the most part.

I also knew that, if I was going to be true to myself and my energy, I would have to let other versions of the self, meaning other people, know the truth about the nature of being and reality. I knew that this would not be easy, for doing so would mean that I would have to articulate what was incorrect about all the various belief systems that existed out there in order to help people see past their attachments and illusions. I knew that this would be terribly challenging, and would most likely not be well received by the majority of people who encountered what I had to say and share, and that most likely, I would have to endure an abiding and rabid backlash to anything I might make available to the public. However, my infinite love for myself, and all versions of myself, demanded that I not take the easy path and not speak up, for it is my desire to help myself, and I cannot do that by remaining silent. Thus I decided to share, and demonstrate, as much as I could through my podcast, articles, interviews, lectures, and books – something that I continue to do up to this day. As expected, people's reactions have been anything but neutral, and as a result, I've become something of a *persona non grata* in the entheogenic community, which, ironically, despite making claims of being open-minded and supportive of "new paradigms," has not reacted well to having their cherished paradigms and assumptions challenged.

Within the entheogenic community, there is what may be identified as a standard paradigm of belief. Though not exhaustive, some of the features of this belief system are as follows (and all of which are beliefs that I have rejected as being projections of the ego): There are astral and spiritual realms of existence that are non-material yet are also objectively true and real; Spirits and non-material entities are real; Entheogens can put one in contact with non-material entities; Contact with aliens and UFOs is a real phenomenon that is objectively true; Cakras, past lives, and karma are genuinely real phenomena; There are many different "Gods" and "Goddesses" at work in the universe and in the human psyche; The individual soul is on a quest for enlightenment and awakening across multiple lifetimes; Enlightenment is equated with becoming a "galactic citizen" through out-of-body experiences and psychedelic states of consciousness; All "wisdom" traditions essentially agree with each other and state the same fundamental and universal truths; Truth is ultimately relative and there is nothing universally true (notice how this contradicts the previous belief); Shamanism is a valid and objectively true practice; Ayahuasca and DMT are the most important and powerful of all the entheogens; Astrology, the *I Ching*, and other forms of divination are valid and real; Channeling and mediumship are genuine and true; Prophecy is a valid form of prediction; Psychic abilities are genuine; Spirit guides and angels are real; Individual consciousness survives death; etc.

However, I see getting the truth "out there" as far more important than my own personal comfort or acceptance and appreciation by others. I've therefore taken to articulating and making my views on the nature of being available in any form that I can, and have given it the collective name of "The Entheological Paradigm." For some, what I have shared has been a breath of fresh air and a clarion call to reality and genuine awakening. For others, all they see is a megalomaniacal fool, spewing information that is clearly wrong because it doesn't agree with their beliefs or how they choose to interpret their experience.

For me, my only goal, at this point, is to be myself, however that is to manifest. Part of being myself is sharing openly and honestly, no matter what others might think or how they may react. I have no interest in trying to be anything for anyone, other than being myself for myself. I'm not going to pretend to be otherwise, and I'm not going to water down what I have to share in order to make others more comfortable. That would be being untrue to myself, and that is something that I no longer do. I did that for most of my life, and I'm done with such self-destructive and self-limiting behaviors. Truth and authenticity are, for me, always the best option.

The difficulty that others have had in receiving the information that I share, and how I go about sharing it, has been reflected in my relationship with Jessalynn. Perhaps at some point she may want to write down her story and share with those who are interested enough to read it, so I won't go into many details here – and to really tell the tale, this book would be far longer than it already is. Suffice it to say that it became abundantly clear early on after my transformation that if Jessalynn and I were to continue on as a couple, she had work to do – she needed to get over her ego and accept that what had happened to me was true and genuine, and no matter how much she thought it was some aspect of my ego, it wasn't – that was just the interpretation of *her* ego, refusing to accept the reality of what had occurred.

Jessalynn found herself simultaneously tremendously drawn to me, and my newfound sense of being, while also refusing to accept reality, and was in an almost constant state of struggle. In one of our more drawn together moments, we married each other in a spontaneous ceremony while out on a hike in a profound act of commitment and union – far more meaningful than my marriage to Phoebe – yet at the same time fearing that I was trying to brainwash her or was somehow manipulating her. As the reader may recall, Jessalynn was raised by a seriously over-the-top New Age mother, and I was confidently and authoritatively dismissing virtually all of the beliefs, practices, and illusions that Jessalynn had adopted from her mother. Jessalynn's ego fought long and hard to maintain these illusions and attachments, and there were times, several, in fact, when she came very close to telling me to leave. But she knew that if she did so, I'd be out the door and I'd never come back, and the deeper part of her, the more genuine part of her, wanted to be with me, and wanted to find the clarity for herself that I had found within myself.

Thus Jessalynn and I spent months working on her and helping her to overcome the many distortions, illusions, and projections that were at work through her ego. It was extraordinarily challenging for her, but she persisted, and eventually we broke through. In the process, I learned how to really work with others as both a reality coach and energetic mirror, and have found that I'm able to assist people in ways that are not available through any other person or means, and since these early days, have had the pleasure of working with hundreds of people who have come from across the country, and the globe, to work with me and find their own inner clarity and true energetic nature. And it was my work with Jessalynn that made this possible. However, it must be made clear that there was nothing I was able to do for Jessalynn, or anyone else, that was not of their own free will and determination to be genuine with themselves. I can serve as a mirror and clear reflection, but each individual must do his or her own work and go through his or her own process, just as I had for myself and my own awakening and transformation. It is all, in the end, up to each individual to do this work for him or herself, and no one and nothing else can do it for them. Each individual is perfectly free, and perfectly capable, of either choosing to remain trapped in the ego, or set one's self free. It is a choice, and a process. In this, there are no magic bullets, no shortcuts, and no saviors. It is personal, challenging, and highly demanding. Only commitment to genuine truth can really assist anyone in this process.

These days, Jessalynn and I are legally married, making our spontaneous union legally recognized this past spring before the birth of our son, Jaden. We're still here in Ashland, and I still work part-time at the university. I do what I can for income, working various jobs and projects – no one thing that I do is financially viable on its own. I write often and share what I write through my podcast, articles, interviews, and books. Everything I've written since 2009 has been with the aim of articulating the Entheological Paradigm, starting with *Being Human,* and continuing through my recent novel, *Beyond Azara.* At this point, I think that I am perhaps the most prolific author on the topic of entheogens that the world has yet seen, with some fourteen books on the subject! I also continue to make and record music rather prolifically, and perform out in public when I can. As of late, I've gotten into fractal art, and have been enjoying showing and selling art throughout this past summer. In many respects, I'm just an ordinary guy, living his life.

Now, in the aftermath of the world-wide delusion of "2012," I'm personally hoping that people will be more open to truth, and spend less time, money, and energy nurturing their delusions of some ego-projected "global transformation" as promoted by authors like Daniel Pinchbeck, Terence McKenna, and countless others. Despite the complete and total failure of "prophecy" to bring about any genuine change, many still cling to their illusions. The ego is profoundly resistant, and it's quite ingenious at finding ways to hold onto its illusions, even when truth is obvious and staring one directly in the face. So, it remains to be seen whether people will take up the challenge to discover reality, or if they'll continue to indulge in their fantasies, or create new, ever-more enticing ones. History has proven that mostly new sets of illusions replace the old ones, and collectively, we don't really get any closer to a genuine, worldwide awakening to reality, but I'm hopeful. It all comes down to free will and personal choice, and I'm hoping that, as we collectively move into the future, more people will be willing to undergo the work necessary to truly learn who and what they are: an infinite being experiencing itself in the form of a human being without any fundamental identity. The ego is addicted to stories, however, and loves to hold onto its special and unique sense of self, so the work that needs to be done won't be easy, but it is possible.

It remains to be seen what, if any, impact my own work will have on the world at large. I've never "made it big" as an author or speaker, and only sell a handful of books any given month, so the realistic reach of my work is probably rather small. What I've sought to do is provide people with a framework for understanding the nature of the self, methods for working with medicines to achieve personal insight and clarity, and provided myself as a model for how it's done and what it really means. I have no personal illusions of being some kind of prophet, or savior, or healer of nations and saver of souls – I'll leave that for the fantasy figures of religion and self-proclaimed spiritual figures that currently dot the cultural landscape. I also know that most people who encounter my work have such strong ego-generated reactions to what I share that they don't even try to understand what I'm sharing and instead resort to emotional reactions, often centering around the thought of "Who-the-fuck does this guy think he is?!" Even many people who "support" my work often don't really understand it – and in most instances, it couldn't be any other way.

Really, what I've been attempting to do is provide other versions of the self with something of a road map to personal awakening, enlightenment, and liberation, and realistically, others can only understand what I've shared if they've experienced it for themselves. Despite my commitment to writing, this isn't really something that can be communicated through language, which is inherently dualistic and always faces a translation problem. What I'm pointing toward is a process that people need to undergo for themselves, and I've set out signs and directions along the way, yet all such signs are potential opportunities for confusion, attachment, and over-intellectualization. The map is not the territory, after all.

But every once in a while I get an email from someone who tells me about how angry and pissed off they were at me when they first found my work, but after some of their own experiences and insights, started to realize that I was simply telling the truth, so it gives me hope that at least a few people might get it, and maybe it will be enough to make some kind of difference in this world of mass delusion and confusion. It's what I hope, anyway, and it inspires me to keep at it. And realistically, I don't really have anything better to do, so writing a book like this is something that fills my time, gives me a project to work on, and satisfies my desire to express myself. And really, that's all that life is all about.

As for myself, my only real goal or aim is to be myself and stay true to my energy, no matter what. Once one has committed to living in reality, it isn't all that difficult, though I do find that I need to explain myself over and over and over again. Living on the west coast of the U.S., and having many connections among the counterculture, everyone assumes I believe in past lives, reincarnation, spirits, entities, alternate realms, angels, ascended masters, prophecy, karma, astrology, the "Mayan" calendar, etc. I've often found that the best route for me personally is just to let people talk about their illusions, but if they ask me what I think, I always let them know, and they're usually surprised, and challenged as well. Egos are pretty much always looking for other egos to play along with their self-created games, and don't react too well when someone refuses to play their games and indulge their personal fantasies and illusions. I do what I can to help others learn to live in reality, and be a model for them of how it's done, and demonstrate what it means energetically. Mostly, I seek to work with individuals one-on-one, as this is the only real way to make progress, so it's slow going, but it is effective, and for that, I am grateful. Overall, most people don't like having their carefully constructed and painstakingly maintained sense of identity challenged or dismissed, and most react defensively and with a great deal of emotion and anger. Some, however, are genuinely ready to go beyond the bullshit they've been living with their whole lives and get down to genuine reality.

It's not easy being God – for anyone. At heart, there is this profound and tragic loneliness. After all, despite all appearances, there is only one being here – thus it has always been, and so it will always be. Loneliness is the heart of universal love, and in some respects, that's what the "illusion" of reality is all about – one universal being that has evolved itself into "separate" forms over vast eons of time in order to not be quite so lonely. That's also one of the primary reasons the ego holds on as tightly as it does – its job, after all, is to convince God that it isn't in fact God, and that there are other beings here to interact with – one great big game of self-delusion.

True nonduality is not the feel-good "we're all one" sentimentality of the spiritual. It's raw, terrifying, and awesome. Forever one, forever alone – that's real nonduality. There is no plethora of beings and souls, evolving through time and space. There's only one – and that one is all the beauty, all the terror, all the joy, all the horror, all the love, all the violence, all the pleasure, all the pain, all the relief, and all the suffering. The full spectrum of being is absolutely mind-blowing, and it is a true and genuine horror. It's what's real, however, and the sooner any individual can accept that, the better off one will be, and the more fully and responsibly each version of the self can be itself. Going to ceremony won't do it. Praying won't do it. Worshiping God or Goddess or Buddha or Allah or Jah or Yahweh won't do it. Sitting around meditating won't do it. Reading self-help books won't do it. Discovering and adopting the next "new paradigm" won't do it. Taking lots of drugs won't do it. Only sustained, relentless self-observation, commitment to absolute truth, and willingness to open up to the genuine nature of energy will do it.

Living in reality is also fundamentally about being right here, right now. It's not some exalted transcendent state. It's not about living in some ephemeral spirit world. It's not about developing magical, mystical powers. It's just simply about being present with what is, and living genuinely with that, free from distortion, projection, and illusion as generated by the relentless ego. It's so simple. It's not about being anything other than present, clear, and true. The ego wants enlightenment and liberation to be something special, something amazing, something radically profound. It isn't. Not really. It's just about being here, and being true to one's self. It is about living life as one desires, and taking things as they come. There's no big esoteric secret or mystery to unravel. There is no great ascension to attain.

On the positive side of things, if my process indicates anything, it is that the ego, and all the limitations and illusions it generates, is primarily and fundamentally an energetic issue, and one that can be overcome through energetic means. As such, entheogens are an invaluable tool, for they allow us to experience our energy in highly amplified form. The upshot is that being religious or spiritual or even a "good person" are not pre-requisites for doing the necessary work, and in fact, such things often get in the way more than they truly help. In many important respects, what I have learned through my process can help others to de-mystify how to become enlightened and liberated from the illusions of the ego. It isn't in any way a spiritual or metaphysical problem – it is just an energetic issue, and one that can be overcome. The process of overcoming the energetic structures and patterns of the ego isn't easy, and requires true dedication to really work through, but it is entirely possible. Hopefully, this realization can help inspire others, and maybe, just maybe, humanity will one day be able to move beyond this child-like and immature stage of needing to be spiritual or religious and become full adults – mature, responsible, and living in reality. Just like children need to eventually accept that Santa Claus isn't real, humanity could only benefit from leaving behind its attachment to religion and spirituality, and the fantasies and ego-projections that are inherent and ubiquitous in these personal and collective forms of expression and sense of identity. Then, maybe, the real party can get started. Coming into adulthood and the awareness and responsibility that it entails isn't always easy, but it is what is real, and everyone is better off living in reality rather than fantasy. Only by living in reality can we authentically deal with the challenges and issues that we face, both individually and collectively, and we have certainly reached a point where this is now required of us, if we are to survive and flourish here on good old planet earth. The choice rests with each and every individual.

Be true, live authentically in reality, and be yourself.

Or be your illusions.

The choice belongs to all of us.

EPILOGUE:

I'd like to wrap up this narrative with one more account of Burning Man.

My final opening and transformation had taken place in the early spring/late winter of 2009. By that summer, I was busy working on my book, *Being Human: An Entheological Guide to God, Evolution, and the Fractal, Energetic Nature of Reality,* and had been busy articulating my views on my podcast. I was also receiving visitors from around the world, at that point, so things were progressing in my attempts to share what I had learned and been through, though negative public reactions were also a regular feature of my experience of trying to help others find clarity.

Something that I had found the year before, at Burning Man of 2008, was that the festival no longer had the same pull on me as it once had. When I had been married to Phoebe, I had lived for Burning Man and my one week of freedom during my otherwise unhappy year. Things started to shift in 2008, but now, in 2009, after having undergone my own radical liberation, Burning Man no longer meant the same to me, as I had learned to be myself in all times and places, no matter what. While I was still looking forward to Burning Man, it no longer dominated my dreams or desires, for overall, I was profoundly happier in my ordinary, everyday life (which at this time, was anything *but* ordinary by any measure!).

Whereas I had previously looked forward to all the profound experiences I'd have at Burning Man, absolutely mind-blowing profundity was a regular feature of my everyday experience now, so Burning Man, if anything, meant perhaps a playful respite from my ongoing work.

Jessalynn had purchased an old and decrepit RV for us for that year, having toughed it out with me in a tent the year before. She was also insistent that we get a generator so that we could run the air conditioner, and this fact started making waves in camp before the Burn even started – specifically, it started making waves with Devon. Before he ever had a chance to hear the generator, he started complaining about how the sound of the generator was going to ruin his Burn and his peace of mind in camp. His attitude wasn't made any better by the fact that Kat ended up leaving him not too long before the Burn.

Devon had also made plans to experience the new rage on the Playa – cardboard yurts – and he and Rod had been working on making these structures available for themselves in our camp. In converging in Black Rock City for 2009, Devon was to bring all of the gear and structural materials for the God Box, which were stored up at his place in Eugene, and Rod was going to be bringing yurt materials up from Santa Barbara.

Jessalynn and I arrived on the Playa first, followed by Rod and his girlfriend, Anne, and then joined by Patrick and Jenny, and for a few days, their friend, Scott Huckabay. Though communications were spotty, word came through that Devon had secured a ride with another fellow who was driving a bus down from Eugene, but they were having engine trouble with no estimated time for when they'd arrive on the Playa.

We thus were faced with a dilemma, as a camp. We could wait for Devon to arrive, we knew not when, or even if, and set up camp then, or we could use the materials that we had on hand and redesign our layout for the God Box and the Lair of the Mystic Toad – all of which was supposed to arrive with Devon. When Monday afternoon arrived and there was still no word from Devon, at my urging, we decided that we would use the materials that had been intended for Devon's yurt as the purification dome and lair for the Toad, and would use

Patrick's shade structure as a replacement for our welcoming dome. We knew that Devon would not be pleased with this, but our grand opening was to be the following morning, and as it was, there was no way we could open without taking advantage of this option. So that's what we did.

Devon arrived on the Playa the following afternoon in a truly piss-poor mood. And despite the fact that one of his previous Playa girlfriends showed up for a private session with the man a mere few minutes after his arrival, it did nothing to improve his mood. He was furious that his yurt had been used to construct the necessary structures for our camp to function, and insisted that everyone take everything down and rebuild from scratch, and despite the fact that we had decided to do this collectively, he thoroughly blamed me as being responsible for his displeasure. Not wanting to be part of the complete reorganization of camp, Jessalynn and I went out on the Playa for more pleasurable company.

In contrast, Hal also showed up on the Playa that afternoon, and though he had good reason to be in a foul mood, he was joyfully ecstatic. On his way to Black Rock City from Ashland, he had run directly into a large elk on the highway in the middle of the night. The elk had gone through his windshield and smashed him directly in the face, completely disintegrating the elk's head in the process. Much to the surprise of the paramedics, it hadn't killed Hal. His face looked pretty fucked up, but otherwise, Hal was better than ever, and was reveling in telling his elk story to anyone who would listen. He credited his experiences with 5-MeO-DMT with his ability to relax and just surrender in the crash – a reaction that probably saved his life.

The last thing that Devon wanted to hear about was 5-MeO-DMT, or anything to do with any form of DMT, for that matter. Whenever someone mentioned either of these medicines, he'd slip further into his funk, telling me that it kept bringing up how much he loved Kat and missed her, and it would take him back to the year before when he tried 5-MeO and displaced all his energy into clinging onto her and telling her how much he loved her. Devon hated the fact that Hal was around camp, telling his story over and over of how 5-MeO had saved his life.

What was worse was that we had scheduled Hal to give a talk about 5-MeO at the God Box, and additionally, I was giving talks at Entheon Village and Center Camp that year, so we had a constant stream of people coming by camp to talk about DMT and 5-MeO-DMT throughout the week – we were even gifted with a generous supply of *changa* DMT cigarettes. Devon took all of this as a personal affront and got madder and madder as the week wore on.

To top it all off, Devon was personally exhibiting the kind of negative reaction that I was getting from sharing my view publically. His overall reaction to what I had been through and discovered, and was now sharing, was along the lines of "Who-in-the-fuck do you think you are?" So virtually everything I said he found personally offensive, and it only escalated with each passing day.

It all proved too much for Devon, and by the end of the week when we were packing up to go home, he essentially threw a tantrum, worked himself into a frenzy, and then literally threw himself off the back of a truck onto the Playa. Much to his dismay, he wasn't getting any genuine sympathy from all of us as we felt that he was just acting out, trying to take everything personally, and making everything about him and his happiness, even when things had nothing to do with him. In many ways, Devon had tried, unsuccessfully, to make the rest of us as miserable as he felt.

And that, my friends, proved to be the death of the God Box, and 2009 became our final year as a camp. After returning home, I soon found that Devon had de-friended me on Facebook, and all communication between us stopped. And that's where things stand today.

Devon had been an invaluable friend and ally over the years, and in many ways, he had served as my life-line to the life I wanted for myself but was too afraid to go out and claim. Yet once I did, he no longer had the same value for me, and that lessened his power and influence over me, in turn. I can't speak for Devon, so I don't know how he characterizes all of this. A strong part of him probably just thinks that I turned into an unbearable know-it-all asshole, as many people have concluded. I'm personally not interested in trying to change anyone's mind, as our thoughts are our own responsibility, so if Devon wants to think I'm an arrogant asshole, that's his choice. I am saddened that through this process I lost my best friend and the only true confidant that I had for many years, but it's a loss I accept. People have to be free to make up their own minds, and I'm not about to change myself, or my behavior, to try and make someone else think better of me. They can either take me as I am, or leave me be and go their own way. I'm not trying to win hearts and minds.

I think of Devon often. He's just a couple hours up the road in Eugene – I presume – since it has been a few years since we've spoken, I suppose he might be anywhere at this point. Maybe's he's back in Australia. I don't know. He's the one personal casualty of my awakening and transformation, and I'd like for things to be otherwise. But things are what they are, and Devon is who he is, and only a willingness and commitment to facing and addressing his own inner turmoil might hold out hope of things becoming otherwise. I wish him the best, and just like the rest of us, he is, ultimately, on his own.

Jessalynn and I went to Burning Man for two more years, with our last trip in 2011. In 2012, at the time of the Burn, we traveled to Europe – my first time, and it was a great experience. This past year, I was down in Santa Barbara visiting Miranda and Ethan during the start of the Burn, and then watched the Man and the Temple burn via web-cast with Jessalynn – something we both really enjoyed in our dust-free home. Maybe we'll get back out there next year – maybe not. As I said, it isn't important to me in the way that it once was, and Jessalynn is not a big fan of the dust. What the future holds is anyone's guess, so we'll just have to wait and see.

In the end, what I have to offer, as a result of my process, is the truth – the truth of being and the certainty that each and every one of us is God embodied – nothing more, and nothing less – one being, many forms of expression. I have no prophecies, either to make or fulfill. I have no miracles. I have no promises of an afterlife or immortality. I have no offerings of astral realms and ethereal beings. There are no UFOs here. No machine elves. No personal godhood. No ancient cultures to glorify. No indigenous wisdom to share. I have no doctrine, and no church. There are no conspiracies to unravel. No mysteries to unlock. No ancient secrets to reveal. No metaphysics to tap into. I offer no ceremony, no ritual, no prayer. There's nothing to worship. There is no DNA that needs to be activated. No promise of a great awakening or collective transformation. No archaic revival. No cakras to be opened. No grand ascension into the galactic community. No karma to be overcome. No unrighteous to punish. No just to reward. There are no commandments. There are no divine guidelines. There is nothing sacred. There is no path. There is no destination.

Just pure, direct, and undiluted truth.

There is only one, and it is you, and it is I, and everything in between.

There is only reality.

There is only God.

That is all.

ABOUT THE AUTHOR:

MARTIN W. BALL, PH.D., lives in Ashland, Oregon with his wife, Jessalynn, and son, Jaden. He is the author of over 14 books, fiction and non-fiction, on the subjects of entheogens, nonduality, and personal awakening and transformation. He also creates visionary fractal art, is an avid musician and composer, and assists others with energetic openings and transformations. His primary webpage is www.martinball.net, and his art can be found at www.fractalimagination.com. For additional details on his nondual approach to entheogens and the nature of reality, visit www.entheological-paradigm.net. His podcast, "The Entheogenic Evolution," can be found at www.entheogenic.podomatic.com

Other works by Martin W. Ball:

- *Tales of Aurduin, Volumes I-IV*
- *Mushroom Wisdom: How Shamans Cultivate Spiritual Consciousness*
- *Sage Spirit: Salvia Divinorum and the Entheogenic Experience*
- *The Entheogenic Evolution: Psychedelics, Consciousness, and Awakening the Human Spirit*
- *Entheologues: Conversations with Leading Psychedelic Thinkers, Explorers and Researchers*
- *Being Human: An Entheological Guide to God, Evolution, and the Fractal, Energetic Nature of Reality*
- *The Entheological Paradigm: Essays on The DMT and 5-MeO-DMT Experience . . . and the Meaning of it All*
- *Tryptamine Visions/The Process*
- *All is One: Understanding Entheogens and Nonduality*
- *God's Handbook for Operating Human Vehicles*
- *Beyond Azara: A Universal Love Story*
- *Speaking of the Nondual: Mystical Poetry and Fractal Art*

28375126R00182

Printed in Great Britain
by Amazon